Culture & The City

Culture & The City

Cultural Philanthropy in Chicago
from the 1880s to 1917

Helen Lefkowitz Horowitz

The University Press of Kentucky

ISBN: 0-8131-1344-X

Library of Congress Catalog Card Number: 75-3546

Editorial and Sales Offices: Lexington, Kentucky 40506

To Dan

Contents

Preface / ix

Acknowledgments / xiii

1 Culture & Society in Nineteenth-Century America / 1

2 The Responsibility for Culture in Chicago / 27

3 The Cultural Philanthropists / 49

4 The Meaning of Culture / 70

5 The City-Wide Cultural Institutions / 93

6 The Settlement House Reformers' Critiques / 126

7 The Administrators' Alternatives / 145

8 The Appraisals of Artists & Writers / 167

9 The Progressive Period / 194

Appendix A   Participation of the Cultural
                     Philanthropists / 229

Appendix B   The Chicago Institutions / 235

Notes / 239

Index / 275

Preface

At the turn of the century, Chicago was a city of contradictory impulses: it was both a commercial center dealing in the basic commodities of an industrial society and a community caught in the winds of cultural uplift. As one commentator put it, the city was "a strange combination of pork and Plato."[1]

A major manifestation of Chicago's drive toward culture was the establishment of the city's great cultural institutions in the 1880s and early 1890s. The Art Institute, Chicago's museum of fine arts, evolved out of the Academy of Design founded in 1869; reorganized in the late 1870s, the museum assumed its distinctive identity and permanent form in the 1880s under the leadership of Charles Hutchinson. The Newberry Library was created in 1885 (when the bequest of Walter Newberry became effective) to serve as a noncirculating library specializing in the humanities. The Chicago Symphony Orchestra was founded in 1891 to bring Theodore Thomas to Chicago. From its opening session in 1892 the University of Chicago established itself as a major university. Originally the repository for exhibitions of the World's Columbian Exposition in 1893, the

Field Columbian Museum developed into a museum of natural history.[2] The Crerar Library, with endowment from the will of John Crerar, opened its doors in 1895 as a noncirculating library taking the literature of the sciences as its domain.

These institutions were a new phenomenon in the city. Whatever the initial impetus behind their founding, they were largely organized, sustained, and controlled by a group of businessmen who served, with considerable overlapping, on their boards of trustees. Yet while privately supported and managed, the institutions were designed for the whole city. Their trustees had turned to cultural philanthropy not so much to satisfy personal aesthetic or scholarly yearnings as to accomplish social goals. Disturbed by social forces they could not control and filled with idealistic notions of culture, these businessmen saw in the museum, the library, the symphony orchestra, and the university a way to purify their city and to generate a civic renaissance.

These ends were hardly attained: Chicago remained the lusty metropolis of the West. But through the attempt to reshape the city, Chicago gained a network of city-wide cultural institutions shaped by the understanding of culture and the social goals of the cultural philanthropists.

I have examined the annual reports of the city-wide cultural institutions for the years from their founding to 1917, and I have read the available printed and manuscript material on the institutions and the men who created and sustained them. To put these cultural endeavors into focus, I have looked more broadly at earlier American conceptions of culture and its social uses and at the development of cultural institutions in eastern cities. To provide perspective on the changes made in the early twentieth century, I have attempted to pinpoint criticism and alternatives posed by contemporaries in the city—settlement house reformers, professional administrators within the institutions, and artists and writers. Finally, I have carried the exploration into the Progressive period, looking at the contradictory tendencies of early twentieth-century development.

While highlighting aspects of the history of Chicago, this investigation has implications beyond its specific locale. It illumines the cultural forces at work in America, forces which were dominant in Chicago at the turn of the century, but which, to some extent at least, were shared by other American cities and have continued into our own time.

Acknowledgments

The study began as a doctoral dissertation at Harvard in the History of American Civilization. Perhaps more than I am aware, many of the questions it addresses came out of graduate study under Oscar Handlin, Bernard Bailyn, and Kenneth S. Lynn. Professor Lynn provided encouragement and direction in the early phases of the thesis. His continuing interest and good conversation has helped sustain my belief in the academic endeavor. Professor Warner B. Berthoff's receptivity allowed a smooth transition, and his careful reading guided revision.

The Harvard University library system and particularly the courteous and efficient Interlibrary Loan Office brought much of Chicago to Cambridge. In the ensuing years I have been aided by the Skidmore College library, the Union College library, the Honnold Library of the Claremont Colleges, and the Huntington Library in San Marino, California. Research trips to Chicago were aided by the staffs of the Newberry Library, the Special Collections of the University of Chicago Library, the Ryerson and Burnham libraries of the Art Institute of Chicago, and the Chicago Historical Society. In particular, I wish to thank

Archie Motley, manuscripts librarian of the Chicago Historical Society, and Diana Haskell, curator of modern manuscripts of the Newberry Library, who expand their institutions' usefulness by the extraordinary aid they give to unknown, but grateful, scholars. Miss Louise Lutz, secretary of the Art Institute, graciously led me to storeroom and files. Mary A. Hagberg, registrar of the Field Museum of Natural History, located important material; while at the Field I had the pleasure of an informative talk with Director E. Leland Webber. I also wish to thank Charles Boardman and Ralph Guthrie at Orchestral Hall. At a critical point Union College provided the funds for travel to Chicago through the Ford Foundation Faculty Development Program in Humanities. Union College also subsidized typing of the manuscript. Scripps College has generously aided final stages of preparation. I am grateful for the assistance at various points of Martha Reid, Peter W. Sage, Cynthia Field, and Judith Smith. I would also like to thank the Chicago members of my family—Ruth Binstock and the late Rabbi Louis Binstock and Sadie and Samuel Horowitz—for their hospitality and their perspectives on the city. *History of Education Quarterly*, in which chapter 6 appeared in slightly different form as "Varieties of Cultural Experience in Jane Addams' Chicago" (Spring 1974), has graciously granted permission to reprint here.

I had the good fortune to have friends, colleagues, and scholars read and criticize my ideas and my prose during a long and uncertain period before publication. It is a pleasure to acknowledge the aid given me by Marvin Lazerson, Frederick C. Jaher, Kenneth S. Lynn, Stephen Thernstrom, Thomas Hines, and Richard Rabinowitz. Both Roger B. Stein and John G. Cawelti responded to the solicitation of one they had never met and read the manuscript with care and extraordinary insight. I am deeply grateful to Neil Harris: his supportive aid during research trips, his comprehension of the manuscript, and his generous help as I sought to find ways to put the study between two covers leave me in his debt. Excellent readings by members of the Frederick Jackson Turner Award Committee, headed by Mary Young, proved useful as well as provocative. Finally, though my dedication says it all, I wish to acknowledge the prodding, aid, good judgment, and example of my husband.

1

Culture & Society in Nineteenth-Century America

As the World's Columbian Exposition drew to a close in the autumn of 1893, Charles Eliot Norton, aging Harvard art professor and the nation's arbiter of taste, scolded the skeptical Henry Blake Fuller, who had criticized Chicago in his novel *The Cliff-Dwellers.* Enthusiastic about the fair, Norton upbraided Fuller for his lack of balance: "I think you should have sympathetic admiration, nay, even affection, for the ideal Chicago which exists not only in the brain, but in the heart of some of her citizens."[1] The full meaning of Norton's remark is the subject of this study. Cultural philanthropy in the late nineteenth and early twentieth century was an effort by some of its citizens to infuse into their city the "ideal Chicago." Certain of their contemporaries, such as Henry Blake Fuller, questioned the results of this effort and the assumptions behind it. And it was Charles Eliot Norton, perhaps more than any other, who had shaped the sense of "ideal" that guided cultural philanthropy and the belief that it was the mission of "some" of the city's residents.

Awareness both of cultural idealism and of the special role of an elite is essential to an understanding of the larger cultural movement in Chicago of which the fair was, in some sense, a part. The origins of both elements lay in the early years of the nineteenth century and need to be sketched. But it was the experience of Norton and his generation in the Civil War and its aftermath that gave the critical definitions.

The first decades of the nineteenth century were ones of significant social, economic, and political change that saw early efforts to make culture the mark of status. The Revolutionary period had weakened but not severed the connections between wealth, social prestige, and political power. American society remained governed by deference. During the nineteenth century the economic opportunities of an expanding and industrializing nation, coupled with the results of political party rivalry, effectively challenged the authority of the old governing elites. At different periods in different regions and locales, men who felt the naturalness of their economic and political primacy were forced to share power with new entrepreneurs and with political rivals whose claim was based on votes, not fitness to rule.[2] For some members of this older elite, the word *materialism* came to have a sharp class edge. Materialism connoted the values of the *nouveaux riches*, men who had not learned how to spend their money with taste rather than ostentation. Many patricians fashioned a contrasting view of themselves as men of cultivation and leisure. For them the pursuit of the ideal expressed an alternative to the economic and political ambitions that seemed to motivate America.[3]

As Americans traveled to Europe they encountered European masterpieces; but for certain patricians, individual works of art were less impressive than the European city. At home the world they knew was being threatened, not only by the rise of newer men but also by the beginnings of mass immigration. Paris and Rome seemed to offer important lessons to American cities. With their parks, boulevards, and fine buildings, with their museums and concert halls, they seemed able to preserve order and protect aristocratic and *haut bourgeois* life. Certain members of the older American elite began to identify the order they desired with the physical environment of the European city.[4]

Both in framing their self-definitions and in thinking about the city, these men could draw on a body of thought about the nature and function of art that—despite vigorous debate—agreed on art's idealistic premises. Cutting across aesthetic controversies and shifts in taste was the deeply rooted assumption that the role of art was to transcend material realities, the stuff of perception and experience, to go beyond the useful to express the ideal. The meaning of "ideal" varied from period to period and from commentator to commentator, but it was always understood by nineteenth-century minds to refer to generalities rather than to particulars, to mental conceptions rather than to raw facts, to beauty rather than to utility.[5]

Enlightenment thinkers had based the well-being of the republic upon the virtue of its people. Devotion to reason and morality could be preserved only through simplicity and restraint. Since art was associated with the luxury and sensuality of Europe, its development in America threatened to introduce germs of the decay that Europe symbolized.[6] But nationalism helped undermine this fear of art. In confronting the European criticism of American cultural achievement and the prediction that, as a republic, America had no cultural future, Americans were forced to defend their accomplishments. In pushing Americans to display their achievements in European terms, nationalism required them to measure their success as a society by the quality of their art.[7]

Neoclassicism, as it was being defined by English

artists and writers, offered a way to satisfy the seemingly conflicting demands for culture and morality. Neoclassicism emphasized the values of simplicity, order, and control. The artist, in imitating nature, was to select and record the essential elements of a scene, which he could come to identify through a study of the artistic tradition. The conventions used by earlier artists enabled him to go beyond the limits of the particulars of an event or scene and to get at its essence. As the audience became familiar with works of art, its taste would be shaped according to the tradition. The ultimate end of art was culture. As one trained and pruned a garden, so through the arts and letters might one tend one's spirit. The essence or ideal captured by art included moral as well as physical perfection. Immersion in art's conventions and identification with its models would help one attain the grace and character vital to citizenship in a republic.[8]

Foreign criticism further encouraged tendencies toward generalization and abstraction. The classical philosophical tradition that defined materialism as the vice of a democracy was often repeated by commentators on American culture. Only an art that expressed ideal values could successfully refute this generality. While cultural nationalists sought to discover or create a particular American tradition, throughout the nineteenth century there remained those who felt art should have an international vocabulary. America, if it would play its proper role in world art, would have to offer images that softened American particularities.[9]

Transcendentalism, America's radical version of romanticism, broke decisively with neoclassicism in its conception of the mind and of the nature of knowledge. In the thought and practice of certain transcendentalists were the seeds that would develop into realism after the Civil War: a reverence for the particular natural fact; an appreciation for Horatio Greenough's architectural theory that form should be derived from the use to which a building would be put; and a firm sense that art was to express the right relation existing between man and nature, not alter it.[10] However, as transcendentalism was translated into popular consciousness, its dominant understandings largely joined and strengthened the idealistic stream of American aesthetic thought. Art was to mirror nature, but in a special way. Nature was an articulation of spirit, and through his intuitive powers the artist could confront the divine behind natural forms; the art he created could, by capturing the spirit, heighten its clarity to others. In contrast to his neoclassicist predecessors, the artist was to stand stripped of literary and artistic convention in treating nature; but like them, he was to select from the sensory data before him in order to separate the eternal from the ephemeral.[11]

Less directly, transcendentalism intensified idealistic pressures by creating a new role for the artist and for art. The writer or artist in the early national period had seen himself as shaping character and patriotism. Through the reflections of romanticism he became seer and priest, "a link between God and man."[12] As romanticism had done in Europe, transcendentalism signaled the beginning in America of that process in which competition between sects, disintegration of tradition, and breaches in metaphysical structures elevated the arts to the role of a secular religion. These developments increased the pressures on art to maintain its idealistic thrust.

While the transcendentalists read English and German romantics and adapted their thought to American purposes, another influential group of Americans, by mid-century, was reading the criticism and reflections of John Ruskin. Ruskin's impact on America was extensive and varied. Initially, Americans rightly read him as one more buttress to idealism. In his early writings Ruskin had attempted to reassert the identification of beauty with order. Art distilled the beauty of nature, enabling man to view with heightened clarity the order of God's creation.[13]   As Ruskin's interest turned from matters of faith to man and human society, art would increasingly become a measure of the health of a nation rather than a map of the divine plan. His own position was both complex and contradictory. In England and in a later period in America, certain reformers would take his insights into the relation of art and society and make them the basis for efforts to alter the economic system.[14] But Ruskin's main influence on nineteenth-century America lay in another direction. In his later writings as well as in his earlier works, his thought seemed to Americans to support the effort to use art to change the society.

Disturbed by the harsh changes of industrial revolution, Ruskin had found in the medieval past an organic, harmonious society capable of great art. In contrast, the aesthetic poverty of the nineteenth century was a judgment upon industrial society. The worker was no longer a creator; he had become a tool, a slave engaging in monotonous, exhausting labor.[15] Americans could extract from Ruskin's critique an analogy between America and the present, Europe and the past. But while Ruskin's thought increasingly connected his interest in architectural style and the development of museums and educational institutions with a hatred of the contemporary economic order, Americans could limit their attention to his aesthetic concerns. Adding the views of Ruskin to their idealism and interest in the European city, some members of the older American elite would reverse Ruskin's sense that the quality of life in a society determined its art. These men would attempt to use art to alter what disturbed them about American life.[16]

Art would not only provide models and soften rough edges; it would not merely inspire through the truth of the artist's vision; it had the power to turn men away from their appetites and to develop their spiritual nature. Idealism now had clear social implications. A more beautiful visual environment could mold better men. Living more harmoniously with each other in a society governed by idealism and learning art from an environment filled with great models, these men would themselves be capable of creating great art. Art became an opening thrust to a spiral of growth.[17]

In the pre–Civil War period American patricians were responsible for important efforts to create institutions of culture in their cities. They established or encouraged museums, libraries, cemeteries, and parks. While contemporaries lumped these institutions together as part of a single effort, there were important distinctions between even the most closely related of these. For example, New York in the pre–Civil War period saw the founding of three associations designed to promote art: the National Academy of Design, the American Art-Union, and the American Academy of Fine Arts. The National Academy was an association of artists formed to provide members of their profession with a school and a place to exhibit. The Art-Union, with its purchase gallery and its lottery and lithographic distribution, was of most important service as a channel through which American art could be distributed. Only the American Academy seems on the surface to have been a museum designed for the edification of the public. Established at the beginning of the nineteenth century by wealthy New Yorkers interested in art, it provided rooms for exhibitions and filled them with works of art and reproductions. There was one basic difference, however, between the American Academy and a museum. With the exception of an annual exhibition, the academy was essentially closed to the public. Rather than being, as it seemed, an institution to uplift the public—to mold its manners and to disseminate the revelation—it was designed to provide the older New York

business and professional elite with aesthetic pleasure and
to confirm their status by identifying them with the
cultivated life. While offering more varied annual exhibitions than the Academy and thus attracting wider audiences and greater revenues in fees, the Pennsylvania
Academy in Philadelphia and the Boston Atheneum seem
to have served similar functions for the patricians in their
communities.[18]

But two new developments were on the horizon. The
pre–Civil War period saw the creation of an institution
with a very different purpose and the development of a
theoretical approach to cultural institutions that would be
applied in the post–Civil War era.

While certain clergymen and members of the older
elite reflected on the function of art institutions in Europe
and on the power of art to mold character and behavior,
the most interesting efforts in this direction came from
the rather unexpected quarter of landscape architecture.
Andrew Jackson Downing, in theoretical statements and in
actual designs for country living, gave detail and substance
to the notion that the visual environment could be manip-
ulated for social as well as aesthetic ends. Beginning in
1848, he promoted the development of an institution
designed to "civilize and refine the national character"—
Central Park in New York City. Earlier voices had spoken
out for a park in Manhattan as buildings began to fill all
available empty spaces, but that generation had promoted
park development only for recreation. Downing, who
thought of his work as akin to that of a landscape painter,
as aiming "to separate the accidental and extraneous in
nature, and to preserve only the spirit, or essence," projected the goals of an idealistic conception of art onto his
work.[19]

This sense of the park was adopted by Frederick Law
Olmsted, the superintendent of Central Park and its
architect (with Calvert Vaux, the successor to Downing's

practice). Olmsted shared with members of New York's older elite an enthusiasm for the city as the generator of possibilities far beyond those of a rural environment. Within the city, Central Park was to offer the values of the country: it would provide visual variety and open up vistas to counteract urban regularity and density. Olmsted's success was hailed by contemporaries as an important breakthrough. As Henry Bellows, the New York Unitarian minister, aptly expressed it, it was "a royal work, undertaken and achieved by the Democracy," a park comparable in scale and expense to those in European capitals. What at the time seemed of crucial importance, though it proved a quite temporary arrangement, was that the people had taxed themselves for the park and then turned over authority to those who could best exercise it—trustees, who happened to include members of New York's older elite, and technical experts such as Olmsted and Vaux. In the years that followed, this proved to be a tantalizing anachronism.[20]

At the same time in one rather distant quarter James Jackson Jarves had begun to think seriously about the nature of the art museum. A former Bostonian settled by the 1850s in Florence, Jarves was a serious collector. Influenced by European students of museums and by Ruskin's approach to art, Jarves presented his ideas in a number of books on art published in the 1850s and 1860s. He argued for a complete museum, historically arranged, that would enable the viewer to comprehend fully the development of painting. Although in 1859 few would have questioned the idealistic premises of his thought, his plan for an art museum was rejected. Before the Civil War the widespread commitment necessary to establish such an institution had not yet developed. Jarves offered to sell his collection of Italian primitives to serve as the nucleus of a permanent gallery in his native Boston. Though Charles Eliot Norton supported his friend's effort, others in Boston were unenthusiastic; the lack of subscription to a matching fund eventually forced the Atheneum to reject Jarves's proposal.[21]

The Civil War interrupted consideration of art and its social uses. Jarves argued that it was appropriate to consider museums in the midst of war, since war was only ephemeral while art was eternal; but it was perhaps only his emotional distance from America that made such a statement possible. While Jarves worked to set out a full rationale for the development of cultural institutions in the city and sought to persuade state legislatures to assist in museum development, those in America who had shared much of his enthusiasm for the social uses of art were turning from their aesthetic concerns to deep involvement in the political struggles of their society.[22]

Totally absorbed in the conflict in which they identified completely with the Union cause, members of the older elite and spokesmen such as Olmsted and Bellows lived at a fever pitch in those years. The Civil War was their great opportunity. They had profoundly wanted to lead, and the nation at war offered them a chance to exert influence and to perform a kind of service that fit their sense of noblesse oblige. Dissatisfied with the Army Medical Bureau, they established the Sanitary Commission to organize the relief of the wounded. In that organization, which became a focus for their loyalty, they found a channel to carry their views on war policy to the executive, a means of exercising their administrative and exhortatory gifts on a national platform, and a way of educating others about the right relation of men to their society.[23] Yet while totally immersed in politics, indirectly they were creating institutions and a climate of opinion that would have an important bearing on civic cultural developments.

Despite their social prominence, the Sanitary Commissioners did not hold local political office. To them, the talk of compromise with the Confederacy by their city's officials seemed treasonous, "the revolutionary schemes which unprincipled men are plotting to accomplish." To regain the local authority they felt appropriate, they organized—in New York, Philadelphia, and Boston—Union League clubs. The origin of the New York club makes its elitist goals clear. Olmsted, brooding in Washington over the state of the Union and of New York City, wrote to Woolcott Gibbs a troubled letter suggesting that through the guise of a men's social club, the trusted forces of nationalism—that is, the "elite of the elite"—might organize to serve as a center of loyalty to the Union within the city and as a stimulant to private efforts to mold public opinion. What emerged from the meetings of the Sanitary Commission officials in their New York office was the Union League Club. Drawing together influential men of wealth, including important members of New York's older elite, the club served as an important focus of Union sentiment during the war years.[24]

As the fortunes of the Union army rose, so did the spirits of the men involved with the Sanitary Commission. Men such as Bellows and Charles Eliot Norton had at the outset of the war seen as its cause the nation's pursuit of material gain. The war could serve as a cleansing agent, and, when battles were lost, as atonement for national sins. But with victory a possibility and their own influence a reality, their faith in America was renewed. Idealism was defeating materialism on the battlefield; the nation, disciplined and uplifted, was becoming what it ought to be.[25] As they looked ahead to a realized America, they saw the need of a national organ to instruct the nation in the way it should go. The best thinkers on all national topics, from Reconstruction to art and literary criticism, should be brought together in such an enterprise. Members of the older elite in New York, Boston, and Philadelphia provided the capital for the *Nation*, picked Olmsted's and Norton's friend E. L. Godkin for editor, and looked forward to an era in which men like themselves would create a rational politics.[26]

The postwar years would be a rude awakening from this dream of political power. The war left in its wake tremendous social problems. The relation between blacks and whites in the South could not be resolved without the kind of redistribution of land that was unacceptable to property-conscious interests. More important in this context, the war and the Republican administration had opened the way to a greatly expanded economy and to a new supportive relation of government to business. Men whose talents the Sanitary Commission veterans hoped to tap turned their full attention to the business opportunities of the industrializing economy. The public, whose numbers swelled with the growing rate of immigration, found other political leaders, a process that consolidated the power of local party machines.[27] The Union League did not fulfill the hopes of its founders. While the confidential prospectus for the club had spoken of the need "to dignify politics as a pursuit and a study; to reawaken a practical interest in public affairs in those who have become discontented," no restoration of direct political power to the older elite was to be realized. Those who remained interested in reform causes found themselves once again without a constituency. Bellows in 1879 best conveyed how this felt. Gone was the clear foe of the Civil War years. In its place came "a secret rot, an enemy with the invisible powers of a pestilence."[28]

What emerges as of critical importance from the experience of these men is not that the postwar world was a letdown, which it was, but that the Civil War involved them in anachronism and fantasy as well as teaching them real lessons. The new faith in America these members of the older elite felt during the war reflected the flush of victory, but it also resulted from the sense that they held political power. Through the Sanitary Commission, the

Union League, and the *Nation*, they created organizations that did influence the public at large and the national administration; but, for the most part, they did not hold elected office. And, with the crisis over, other interests intruded: Norton and Bellows immediately left active life to travel in Europe; Olmsted had resigned during the conflict and entered a private venture in California.[29]

Yet in a different sense the Civil War experience had both real lessons and symbolic power. The war organizations had brought together for the first time members of the older elite who shared a personal interest in art and a concern for its social uses. It had raised certain of their number to positions as national spokesmen, positions that could be translated to other ends. It had showed the power of an organization outside the formal channels of government. It created an ideal of social harmony and sounded a chord of hope that intensified commitments to a vision of America.[30]

Some of the responses of the older elite to the postwar era are well known. Experience with the Sanitary Commission led some directly into the effort to apply its lessons of organization and efficiency to charities in the city. Those who had been most closely involved in the elite organizations of the Civil War became liberal reformers. With close ties to the business community and with a firm belief in principles of classical economics, these independent Republicans or Mugwumps defined the problem as one of political corruption and the danger as government involvement in the economy. They sought to restore order through the installation of elite leaders and through civil service reform that would staff the government bureaucracy with talent rather than with political payoffs. Some Mugwumps remained interested primarily in politics, though serving largely as publicists and advisors rather than as officeholders, but others returned to the private and professional concerns of the prewar years.

Bellows turned his organizational gifts to his Unitarian church. Olmsted quickly developed an expanding and highly influential landscape-gardening practice. Charles Eliot Norton returned to the literary and aesthetic life.[31]

Norton's life is pivotal. The grandson of a leading Boston merchant whose daughter had married Andrews Norton, the most influential voice of conservative Unitarianism in Boston, Charles Eliot Norton began in business only to find himself unsuited. He experimented in philanthropy as a young man, but by the early 1850s was turning toward the scholarly life. His deeply conservative pamphlet *Considerations on Some Recent Social Theories* conveys how far removed he was from a society that did not recognize clear and fixed social orders:

> the people sit in the dark night of ignorance. . . .
> It is not, then, to this people that we are to look for wisdom and intelligence. . . . They could not, if they would, rescue themselves from evil, and they have no help for others. But their progress must be stimulated and guided by the few who have been blessed with the opportunities, and the rare genius, fitting them to lead.

Fond of travel, Norton returned to Europe in 1855 in what his biographer calls "a search for his spiritual home," and was accepted as a member of the network of English men of letters. Through Ruskin, Norton found the medieval cathedral to be the epitome of art, expressing the right relations among men in a unified, democratic society. He gathered literary manuscripts in England for the newly founded *Atlantic Monthly* and returned to the United States at the end of the decade to publish his translation of Dante's *Vita Nuova*, write essays and reviews on art and scholarship, and begin his critique of American commercial culture.[32]

The war broke into this way of life. Norton found himself deeply involved as a supporter of the Sanitary

Commission, an organizer of the Boston Union League, and the full-time editor of the Loyal Publication Society. Writing now not for the cultured few but for the Northern public at large, Norton came for the first time in his life to identify with the American people. He loosened his hold on the belief in the necessity of elite leadership and placed a "new trust in the political instincts and intentions of an instructed and intelligent people." "We are getting beyond leaders in America" and beyond the need for formal religion. There was no longer the split between the ideal and the real. One could see "in actual vision" that America was becoming the promised land.[33] Perhaps Norton's most interesting statement was the restrained, indirect response to Ruskin's comments about the new optimism of his American friends. Norton wrote to Miss Gaskell that Ruskin "fancies that our happiness is a delusion, our efforts vanity, and our confidence folly. I believe that we have really made an advance in civilization, that the principles on which our political and social order rest are in harmony with the moral laws of the universe. . . . The war has given us a right, such as we had not before, to trust in the fidelity of the people to the principles of justice, liberty and fair play." It was Lincoln, "the great net gain of the war," who inspired such confidence. His rusticity had at first only excited Norton's and his colleagues' contempt, but it came to symbolize to them the raw power and eloquence of America.[34]

It is difficult to pinpoint in time Norton's disillusionment after the war or to separate it from the personal tragedy of his wife's death. But it is significant that Norton, like Olmsted and Bellows, withdrew from involvement very quickly at the war's end. In 1868 Norton sailed for Europe with his family and remained there five years. By the time of his homeward journey in 1873 he was thoroughly disillusioned with America. His negative reactions to Ralph Waldo Emerson's optimism as they con-

versed on shipboard were a measure of his return to a
sense of alienation from American life, with its accompanying judgments on American culture and an intensi-
fying sense of elitism. In Europe Norton had deepened
his appreciation for the medieval past and for European
standards of taste. With his return to America he took
up again his earlier career as essayist, reviewer, and cultural
critic and began a career as teacher and scholar of art
history at Harvard.[35]

In the last decades of the nineteenth century Norton
assumed a role that no American had previously played:
he became the cultural arbiter of the nation. The economic
and social changes that followed the Civil War were
making the United States a nation in a new way. Regional
economies were linked by transportation networks and
then by growth and consolidation. Business leaders attained economic power on a national scale. While regional
and local differences remained important, there were now
national models. As the successful businessman became
the voice of economic authority, the nation looked for men
to assume that role in other spheres, to articulate national
standards. Norton was ready. From his pulpit at Harvard
he preached the doctrines of aesthetic idealism given flesh
in the masterpieces of the past. The imagination could
"conceive that which nature and experience suggest but
never completely attain or afford—the ideal which is the
essential truth and reality that lie concealed within the
husk of the actual."[36]

Medieval Italy was for Norton the high point in the
history of art. Unified by the Church, social classes were
linked together in a republican spirit and became awakened
to the sense of beauty. The artist of such a medieval city
as Florence became an "interpreter to itself of his own
generation." He was "in the fullest sympathy with his contemporaries, because the sources of his inspiration were the
natural sources of spiritual life common to them and to

him, but from which he drew more deeply than the rest."[37] Norton could use his understanding of the past as a standard by which to judge American culture. By the late nineteenth century he found it "of all civilized nations . . . the most deficient in the higher culture of the mind, and not in the culture only but also in the conditions on which this culture mainly depends."[38]

Norton's words found a resonance in the writings of certain of his contemporaries and friends whom we have come to call the genteelists. Less systematic than he and more closely linked to the world of publishing and to New York City, such poets, essayists, critics, and editors as Bayard Taylor, Edmund Clarence Stedman, George William Curtis, and Richard Watson Gilder attempted to promote literature and culture in a society they regarded as hostile to the arts. The first generation of professional writers in America, they were supported by *Harper's*, the *Century*, and similar periodicals, which had grown to satisfy a middle-class, largely feminine, reading audience. The goal of the genteel writers was to shape the taste and manners of Americans. They maintained publicly, whatever their private doubts, that art was to express the beautiful, that its province was elevated emotions and noble deeds, and that it should not offend the standards of decency of its audience. The genteelists' strength as a cultural force came not only through their literary and critical writings but through their close alliance with the publishing business. Acting as judges and censors, they screened the literature and illustrations of the day for any suggestion of language or image that might offend. As they attempted to write and encourage works that portrayed the ideal, they lent diffuse, but effective, support to the notion that art should be used to elevate the society.[39]

While profoundly influenced by Norton's views on the value of art, late-nineteenth-century critics added, some-

what unsystematically, notions from German idealism and
Matthew Arnold that gave further theoretical strength to
the power of art. Such ammunition was needed; for, while
idealistic notions of art had always been questioned by
practical-minded Americans, in the latter part of the nineteenth century idealism was being put on the defensive by
writers for the first time. Walt Whitman had voiced an
objection to the timid and precious work he saw passing
for art and literature as early as 1871, but it was in the
mid-1880s that Norton's friend William Dean Howells
was developing a firm theoretical structure for realism, the
kind of writing that he, Mark Twain, and others of their
generation were doing. Art was to give expression to
reality at the level on which it was experienced, with all
its irregularities and ugliness. Literature was useful mainly
as it made men aware of the social world around them and
lent the appropriate democratic respect to all aspects of
all men's lives. Seeing men as products of historical forces,
the realists denied that art could change man's nature.
Idealism (or, in their terms, romanticism) was merely the
effort by critics to impose elite standards on a democratic
people.[40]

Hegelian notions filtering in through popularizers
offered a way to reestablish and reassert art's role. It posited
a Platonic order of absolutes "whereof phenomena are
merely the gross shadows." Art was the "essence . . .
revealed in a concrete form, as individual beauty. . . . the
external manifestation of the idea, the revelation of the
invisible reality through the senses. It is 'eternity looking
through time.' "[41] Art was therefore no longer a refinement
over reality, a spiritualization of natural forms. It was,
in fact, an alternative, a counterworld.

The writings of Matthew Arnold shifted the emphasis
of concern from the creation of art to its value in perfecting
the individual and society. The nineteenth century had
always seen art as a spiritualizing force, offering models to

neoclassical minds, revelation to romantics. But increasingly the approach to art that Bellows had represented in the prewar period, the interest in the power of art to develop the soul, began to dominate late-nineteenth-century thought. Art could provide a means to strengthen men's spirits against their bodies. In the first book on aesthetics written in America, John Bascom gave this view cogent expression, more important for its representativeness than for its influence. The enjoyment of art "does not belong to our animal nature, neither to the appetites or passions, but as a higher and more spiritual enjoyment, can be thrown into the balance against these. . . . In the contest between the spiritual and physical which is waged in every man's nature, beauty arrays itself on the side of the former." Hegelianism intensified this understanding and separated it from explicit moral content. As the incarnation of the ideal, art could, in and of itself, lead to the "enfranchisement of the soul." But this was not to require of each poem that it be a sermon. "It is not the function of the artist to preach morality, to inculcate virtue. The laws of art are proper to itself. And they are the laws of beauty." Building on this sense of art's purposes, Arnold added encouragement that the cultured few could serve as the saving remnant of society. These men, involved in "a pursuit of our total perfection by means of getting to know, on all the matters which most concern us, the best which has been thought and said in the world," could break away from their class to express in their best selves the interests of humanity. They could then serve as a center through which sweetness and light would redeem the rest of the society.[42]

The difference that this more rarified idealism made can perhaps be seen in the understanding of the European past. Medieval architecture had been the culmination of culture for Norton. The Renaissance, with its contrived quality and its link to aristocratic patronage, signaled the decadence of art. The late nineteenth century rediscovered the Renaissance. In contrast to the organicism and exuberance that had seemed to define the Gothic, the Renaissance values of order, proportion, and balance were associated with the world of essences, and thus they defined beauty. Renaissance art was the purest example of that counterworld that would spiritualize man. The Renaissance prince no longer called up negative images of aristocratic control but served as a model for the wise use of wealth and power.[43]

Inherent in one stream of the idealistic understanding of art was a belief in its international quality. Jarves had written in 1864 against the notion of an American art. "No one dreams of it in science, ethics, or physics. Why then propose it in art? We are a composite people. Our knowledge is eclectic."[44] Similarly, there was no strict division between past and present. But the uses of the past for the present changed in the late nineteenth century. While Ruskin and Norton appreciated medieval art and architecture largely for what it had meant in the past, admirers of the Renaissance sought to fashion contemporary buildings, sculpture, and paintings by Renaissance canons.[45]

These changes in the theoretical understanding of the nature of art and its social uses, in contrast to those in the decades before the Civil War, were inextricably enmeshed in the development of cultural institutions. The older urban elite who had been patrons and theorizers before the war failed to gain positions as governors of the society in the postwar world, and some of these turned to the arts as a means of continuing their involvement in public affairs. Norton was their spokesman. In local communities men who had shared elements of his experience sought ways to bring the fine arts into the life of their cities. The second half of the nineteenth century saw the establishment of museums of art and of science, libraries, orchestras, and expositions. While some of them perpetuated the clublike functions of the pre–Civil War cultural institutions and even heightened their status-confirming role, the distinctive development of the post-war years was the institution designed to serve the whole population of the city and backed by adequate capital to do so.[46]

The question of wealth and its uses was critical. Necessary to the establishment of museums was the belief that wealth should be used for the support of the arts. Henry Ward Beecher, the influential minister of Plymouth Congregational Church in Brooklyn, had long pondered the relation of art to morality. As he attempted to guide the members of his prosperous congregation, he eased their minds about the possession of wealth. His words helped shape a different commitment in the years after the Civil War.

Beecher saw society organized in a hierarchy of classes: wealth confirmed quality, but there was in each generation opportunity to rise. Beecher saw the need for the expression of riches both in private houses and in public institutions. The handsome dwelling would serve as an example and as an inspiration to the less fortunate. The art it contained could and should be shared: "Nothing can make others so rich, without diminishing our own means, as generosity in the use of art-treasures, or materials of beauty."[47] Cultural institutions would work to improve society, to engage its elite directly, and, in so doing, to elevate others. While an observatory might seem to have nothing to do with people in a community, those who used it would become "broader and deeper and better. Through them, but diluted and not recognized, the next class below will be influenced—not by *astronomy*, but by the moral power of men who have been elevated by astronomy. . . . There never can be too many libraries, too many cabinets, too many galleries of art, too many literary men, too much culture. The power of mind at the top of society will determine the ease and rapidity of the ascent of the bottom. . . ."[48]

It was with the founding of the Metropolitan Museum of Art in New York that these threads—the understanding of the role of art and the development of an elite committed to culture and ready to use wealth in its support— came together for the first time. While there were pressures for the founding of a museum from a variety of sources, the effective cause was the Union League. In 1869 John Jay gave a Fourth of July speech to the Americans gathered in Paris to prepare for the Exposition in which he suggested that it was time for America to have a permanent gallery of art and history. The speech was relayed to the Union League, of which Jay was president, as the association best able to bring the museum into being. While important New York artists were members of the club's art committee, of greater significance was the fact that the club had brought together the important patrons of art in New York City who, despite the aims of the Union League, remained outside local political office. The Union League called a meeting with representatives of other organizations in the city out of which came the initial plans for the Metropolitan Museum of Art.[49]

The plan of the museum and the address at its opening by George Fiske Comfort make clear its idealistic premises as well as the degree to which Jarves's sense of a museum had become accepted. Comfort argued that "true art is cosmopolitan. It knows no country; it knows no age. Homer sang, not for the Greeks alone, but for all nations and for all time. . . . And Raphael painted, not for the Italians alone, but for all, of whatever land or age, whose hearts are open to sympathy with the beautiful in art. An ideal museum must thus be cosmopolitan in its character; and it must present the whole stream of art-history in all nations and ages." The museum "should illustrate the history of the origin, the rise, the growth, the culminating glory, and the periods of decline and decadence of all the formative arts." Like its counterpart in Boston, the New York museum anticipated achieving this not through a large collection of original masterpieces, but through the use of plaster casts for sculpture, models and casts for architecture, and copies and reproductions of great works, though there would be some cautious purchasing of originals when they became available.[50]

Central Park was the closest parallel in the prewar period to the cultural institutions in the latter part of the nineteenth century. But the difference is instructive. The government of the park by commissioners, enabling New York's older elite to have control over park decisions, did not survive the postwar decade. Olmsted, who had returned to the superintendency after his California venture, left once more as he saw his plans being altered by city officials to fit a different conception of an urban park system. In his park work throughout the country, Olmsted continued to advocate the commission form of park government as delegating decisions to a "small body of select men" who could act like a "board of directors of a commercial corporation," free from the pressures and temptations of politics. As his colleagues established cultural institutions in American cities, they developed a form close to Olmsted's model but much more loosely tied to municipal government. Only after they formed corporations endowed through private philanthropy did they go to the city for land and some support. Through this device, the trustees, while dependent on city government for resources, were able to establish an area of control where they could make decisions independent of local politics.[51]

Comfort framed his speech at the opening of the Metropolitan Museum of Art not in terms of the particular

situation in New York, but of the national context, pointing to what seemed to be a movement coming out of
"the great intellectual awakening which has followed our
late national convulsion," a realization of the lack of
"institutions for the promotion of aesthetic culture." He
spoke of the needs not only of the largest cities, but also
of those of the scale of Buffalo or New Haven. Other
writers in the 1870s similarly felt that a museum movement
was under way. This sense was promoted by such national
periodicals as the *Nation*, which carried articles on art and
its promotion and reported on cultural developments in
American cities.[52]

While important institutions were established, rhetoric outran achievement in these years. The foundings
were limited in number and in support, as they have always
been in America. Yet the end of the nineteenth century
did see more museums, extensive endowments, and a new
sense of the bond of common interest among the different
cultural institutions of the city. While clearly related to
industrial growth, which was enabling some businessmen
to garner the huge profits on which philanthropy depended,
these developments were also linked to the changing sense
of art and its uses.

The museum movement in the 1870s had been closely
tied not only to the sense that art would contribute to
public taste and morality, but also to the hope for the
education of artists and craftsmen. Comfort in his address
agreed substantially with C. C. Perkins, who had had an
important influence on the development of the Museum
of Fine Arts in Boston, that the museum, by showing
examples of the decorative arts, would foster craftsmanship
and industrial design.[53] Ruskin and Norton could not
have wished for closer adherence to their goals. Housed
in buildings reflecting the Gothic spirit, the museum could
serve as the force that would help spiritualize American
society. But as art's power came to be linked to the

formal qualities of the masterpieces rather than to their content, and as concern for art's effect focused on the appreciators rather than on craftsmen and artists, Renaissance design replaced Gothic, the industrial rooms were allowed to lie dormant, and original paintings of the great masters were sought to replace reproductions.[54]

The idealism that supported these developments in art museums linked the visual arts to music and literature as varied expressions of the ideal and hence as equally useful tools for personal and social regeneration. By the end of the century the realm of the ideal was large enough to embrace scholarship and science as well. No clear distinctions were made between aesthetic appreciation and intellectual understanding. Both were approaches to the world of the spirit, countering the materialism that increasingly seemed to threaten America. Academic scientists had wrestled with the relationship between their work and the technological improvements supporting America's growing industrial power. In their definition of pure science, based on scientific method and leading to research for its own sake—as opposed to the practical studies associated with economic gain—they found the formula that would prove attractive to patrons of culture. The science that "ennobles and purifies the mind" would be the science that was worthy of philanthropic support in universities. This rationale would also buttress the former cabinet of curiosity as it attained a new status as museum of natural history. Gentlemanly exploration would merge with scientific discovery on behalf of museums that became dedicated to the systematic portrayal of the natural world. Thus the American Museum of Natural History in New York City and the Metropolitan Museum of Art were founded almost simultaneously.[55]

The Boston Public Library was the first full expression of the late nineteenth century's understanding of culture. Sharing a square with the Museum of Fine Arts and Trinity

Church, the library was intended to be "the visual expression of the civic consciousness of Boston." The library trustees called the most important architects and artists of the day to design the Renaissance palace and decorate it with sculpture and murals. These artists were to gather again in Chicago to project this conception of the unity of the arts and their harmony with science and scholarship in the period's most compelling cultural symbol, the World's Columbian Exposition.[56] The theoretical understanding of art and its social uses which lay behind the development of museums could now be applied to libraries, symphony orchestras, expositions, science museums, and universities.

Thus, to the generation of men awakening to civic concerns in the Chicago of the 1880s and 1890s, there was available a distinctive form of civic activity with a developed rationale—cultural philanthropy inspired by the vision of an "ideal Chicago . . . in the heart of some of her citizens." When political and social developments in their city continued to impose the frustrations experienced by such men as Charles Eliot Norton in the years after the Civil War, this later generation would turn to the creation and support of cultural institutions.

2

The Responsibility for Culture in Chicago

When Chicago was chosen as the site of the World's Columbian Exposition, eastern reaction was expressed bluntly. Chicago, the meat-packer and grain dealer, would embarrass the nation by a vulgar, materialistic display worthy of a state agricultural fair. Representing all that was crude in American life, the city was incapable of reflecting deeper values. Sheer jealousy partly explained these remarks—New York had vied with Chicago for the fair and had lost. But the terms in which the condemnation was cast played on the stereotype by which the city was recognized and labeled in 1893, a stereotype that was, to some extent, accurate.[1]

The shock that the fair engendered was genuine: Chicago, the emblem of the raw West, had produced the White City, to many observers the supreme flower of nineteenth-century culture. "The wonder that these noble, artistic conceptions [of the fair] were realized at all is increased by the fact that they were realized in Chicago. It would have seemed possible in ancient and

opulent cities . . . but Chicago! The original suggestion
of the name was received with mingled derision and dis-
dain. Its competitors affected incredulity. It was not
serious. It was a frontier joke, an advertisement, a bid for
notoriety."[2] At the time, the fair seemed like a biological
sport, a result that had no perceivable relation to its cause.
But there were those who realized that they would have
to take a new look at the city and perhaps revise their
understanding of the values that informed its life. When
they did, they saw that the fair was not an isolated phenomenon but was related to other cultural efforts in the
city.

It cannot be denied that in many respects Chicago in
the 1890s fit its reputation for materialism and roughness.
It was a new city built on the foundations of commerce
and industry. Founded at the point where the Chicago
River meets Lake Michigan, it was, from the very beginning,
in a strategic location to profit by the westward movement
of the population and the development of agriculture. Its
position was only enhanced by the growth of the railroad
system. Through location, luck, and aggressive promotion,
Chicago became the center from which radiated the great
trunk lines east, west, and south. Here increasing amounts
of grain, lumber, and meat were shipped for processing
and distribution to the East. Here manufacturers were
gathered and produced to supply the consumer needs of
the West. The great department stores with their wholesale houses expanded to service the growing supply and
demand. Banks and investment houses sprang up to
finance the enterprises and to generate speculative gains.
And as the economy of the area developed, the population
was growing and requiring more goods and services.[3]

The process was hardly automatic. There were other
cities with strategic locations—Saint Louis on the Missis-
sippi and Cincinnati on the Ohio. But Chicago also had

a peculiarly aggressive and able group of entrepreneurs who seized or created opportunities for growth and profit. Cyrus Hall McCormick joined business ability to inventive capacity in producing his rapidly expanding reaper works. Marshall Field organized his highly profitable dry goods establishment by limiting certain floors to selected classes of goods, creating the department store.[4]

To an unusual degree, Chicago entrepreneurs were willing to cooperate to attain common ends. In 1864 the Union Stock Yard was incorporated. Organized and financed by railroad men and packers, it yielded almost immediate economic gain. However, cooperation was not limited to enterprises offering clear return. A dramatic instance was the decision in the 1850s to raise the ground level of buildings above the low water level of the river. Each property owner engaged the services of a work crew who slowly raised the building as each man gave his jack screw a half-turn. The most significant cooperative moment before our period was the response to the Great Fire of 1871, which completely devastated the entire downtown area: the unquestioned willingness to stay and rebuild in a spirit of optimism was called by residents and outsiders alike "the Chicago spirit."[5]

Chicago's location and the vigorous activity of its entrepreneurs attracted a population eager for opportunity. With the exception of the 1870s, every decade after 1840 saw the city's population double; it totaled a million in 1890.[6] Some migrated in emulation: they hoped to build their lives on the pattern of the successful, to find in this dynamic setting a need or a process upon which they could base their fortune. Those who succeeded provided Chicago with a new generation of business leaders to join the sons of the old. Others gained only a competence, while many moved on or became part of the swelling working force of the city. These latter were joined by perhaps the bulk of Chicago's newcomers—those escaping from dire need and seeking not fortune, but employment. To them Chicago offered no more than they could find elsewhere, far too little with which to live comfortably and securely.

Chicago's laboring class in the latter part of the century was largely made up of the foreign-born and their children, who represented 78 percent of the city's total population. Of these, approximately one-third came from the German states, another third from Britain, and the rest from the remaining countries of the Continent, though the increasing influx from Eastern Europe was shifting the proportions. While to those within, the hold of custom and family and the ties of neighborhood and of religious and fraternal organizations gave a sense of place and order, to the outsider these immigrants added to the confusion of the city. Their strange tongues and customs seemed evidence of chaotic conditions. The poverty and deprivation that some observed were real; yet real, too, was the possibility of opportunity. While the men of great wealth were predominantly of American parents, a few immigrants had joined their number. Of greater significance were those who in their own lives or in those of their sons had gained a foothold through small business, politics, skilled labor, or the professions.[7]

All of these—wealthy, middle class, and workers, native-born and immigrants—entered into and swelled the mix that was Chicago. By their very presence as well as by their activities they contributed to the central aspect of Chicago's self-definition, the sense of growth and change.

To residents of Chicago in the 1890s, change seemed overwhelming. The experience of pioneer beginnings was within living memory. The raw village of 350 persons, incorporated as a town in 1833, had become a city covering roughly 170 square miles by 1890. Its society had grown incredibly complex and heterogeneous. While one's neighborhood was familiar, nearby was a seemingly separate community, speaking a different language, practicing its own ways. The powerful businessmen who had governed the city in the beginning had given way to representatives of the ethnic communities and to the professional politicians who had worked their way up through the party hierarchies.[8]

The change in numbers and wealth had meant a change in scale and pace. Massive buildings were altering the face of downtown; having broken the limits on height, they seemed to proclaim boldly their utilitarian purpose and their owners' power. Factories sent forth billows of soot-laden smoke and deposited refuse that polluted the Chicago River. The street railways and the sheer number of people generated a new level of noise. Any factor alone would have made its impression. Together they created an atmosphere that was, for many, bewildering.[9]

Neither economic development, population growth, nor change was unique to Chicago in the late nineteenth century. They are the common characteristics of industrial cities in the period. Yet Chicago seemed special in nineteenth-century eyes. It was its similarity to the rest of the country that, paradoxically, gave the city its hold on the American imagination. Chicago seemed to epitomize America. It was as if those qualities which characterized America were embodied in the city in a concentrated form.[10] This view of Chicago contained much truth. The shortness of the city's history and the rapidity of its growth meant that change ran deeper and tradition provided less of a countervailing force than in other cities.

But such a view tended to obscure an important current of Chicago experience that seemed to be running in a different direction, the city's cultural life. Throughout Chicago's history, living alongside the entrepreneurs, clerks, and laborers were those who had sought to express themselves through artistic creation. Others had, in a more desultory way, tried their hand at writing or painting for recreation or self-improvement. Countless more enjoyed listening to music or looking at paintings or fine architecture. Most relevant for our concerns here, many of the latter had joined together in associations for the study or promotion of literature or one of the fine arts. When Chicago was characterized, however, these activities were ignored.

Yet the same elements involved in Chicago's distinctive economic and population growth had taken an active role in the promotion of culture. By the 1880s the city abounded in schools, concert halls and performances, libraries, and galleries. These had been established by municipal authorities, entrepreneurs of various kinds, and by the ethnic and native communities. They had arisen largely to meet quite specific needs of the city as a whole or of segments of the community.

The Chicago Public Library was founded after the Fire as the repository for books donated by England and other nations. It was designed quite consciously as a municipal institution representing the diverse elements of the population, their geographical spread, political affiliations, and ethnic organization. The library board included an Irishman, a German, and a Jew among its nine members. Chicago's national groups openly solicited books from their homelands. The library's underlying philosophy mirrored that of the city's political structure. Responsive to the public's needs, it took as its mandate the existing demand. Its function was to provide the people with light literature and with resources for economic betterment. The first report of the Chicago Public Library board sought funds for "novels, biography, history, or in other words, the cheaper literature of the day." From the beginning the library enjoyed a warm, popular response.[11]

Many commercial ventures into culture shared the public library's orientation to existing demand. Opera and theater productions (which few contemporaries would have called culture) had a known market and appealed to an established taste, while schools of music and orchestras sought support for an existing skill or service, perhaps in spite of an obvious absence of demand. Such efforts differed in form and quality, but what characterized them all was their ultimate dependence upon the market. Good, bad, or indifferent, they stood or fell by their box office receipts. Some sense of their extent can be surmised from *The Chicago Musical Directory, Season 1884-85,* an alphabetical and classified list of performers and music teachers, which ran to 108 pages. A significant example was the Philharmonic Society organized in 1860, which brought Hans Balatka from Milwaukee to head the orchestra. After eight years of concerts frequently attended by Chicago's social leaders, the orchestra folded, insolvent. This was only the last in a series of orchestral failures.[12]

Seemingly different from the commercial ventures were associations of artists such as the Vincennes Gallery of Fine Arts, formed to display paintings. But these societies differed only on the surface. In reality the artists' groups shared a market orientation, if one step removed. They subsisted not from box office receipts, but from the support of artists who needed display space and promotion to sell their paintings. If the galleries failed to attract eventual customers over too long a time, there was little reason to continue support.[13]

Ethnic groups within Chicago were vital centers for cultural interest and expression. Scattered throughout the city were associations of Germans, Scandinavians, and other national groups which met to share their cultural heritage. Their singing groups, especially, brought considerable numbers into active participation in the arts. The Orpheus Gesangverein, for example, had over three hundred members from among the city's German population as early as 1875. Local church choirs drew on their own communities, as did the best-known musical organization in the 1880s, the Apollo Club. Patterned after Boston's male chorus of the same name, the Apollo Club was organized in 1872 by Silas Gamaliel Pratt, a former Bostonian, and by the music critic George P. Upton. It drew its membership from the sons of native-born Protestants of predominantly British descent. Its primary purpose seems to have been the pleasure that similarly situated men had in singing together. While the society gave concerts, these were secondary, giving structure to choral practice and confirming the importance of the group to the community.[14]

Just as the Orpheus Gesangverein was only one of the many German organizations of the city, so the Apollo Club was just one of the many bringing together Chicago's native-born. In the predecessor of the Chicago Public Library, the Young Men's Association, men sharing these origins came together to form a subscription lending library. Those with an interest in Chicago's short past formed the Chicago Historical Society. The Chicago Academy of Sciences, with its small museum, was established by those who shared an enthusiasm for natural science.[15] All these organizations were created by members of some specific social group which shared a particular cultural interest. Although the musical associations gave concerts and the library and museum were open to all, they were intended primarily for the direct satisfaction of the men who initiated and sustained them.[16]

While the Chicago Academy of Sciences was like the Orpheus Gesangverein in that it brought together men of similar background in a common expression of interest, the two associations differed in a critical respect. The Gesangverein drew its membership from the German population; the Academy of Sciences, from the native born. J. Young Scammon, the president of the Marine Bank, and Eliphalet Wickes Blatchford, a wealthy lead manufacturer,

were among the native sons who joined together in 1856
to form a society for the promotion of scientific investigation. While not all their fellow academicians would share
their business success, the ethnic group to which Scammon
and Blatchford, as Protestants of British descent, belonged
would provide Chicago with most of its business and
professional leaders in the nineteenth century.[17] Yet the
difference between the members of the two cultural
organizations was not merely one of economic power. As
important were the less tangible distinctions of identification and prestige. Blatchford had arrived in Chicago
only in 1853; yet he nonetheless thought of himself as
part of the essential Chicago. He joined with other newcomers and the descendants of the first settlers in associations that would preserve the city's past and explore its
terrain. Others in the city recognized the claim of the
members of Blatchford's group: only those who were
Protestants of British (or possibly Huguenot) descent could
count socially within the city. These men and their
families formed a self-appointed elite who were recognized
by others as prominent citizens and social leaders.[18]

     Certain of the associations of the elite assumed a
responsibility for the whole community. These men
organized the Chicago Relief and Aid Society not to
provide direct security for members of their own group but
to organize help for all Chicago citizens. In 1857 it became
incorporated so that, unlike other such organizations, it
could receive support from the city council; moreover, it
had the use of city land rent-free. During the national
emergency of the Civil War, Blatchford called a meeting
to organize a northwestern branch of the Sanitary Commission to provide the Union army with medical facilities
and supplies. While Blatchford served as treasurer, the
prominent lawyers Mark Skinner and E. B. McCagg served
successively as president. Scammon joined with Walter
Newberry and W. B. Ogden, two of Chicago's wealthiest

and most prominent citizens, in contributing significant sums for the Sanitary Commission's work.[19]

Neither the statements of leaders of the northwestern branch nor its activities suggest the conscious elitism of the national leadership of the Sanitary Commission. In fact, the western organization's leaders were often at odds with their eastern counterparts.[20] Yet at a different level, elitism pervades. Blatchford, Skinner, and McCagg presumed that organizing aid for Union soldiers was their task.

At the end of the Civil War these men gradually began to extend their assumption of civic responsibility into culture. Walter L. Newberry, who had gained a fortune in real estate and railroad promotion, had been active in the Young Men's Association and the Chicago Historical Society and had been, as well, a collector of art and books. At his death in 1868 he left one-half of his estate to establish a library in Chicago and named Mark Skinner and E. W. Blatchford as executors. The provision of life use by Newberry's wife delayed the founding of the library for seventeen years.[21] During this time a new cultural climate was created.

The Great Fire of 1871 was partly responsible. In two days much of the city lay devastated. Included in the loss from the fire were private collections of art and books and the slender resources of organizations such as the Young Men's Association and the Chicago Academy of Sciences. After the immediate provisions for medical aid, shelter, and food came the need to rebuild. Chicago's recovery was extraordinary: within a year a new city of brick and stone had arisen. The heroism and communal spirit of the fire days became a matter of legend, and they rekindled memories of the pioneer past and generated a new burst of civic enthusiasm.[22]

There was talk of a jubilee to celebrate the city's recovery from the Great Fire, and there was great interest in promoting Chicago manufactures. The two motives were combined in the Inter-State Industrial Exposition. Financed by subscription, it attracted money from some of the city's most prominent businessmen. The relatively obscure original promoters, John B. Drake, George S. Bowen, and John Irving Pierce, withdrew to the background as Potter Palmer, Chicago's leading hotel owner and real estate dealer, headed a board of directors that included bank presidents and merchants. In its first years the exposition was, as its name suggested, an industrial fair, highlighting equipment and inventions. But within the Inter-State Industrial Exposition were seeds that would prove significant for the development of the city's cultural institutions.[23]

First of all was the mode of its promotion. The men behind the exposition attempted to sell the shares of stock by billing them as a civic as well as an economic investment. Seeking the widest possible support among those able to contribute, they argued that the fair would not only bring profit, it would contribute to the city's general well-being. A measure of the success of their promotional campaign was the exposition's location. Convinced that the corporation was of a public nature, the city allowed the exposition to build on city land in the lake front area that had been set aside as a park.[24]

The fair became an established Chicago institution, held in September of each year. By 1877 it was paying its stockholders a 6 percent dividend. But more important for our purposes, its nature had begun to change. While industry still held primary interest, there was a natural history exhibit prepared by the Chicago Academy of Sciences and an art department. Organized by the dynamic Sara Hallowell, a Chicagoan living in Paris, the annual exhibition of paintings displayed the work of prominent American artists and brought to the United States paintings by the Barbizon School and the Impressionists.[25] But it was the form of the art department, not the art displayed, that commands attention. As a part of a larger profitable enterprise, the show did not have to pay its way. A lay board could hire an expert to exercise his own judgment in selecting works of art, free from the necessity to attract or please an audience. The exhibition was, in fact, a popular part of the exposition, but it did not have to be.

Miss Hallowell was supported by the art committee of the Inter-State Industrial Exposition, whose membership by the early 1880s reflected a new development in Chicago's cultural life: the board was composed of men who had taken charge of the Chicago Academy of Design and were moving it in new directions. The academy, an artists' association that had been incorporated in 1869, had established a class of membership without power for those willing to pay. It was here that the assumption of communal responsibility for culture by members of Chicago's elite first surfaced. By 1874 leading business and professional men had contributed $100 each to become fellows of the academy: William T. Baker, John M. Clark, R. T. Crane, James H. Dole, Nathaniel K. Fairbank, E. B. McCagg, and Mark Skinner were among the prominent names. In 1878 the academy reorganized with some of these men joining others newly involved to form the board of trustees. When they discovered in 1879 undisclosed debts owed by the academy, the trustees resigned as a body and called a meeting to organize a new society "for the general objects and purposes embraced within the aim and scope of the old organization" but unencumbered by financial obligations and artists.[26] Maintaining responsibility for an art school, in 1882 the new trustees elected Charles L. Hutchinson president, changed the association's name to the Art Institute of Chicago, moved to a handsome building, and signaled their "intention of establishing a permanent Museum of Art."[27]

The Inter-State Industrial Exposition was housed in

what was for the time an enormous structure of brick
and glass. It had literally acres of exhibition space. While
the fair itself lasted only two weeks of the year, the building remained—an open opportunity. What its use was to
be, however, was unclear. After a fire at Field and Leiter,
Marshall Field (one of the exposition stockholders) got
the directors' permission to use the building as a ware-
house for his goods, despite some question whether such
private occupancy was appropriate. But certain stockholders, interested citizens, and entrepreneurs foresaw a
different kind of use, one that did not have to argue its
legitimacy. In 1877 the Theodore Thomas Orchestra
began its annual summer garden concerts, playing to delighted Chicago audiences a combination of light and
symphonic music. Four years later a different kind of
enterprise was undertaken, the Chicago Biennial Musical
Festival Association. Designed on the pattern of similar
New York and Cincinnati festivals and drawing on the
talents and popularity of Theodore Thomas, musically it
was a new departure for Chicago. Its officers were those
men of the native-born elite who were assuming a responsibility for culture: Nathaniel K. Fairbank, lard manufacturer and stockholder in the Inter-State Industrial
Exposition, served as president; Philo A. Otis, a leader in
the Apollo Club, as secretary. They successfully sought
subscriptions to the association from George E. Adams,
William T. Baker, Marshall Field, Lyman J. Gage, Charles
D. Hamill, Charles L. Hutchinson, and Franklin Mac-
Veagh, among a host of others.[28]
     Festival backers lost money in 1882 and again in 1884.
The festival closed, but seemingly not because of its
deficits. Rather the exposition building proved too cold
and drafty for performers and audience alike. But in
contrast to what happened after the earlier failures of
musical enterprises, the group behind the festival did not
withdraw. Many of the same sponsors united to establish

another musical series, the Chicago Grand Opera Festival. The principal promoter was Ferdinand W. Peck, a youthful son of Chicago wealth. His interest was, at least in part, commercial. What he had in mind and executed was a vast opera house built within the Inter-State Industrial Exposition building. At the cost of $60,000, Dankmar Adler and Louis Sullivan designed the inner structure. The initial opera season of fourteen consecutive performances proved a commercial success, bringing a handsome profit to its backers. At the annual meeting of the Festival Association plans were broached for a consolidation of these gains, the construction of a great hall for the performing arts. Four years later Chicago celebrated the dedication of the Auditorium.[29]

At a cost of four million dollars, the Auditorium provided a physical setting for Chicago's cultural life. Located on Michigan Avenue near the exposition building, the mammoth stone structure designed by Adler and Sullivan housed an assembly hall seating 4,000, an office building, a hotel, and banquet facilities. The Auditorium was promoted as a profit-making, as well as a philanthropic, enterprise, and it was. But significant for our purposes, it drew together a wide body of stockholders who were to unite again and again for less-commercial-minded endeavors.[30]

From a base of Chicago Opera Festival Association members, Ferdinand Peck extended his net to the Commercial Club, a body of the leading civic-minded businessmen in the city. Speaking at an 1886 meeting, he discussed investment in the Auditorium and got strong support. Five hundred leading citizens and firms subscribed. Though the base of the Auditorium Association was much broader, the list included those businessmen who were trustees of the Art Institute, backers of the Biennial Musical Festival, and active members of the cultural associations of the native-born elite.[31]

Within the next three decades groups of these men would come together to establish, support, and direct the Chicago Symphony Orchestra, the University of Chicago, the World's Columbian Exposition, the Field Columbian Museum, and the Newberry and the Crerar libraries. At the end of the period the most active among them would be aware that they were a part of a group engaged in a common cultural and civic endeavor.

The founding of the Chicago Symphony Orchestra came directly out of the Biennial Musical Festival and the special work of Charles Norman Fay. A member of a family with strong musical traditions and the brother of two accomplished musicians, Fay was an early telephone executive. Beginning in 1879 he encouraged Theodore Thomas to bring his orchestra to Chicago; but it was not until Thomas had despaired of establishing a permanent orchestra in New York and there was a corps of men in Chicago willing to guarantee support that Fay's offer was taken seriously. Whether pledges were taken at a Commercial Club outing or less dramatically through separate solicitation, the group pooled was the same: Commercial Club members led by those active in the Biennial Musical Festival. Fairbank again served as president, now of the Orchestral Association; and Otis began his long tenure as secretary.[32]

The University of Chicago is a special case and one that reveals the developing sense of responsibility for culture among the city's elite. Baptist leaders in the Chicago area were unwilling to accept the failure of their college, Chicago University, and kept alive the hope of establishing a strong, financially stable institution in its stead. Enlisting the enthusiasm of a young Chautauqua official and professor of Hebrew at Yale, William Rainey Harper, they successfully channeled into the endowment of such a school John D. Rockefeller's wish to put some of his resources to the service of his faith. Cautious businessman that he was, Rockefeller gave no money out-right, but demanded that his gift be matched. From the beginning it was understood that campus buildings were the responsibility of Chicago donors. The initial response of the Chicago Baptist promoters was to go to their denomination for support. But apathy and the limited resources of the Baptist community forced a new approach, a turn to Chicago's largely non-Baptist business com-munity, requiring the redefinition of the university as a Chicago, not a denominational, enterprise.[33]

The first intimation of success came when the pro-moters called on Charles L. Hutchinson, in 1889 president of the Commercial Club (as well as of the Art Institute), who promised that the matter of the university would come before the next meeting of the club. As Thomas W. Goodspeed, the secretary of the Baptist Convention, wrote to his sons, "We feel that this is a great triumph and will open the door to that class of men into whose sympathies we have been for two months trying to devise a plan of entrance." The results were successful. Chicago businessmen joined local Baptists in contributing the $400,000 necessary to secure Rockefeller's gift.

The change in the university's constituency was to be a permanent one. Quite consciously the selection of the board of trustees brought together the non-Baptist Chicago business community with Baptists from Chicago and elsewhere. A non-Baptist, Martin Ryerson, the in-heritor of a fortune made in lumber, was chosen president of the board as a man "universally respected, with plenty of leisure, with great wealth, liberal, very close to the wealthiest & most liberal citizens." "They [influential people] think it will do more than anything else we could do to help us in our coming appeal for the building fund."[34] As Goodspeed summed up the situation, "We shall have in the responsible financial positions three of the lead-ing young business men of the city. — Ryerson, Peck, &

Hutchinson, & we shall then have a pull on the wealth of Chicago that we can get in no other way. Those three men can raise more money than any other three men in Chicago."[35]

The World's Columbian Exposition offered the first, often surprised, view of these developments to outsiders. The demonstration was graphic: those brave enough to keep their eyes open on the Ferris wheel could see the buildings of the University of Chicago emerging from the mud. Within the city, the fair served largely to confirm and reinforce the assumption of responsibility for culture by Chicago's elite begun with the Newberry bequest. The wealth of the city launched the fair by pledging ten million dollars and by purchasing blocks of stock (85 percent of which turned out to be contributions). The body of stockholders chose the Directory, a board whose powers included authority over everything but the nature of the collections within the buildings and the awarding of prizes. Most significant for Chicago's cultural institutions, despite their large investment many of the older business and civic leaders withdrew and turned responsibility over to the younger and more energetic business and professional men who were emerging as leaders of the Art Institute, the Chicago Symphony Orchestra, and the University of Chicago.[36] The fair was a critical moment for these men, for it seemed to announce that Chicago had arrived as a cultural center. The men involved in cultural endeavors were quite anxious that they not be embarrassed by Chicago's show. Charles Hutchinson, visiting in New York City, noted in his diary, "How much beyond Chicago, was new York." He felt that "perhaps after all we had made a mistake in undertaking the 'World's Fair.' "[37] The existence of the national Commission competing for authority and the need for speed forced the concentration of power into the hands of a capable administrator, Daniel Burnham. Active work was limited to a small board of representatives from the Directory and the Commission. But Burnham was close to members of the Directory, and the results of his work fully harmonized with the Chicago backers' hopes and confirmed a sense that the fair's achievement was theirs.[38]

The foundation of a permanent collection drawing on the scientific exhibits of the exposition was discussed from the earliest planning stages. As the fair came to a close, serious consideration led to action, and a meeting was held to elicit public support. Harlow Higinbotham, the president of the Directory, argued successfully that a new institution be created, separate from the existing Chicago Academy of Sciences. The issue was not insolvency resulting from artist or denominational control, as in the case of the Academy of Design or the old Chicago University, but stagnation from a lack of momentum. The Academy of Sciences was still run as a gentlemen's scientific club by the older generation of business and civic leaders, who were now being outdistanced by the drive and economic resources of younger counterparts. Ezra B. McCagg expressed his sense of the generational difference in a letter to Charles Hutchinson, who had written the older man to encourage his support of the Art Institute: "It has seemed to me that the work of this kind to be done in this city . . . must devolve upon younger men than I am and to a large extent upon men who have not had their enthusiasm burned out of them. The fire of 1871 destroyed whatever I had set my heart on as however weak in itself yet perhaps the seed corns which in the end would bring a harvest, and left it all to be begun over again, and lame and weary and nearly hopeless I dropped out—and I think may not begin again."[39] For McCagg the issues were the Great Fire and age. But as important as these in causing the change in leadership was a new element called into being by the new purposes the cultural

institutions were being designed to serve: active involvement demanded economic resources greater than many
of the older generation of leaders or their sons could supply.

In two institutions this does not seem to have been
the case. To a greater degree than elsewhere, the Newberry
and the Crerar libraries drew on the services of the older
generation or men like them—prominent men of substance,
but not necessarily among Chicago's most wealthy: since
both libraries were funded by sizable bequests, there was
no necessity to seek financial contributors as trustees.[40]
This difference between the libraries' boards and those of
other institutions would be reflected in the libraries' distinct tone and programs.

That responsibility for culture was, like relief or medical aid to Union soldiers, assumed to be the prerogative
of the city's native-born elite, can be seen in the choice of
trustees. Only rarely does a name appear of one outside
the relatively small group of Protestant native-born sons
of predominantly British descent.[41] Selection was hardly
a matter of chance. The executors of the wills of Walter
L. Newberry and John Crerar chose the libraries' boards.
For the institutions without such arrangements, choice
could still be within a few hands. Edward E. Ayer, whose
fortune was made in supplying lumber for railroad ties,
helped Sidney C. Eastman, the secretary pro tem of the
future Field Columbian Museum, make out a list of
trustees. If men such as Norman Ream, Marshall Field,
Martin Ryerson, and George Pullman on Eastman's list
failed to accept, Ayer suggested in their stead "John
Mitchell, of the Ill. Trust & Savings Bank, John Black,
the banker, John Walsh, H. H. Patterson, of the Tribune,
and Mr. Kohlsaat of the Inter Ocean." Unlike the board
members of the Chicago Public Library these men were
suggested not because they represented diverse groups
within the community, but because they were known and
respected within one group, the native-born elite.[42]

Yet not all Chicago business or professional men with the proper ethnic and economic qualifications were considered. For example, one does not see the name of Gustauvus Swift on a list of potential trustees. Perhaps his exclusion was his own choice, for men did refuse positions. Martin Ryerson and Marshall Field, for example, initially rejected the appeals of the Field Columbian Museum only to become major contributors later. And Cyrus McCormick and E. B. McCagg, who had served in other institutions, were unwilling to become Newberry trustees.[43] But expected refusal is not enough to explain why some men were not chosen. A certain kind of man was asked even if his acceptance was unlikely. For example, though it was anticipated that George Pullman would not accept a position as trustee for the Field "on account of his being too much occupied," it was suggested to Ayer that "it would be a matter of good policy to extend the invitation to him."[44]

It is clear that the native-born elite generally felt a special obligation to provide culture for the city and that there was also a process of selection going on, determining who among this group were acceptable candidates to assume the responsibility. Moreover, by the late nineteenth century certain men were in a position to do the choosing. They were relatively few in number and, like Ayer, tended to be active in organizing, promoting, supporting, and directing a variety of cultural endeavors. By the turn of the century these few men had a sense of mission, as a special fraternity working for culture in Chicago. Such a sense was conveyed to Andrew Carnegie, who wrote to Charles Hutchinson: "Our friend Mr. Ayer was fellow passenger & filled me with interest and admiration for the good work a band of you—all cordial friends— are doing for Chicago. . . . Your name was often mentioned by Mr Ayer as one of the elect."[45]

There are many parallels between the new cultural

enterprises and the ethnically based societies such as the Apollo Club or the Chicago Academy of Sciences. The Apollo Club's membership appears to have been restricted. Clublike and group-affirming aspects were never to be absent from cultural undertakings; and, if anything, the restrictive quality of cultural involvement was to grow more pronounced in the late nineteenth century. Nor was the ability of the Apollo Club to set aesthetic standards, to base its selection of works upon an understanding of what was of value, lost to the later generation. Yet in an essential respect the institutions established in the late nineteenth century differed: those who created and sustained them felt a sense of community responsibility for culture. Although, as we shall see, there were limits to their conception of the public, the trustees of the Art Institute and the Chicago Symphony Orchestra designed the institutions to offer culture to the wider community for what was thought to be its benefit.

While it would seem that the Chicago Public Library with its direct appeal to the masses could have served as a model for the newer enterprises, the library had a fundamentally different relation to the community. Its leadership, in its ethnic and neighborhood diversity, reflected the political forces at work in the city, in sharp contrast to the Art Institute's exclusiveness. Moreover, the Chicago Public Library felt a commitment to meet its constituents' demands, and thus abdicated any responsibility for shaping cultural choices.

The commercial ventures into culture, because of their need to make a profit, seem at the farthest remove from the philanthropically supported cultural institutions. But as the sense of communal responsibility for culture took shape in the 1870s and 1880s, it was these entrepreneurial undertakings that provided the dynamic force. The Inter-State Industrial Exposition, the Chicago Academy of Design, the Biennial Musical Festival, and the Auditorium established a core of leaders with resources and commitment to bring a new sense of scale and importance to the cultural enterprise. No longer content with enjoying their taste within their own group, certain members of the native-born elite assumed responsibility for shaping the cultural opportunities of Chicago as a whole.

Establishing museums, libraries, a symphony orchestra, and a university involved more than the simple extension of civic obligation. The band that included Edward Ayer and Charles Hutchinson shared significant elements of background and common experience in the Chicago of the late nineteenth century. Cultural philanthropy became an instrument these men used to come to terms with the hopes and fears they held for their city.

3

The Cultural Philanthropists

It was Charles L. Hutchinson above all whose career epitomized cultural philanthropy. By the twentieth century he was recognized as the leader of the men who were financing and setting policy for the city-wide cultural institutions of Chicago.[1] His position did not arise from any special qualities or unusual degree of personal magnetism. Rather Hutchinson's was a primacy among peers. Unusual only in the inclusiveness of his involvement in culture, Hutchinson shared background, experiences, and way of life with the other business and professional men involved in cultural promotion. To understand why these men went beyond their ethnic associations to establish and support city-wide institutions, we must look not only at their personal interests but also at their special position in Chicago.

Charles Hutchinson was born in Lynn, Massachusetts, in 1854, the eldest son of Benjamin and Sarah Ingalls Hutchinson, both natives of New England.[2] Business reverses and the hope for broader economic opportunity drew Benjamin Hutchinson to Chicago, where he moved with his family in 1858. Within a short period he was established as a grain trader, meat-packer, and banker. He was one of the principal owners of the Chicago Packing and Provision Company, an organizer of the Traders Insurance Company, and the effective owner of the Corn Exchange Bank. It was as a speculator that Benjamin Hutchinson gained his greatest prominence. Known as "Old Hutch," he became legendary for his ruthlessness and skill. In September 1888 he cornered the wheat market, bringing in what was estimated to be over a million dollars. Recognizable by his distinctive slouch hat, he was the first man on the floor of the Board of Trade each day and the last off. Hard-driving, hard-drinking, he was an extreme example of the aggressive, single-minded business-man of the Gilded Age.[3]

In the 1870s and 1880s Benjamin Hutchinson passed over his enterprises to his son Charles. In 1874 he estab-lished the firm B. P. Hutchinson and Son, Commission Merchants, and Charles Hutchinson became a member of the Board of Trade. (When the firm was dissolved in 1888–1889, the younger Hutchinson remained on the Board of Trade and served as its president in that year.) Increasingly, however, Charles was shifting his interest to another of his father's enterprises, the Corn Exchange Bank. After a term as assistant cashier, he became pres-ident of the bank in 1886, a post he was to hold for the next twelve years. Like other businessmen of the period he also served as director or officer in a variety of other corporations in the city.

The elder Hutchinson could give to his son his eco-nomic enterprises, but not his own spirit. Charles's early desire to follow his intellectual interests was thwarted when his father refused to let him attend college, insisting that he remain in Chicago and enter business. But as the youth grew to be a man, there was little his father could do to change his quite different nature. When he came of age Charles received $25,000 from his father and

invested it. He lost part of the capital but learned a lesson
he never forgot. During the time his father was risking
his fortune on the Board of Trade, Charles Hutchinson
turned away from speculative enterprises and, for the rest
of his life, remained a cautious, conservative investor.
This was of a piece with his business career. Though
active for several decades, Hutchinson was a singularly
undramatic trader, investor, and banker. There were no
grain corners, no big wins or losses. It was a career
dedicated to conserving, rather than making, money; and
it was a career dedicated to giving it away.

As the years passed, Hutchinson became increasingly
involved in philanthropic endeavors. The extent of his
contributions is staggering. After Hutchinson's death
Thomas Wakefield Goodspeed went over a list of Hutchinson's organizational ties: of at least seventy separate
organizations (and Goodspeed felt that the number was
too low) "he was a contributing member or an officer. Of
half a dozen he was president. Of twenty or more he was
treasurer. He was a director or trustee of more than forty."
These organizations ranged from religious to charitable to
cultural. To them Hutchinson gave his time and money.
It has been estimated that Hutchinson gave away each
year over half his income. In 1898 he resigned as president
of the Corn Exchange Bank to assume the less-demanding
office of vice president, giving himself more time for
philanthropic activity.[4]

Of Hutchinson's many and varied endeavors, it was
his work with cultural agencies that distinguished his
career. When the Chicago Academy of Fine Arts was
reorganized in 1879, he became one of the trustees. Three
years later he was chosen president of the Art Institute,
as it was renamed. He was to hold this office during the
crucial years when the institution shaped its goals and
assumed definite form, relinquishing it only with his death
in 1924. Hutchinson was also a member of the art com-

mittee of the Inter-State Industrial Exposition.[5] When the Chicago Symphony Orchestra was organized in 1890, he was one of its backers. Among the first non-Baptist enthusiasts for the University of Chicago, he joined its original board and assumed the office of treasurer. As a supporter of the World's Columbian Exposition, Hutchinson naturally headed the Fine Arts Department of the Directory, as well as serving more generally as subscriber and guarantor. He was an original organizer of the Field Columbian Museum.

Hutchinson was most closely identified with the Art Institute. Its oversight became, by his last decades, the most important activity of his still busy day. Years later the museum's director recalled Hutchinson's schedule. Arriving at the museum at nine, he met with the director and then took a tour of the galleries and school. At eleven, he went to the Corn Exchange Bank, largely to transact his other philanthropy. He generally returned to the Art Institute in the afternoon, and frequently in the evening as well, for committee work, lectures, or social events.[6]

In Hutchinson's enjoyment of the fine arts his personal and public life merged. He had married Frances Kinsley, the daughter of Chicago's famous restaurateur, a woman who shared many of his interests. Childless, the couple traveled a good deal, frequently with Hutchinson's closest friend Martin A. Ryerson and his wife. Together the two men would search for acquisitions for their personal collections as well as for the Art Institute and the Field Columbian Museum. Once back in Chicago, Hutchinson could enjoy his choices as he went through his daily routine. He formed other close friendships with similarly inclined men of his social circle, such as the lumber dealer Edward E. Ayer, who had a superb collection of Indian antiquities and Americana and was active in the Art Institute and the Newberry Library, and the wholesale grocer Albert A. Sprague, who was a trustee of the Art Institute and a member of the Orchestral Association. In his daily round of business affairs, organization meetings, and receptions, followed by dinner and a concert or play. Hutchinson would encounter men who shared his social background, business involvement, and cultural interests.[7]

Moreover, Hutchinson and others like him could socialize with artists and scholars in the Cliff Dwellers, a private club that brought creators and philanthropists together. But long before its founding in 1907, Chicago's culturally inclined businessmen included local artists in their social gatherings. Robert Morss Lovett recalled "the hospitality of a section of the merchant aristocracy" during his early days at the University of Chicago: "Families of Spragues, Bartletts, Glessners, McCormicks exercised a kindly patronage." Charles Hutchinson had the novelist Henry Blake Fuller to dine and enjoyed a continuing relationship with Robert Herrick. In the twentieth century some of the children of those active in cultural philanthropy would bridge the two worlds, and the heirs would become artists, as did Frederick Clay Bartlett and Mary Aldis.[8]

What motivated Charles Hutchinson to lead this kind of life? The simplest part of the explanation is that he had an abiding love for the fine arts, especially painting. He was no connoisseur, nor was he avant-garde; but throughout his life, under the tutelage of Ryerson, a man of excellent taste and judgment, Hutchinson tried to learn about art and to broaden his appreciation. Refined taste did not come naturally. Hutchinson's father hardly shared his son's aesthetic interests. He was said to have commented on Charles's purchase of a French painting of a sheep meadow: "Think about him! A son of mine! He paid $500 apiece for five painted sheep and he could get the real article for $2 a head!"[9]

Whatever Hutchinson was to learn about art came

through his mother's influence and his own efforts. His wedding trip through Canada to New York City and Boston, like the regular tours of Europe, North Africa, and India later in his life, was an exercise in the acquisition of taste. In the United States or abroad, organized cultural institutions—museums, galleries, parks, cemeteries, churches, and concert-halls—were his primary teachers. On his honeymoon Hutchinson would go to the Metropolitan Museum, Central Park, and the Lenox Library in New York; in Boston he would visit the Museum of Fine Arts, Trinity Church, and Forest Hills Cemetery. In Paris it would be shops, galleries, and the concert-hall, as well as the studios of Mary Cassatt and other painters. At least to some extent, Hutchinson's involvement in the cultural institutions of Chicago was an expression of his aesthetic yearnings. It was, at the same time, a measure of the distance the son had traveled from the father. From early in the nineteenth century patricians had distinguished themselves from the newly rich by the mark of culture. For the son of an eccentric speculator who wished to see himself, and to be seen, as a gentleman, the route was clear. Each trip taken, each painting acquired, each book read testified to the son's established position.[10]

Hutchinson was unusual both in the degree of his appreciation of the arts and in the extent of his leisure. At the other end of the spectrum were the self-made businessmen whose lives had been, in large measure, devoted to establishing themselves. Yet many of these men wanted involvement in the cultural life of their time and city. They shared with Hutchinson a sense of their position which encouraged their support of the arts. While the image of the industrial buccaneer spurred the popular imagination, these men were actually modeling their lives after a different ideal. They held up for admiration the businessman who was honest in his dealings, bound by strong domestic ties, and unselfish in his dedication to

public causes. To add to this portrait refinement of taste
and interest in the arts and letters would only give the
final evidence of personal worth. These men offer a
striking challenge to the usual judgment that culture
was a feminine preserve in nineteenth-century America.
P. D. Armour may have indeed offered the often-quoted
pronouncement, "My culture is mostly in my wife's name";
but such was the way of one outside. While women took
active roles in cultural affairs in Chicago, their husbands'
positions as trustees came naturally as an expression of
masculine responsibility for culture.[11]

The sense of the good life of these businessmen
carries with it strong New England overtones—the feeling
of an established elite that might be expected among
Boston's older merchant families. To some extent it is
explicable from the New England origins of many of
these businessmen. Of those whose family histories are
known, approximately one-half trace their beginnings back
to New England. In the inner circle of the ten men most
active in cultural affairs in Chicago, four had permanent
summer homes in New England.[12] Education at Harvard
or Yale may have had a strong shaping force, both initially
and as alumni ties were kept alive. George E. Adams
was graduated from Harvard College and Law School in
the 1860s and at the turn of the century served as Overseer.
After an education in Europe, Martin A. Ryerson received
his law degree from Harvard in 1878. Franklin MacVeagh,
Albert A. Sprague, Edson Keith, and George Manierre
were Yale graduates. William Rainey Harper, who played
a variety of roles in Chicago's cultural life, came to the
University of Chicago presidency from a Yale professorship and held a Yale doctorate.

In addition to this direct contact and identification,
members of Chicago's first generation (many of whom had
come from New England) exerted their influence on
the city's new men. Paradoxically, it was the very forces

making for change in the city which strengthened the hold of this older tradition. The businessman of American-born parents who came to Chicago around the time of the Civil War and made a fortune in one of Chicago's great industries quickly identified with his new city's established elite. Whatever difference this new generation of businessmen felt between itself and the old guard was lost when it confronted the other latecomers to the city.[13] Even when its population reached the million mark, Chicago had a small-town feeling. One observer commented that the city had not broken with its early days when "Chicago folk knew one another and, to a decent extent, one another's business." This atmosphere existed because the "Chicago folk" to which he was referring consisted of only one-fifth of the population, those who were of native-born parents.[14]

The successful businessmen of this fifth were brought closer together by Chicago clubs, the social and semi-political organizations whose names crowd individual biographies of the period. Such clubs as the Union League, the Iroquois, the Chicago, the Calumet, the Commercial, and the University did not serve as means of withdrawal from public life. Rather, by bringing their members into webs of relationships, they spread the values of the old guard to the more recently arrived who might otherwise have remained totally absorbed in business. In so doing they won acceptance for a model of the good life which included respect for the arts and letters as well as for public service.[15]

The extent of membership among those most involved in Chicago's cultural institutions is astounding.[16] All belonged to these clubs; and they averaged nearly eight memberships apiece. Whereas membership in the large and prestigious Chicago Club was almost universal, it may have been the Commercial Club that played the most significant role in cultural development. Not only

were two-thirds of the men most active in cultural philanthropy members, but over one-third served as president.
The club directly sponsored the creation of the Manual
Training School in 1882 and after the Haymarket Riot
gave land for a United States army base near the city.
Until the twentieth century, when it underwrote the
development and early promotion of the Burnham Plan,
the Commercial Club was not to be directly engaged in
culture. But its monthly programs served as a forum for
spokesmen seeking support for cultural institutions from
1880, when the subject for consideration on one program
was "Should not the commercial prosperity of great cities
be attended by the cultivation of art, literature, science,
and comprehensive charities, and the establishment of art
museums, public libraries, industrial schools and free
hospitals?" The plan for the Auditorium was first put
forth at a Commercial Club meeting in 1886; the proposal
that a permanent building be erected for the World's
Columbian Exposition to become the future home of the
Art Institute was a subject for discussion in 1890; the
University of Chicago came before the club in a critical
move for local support; and the Commercial Club may
have been the gathering place where initial backing of the
Chicago Symphony Orchestra was won.[17]

Those businessmen who loved the arts and letters and
those who saw them as a part of the good life joined
together in associations for their promotion. In itself, this
impulse was not new in 1890; it had sustained the cultural
organizations of various groups for decades. The membership of the Apollo Club, the Academy of Sciences, and
the Chicago Historical Society was composed of those of
the native-born elite who valued culture and sought the
satisfactions of companionship and self-expression according to their accepted canons of scholarship and taste. But
the Art Institute was not an institution like the Chicago
Academy of Sciences. It accepted standards, to be sure,

but it was designed for the whole city, not for the select few. Charles Hutchinson went to the art museum not only to meet friends and to share in aesthetic experiences; he went also as the head of a sizable enterprise that sought ever wider support and ever greater involvement in the community. To understand what motivated him and the others like him who served the varied cultural institutions of the city, one must look beyond aesthetic yearnings and sense of the good life to explore those aspects of the social situation that channeled the drive for culture into civic institutions.

The businessmen active in Chicago's city-wide cultural institutions were, like Charles Hutchinson, men of substantial wealth. Their contemporaries regarded them as among the economic leaders of the city. Most of them were in the great traditional business establishments of Chicago: the gathering, processing, and channeling of agricultural products; the distribution of manufactures; and the supply of credit, real estate, and basic goods to Chicago's enterprises and to its residents. For example, Charles L. Hutchinson and Watson F. Blair were in grain and banking, Martin A. Ryerson and Edward E. Ayer in lumber, N. K. Fairbank in lard and banking, Harlow N. Higinbotham in department store retailing, Albert A. Sprague and Franklin MacVeagh in wholesale groceries. These enterprises had a distinctive identification with Chicago. The city's geographical location, both as the center of a vast agricultural hinterland and as a focus of transportation lines, supported the concentration of processing and distribution that emerged. Especially after the railroad lines were built, Chicago seemed uniquely suited for the kind of enterprise in which it excelled. For example, New York could not serve as a gathering point for western meat; nor until the end of the century could Kansas City or Saint Louis offer Chicago's speed, convenience, and credit to an eastern purchaser. Neither could New York distribute finished goods to western consumers.[18] Chicago was in a special position as the primary link between East and West.

The newer manufactures and forms of power would continue Chicago's favored situation into the twentieth century. As the port to which Minnesota iron could best be brought to Illinois coal, Chicago was the ideal spot for the processing of steel; and when electricity came into use, Chicago became the center of the regional power pool.[19] Perhaps Chicago's special advantages were the basis of what seems to have been the unusual economic security of its businessmen in the traditional industries. Though sources on wealth are relatively sketchy, the men who became active in cultural institutions seem to have been able to sustain their philanthropy in what were for many rather unstable times. And who could predict the future? With Chicago's population growing at such a rapid rate, perhaps the city might overtake New York to become the economic—and cultural—capital of the nation.

Yet a new dynamic was at work in the late nineteenth century, altering the nature of the economy and creating tensions between local and national ties. Combination was generating a national economic leadership at a wholly new level of economic power. Some of the men who emerged at the head of business empires built from a base in Chicago: Cyrus McCormick, Marshall Field, George Pullman, and Gustauvus Swift. But for most of the businessmen in the traditional Chicago industries, combination was a mixed blessing. On the one hand, they were in a position to profit from a merger or take-over by another company or from the investments that some of the new combines offered. To a considerable degree the businessmen took advantage of these opportunities, as their positions as directors, for example, of the Great Northern Trust and the Pullman Company would indicate. Yet despite the economic rewards, by creating a rung higher than they could climb, consolidation may have threatened some Chicago-based businessmen with a relative loss of prestige. Moreover, the establishment of national offices, frequently in New York, was draining economic leadership from the city: the address list of the Commercial Club gives evidence of the movement of some Chicago businessmen to New York.[20]

But more important, involvement in national combinations may have created a conflict between local and national ties. Unlike those who did leave the city, those businessmen who became active in culture were wedded to Chicago. Not only were their businesses strongly linked to the city, but also their prestige was based on their role in the city as economic and social leaders. Their identification with Chicago was not a historic or family one: only one of the businessmen who became active in culture before 1900 was born in the city. Most came to Chicago in their young manhood and made their fortunes there. Yet the city was more than just a place to transact business, for while others were migrating to the elegant suburbs developing to the north, these businessmen chose to remain within the city. They built lavish residences on and near Prairie Avenue just south of the business district and on the increasingly fashionable streets of the Near North Side. Significantly, in the years after 1900 when Prairie Avenue was losing its prestige and its value as real estate, many of these men chose to remain rather than join the movement outward.[21]

The feeling of strain between their own positions as business and social leaders within Chicago and the pressures of consolidation may have created a need within them to identify ever more strongly with the city. This need may have been a chief support for the boasting for which Chicago was well known, but it also was a motivating force behind the drive to make Chicago meet their boasts. The city would be best in all areas, including its cultural

life. The loyalty of these men was one impetus behind
the establishment of city-wide cultural institutions.

Along with economic growth, Chicago's most striking
characteristic was its ethnic heterogeneity. Some of the
immigrants and their children were achieving success in
business, including a few, such as the German Jewish meat-
packer Nelson Morris, whose wealth was on a par with
that accumulated by the heads of other Chicago houses
of the great traditional enterprises. Those businessmen
who became actively involved in cultural philanthropy in
the late nineteenth century, however, were almost exclu-
sively white Protestants whose ancestors were predominantly British. To designate the businessmen as an elite
then is to point both to their relative wealth and to their
ethnic background, which in the Chicago context contributed to their economic and social power.[22]

In the Chicago of the 1890s the economic and social
power of the business leaders could not be translated
directly into local political power. In the 1840s business
leaders had headed every phase of Chicago life, including
politics. They were the constitution builders and the first
city officials. However, as the early issues were resolved
to their satisfaction and as economic activity demanded
more of their time, these men withdrew from the political
arena, giving way to the representatives of the newer ethnic
groups in the city that were seeking political recognition.
The consolidation of city machines limited the role of
amateurs whose vocation lay in business rather than politics.
While at various points the businessmen banded together
to support one of their own (most notably in 1881 when
five hundred backed the candidacy of leather manufacturer
John M. Clark), such attempts to gain office required
alliance with machine bosses and were rarely successful.
In their own wards prominent business or professional
leaders of native-born parents might win seats on the city

council as "silk stockings," but they would find themselves outnumbered by the representatives of other wards. On a state or federal level they might hold elective or appointed posts: George E. Adams served as United States senator and congressman; Lambert Tree was minister to Belgium and Russia. But government in the city was largely in the hands of the professionals, often Irish and German, who served the ethnic groups of their wards.[23]

The implications of these local political developments were profound. In the late nineteenth century, officials in municipal government were making decisions of crucial importance to business. Changes in urban life had created a new level of needs that a new technology was increasingly able to meet. As roads were paved, streetcar lines built, municipal buildings and schools erected, Chicago's existing companies and those designed for the purpose sought contracts and franchises to provide the desired goods and services. In the process they competed for privileges with each other and with the public interest. The control of city decisions became a matter of economic importance. Some businessmen able to command great resources, but cut out of legitimate political representation, could buy political decisions on matters that vitally affected their purses. The corruption they supported turned democratically elected representatives into their personal tools and created an atmosphere that other businessmen were finding intolerable.[24]

Furthermore, the changes that brought increasing wealth and a swelling labor force left in their wake immense social and economic problems. For many this meant deprivation and economic insecurity. Business leaders in the late nineteenth century experienced the pervading fear that the population would go out of control. The labor strife that began in the 1870s gave credence to these fears. Riots in 1877 brought business in the city to a momentary standstill, and violence against property and persons panicked members of the employing classes. The Citizens Association, a reform organization formed in 1874 to promote fire protection, raised $30,000 for the local militia and urged passage of laws providing adequate tax support for such forces. Two-thirds of those most active in cultural institutions in Chicago were in the Citizens Association and some held its highest offices. With the agitation for the eight-hour day that culminated in the Haymarket Riot, the Commercial Club gave the federal government the site for Fort Sheridan thirty miles outside the city and the Citizens Association, members of which formed a committee that met daily during the crisis, offered the city its services.[25]

Out of public office, business leaders felt hampered in their power to control a situation that troubled them. Their frustration was increased by the tone of political discourse. Carter Harrison, five times a successful candidate for mayor, proudly identified with every ethnic group. To various nationalities he pictured himself as a descendent of the Vikings, a defender of Irish rights, a visitor to Bohemia, and a guest of Bismarck. One writer quipped that if there were Chinese voters in Chicago, Harrison would convince them he had just cut his pigtail. That Harrison was actually of a distinguished American family of British ancestry only made such courting of the ethnic vote the more deplorable in the eyes of the native-born elite.[26]

For such businessmen as were moved to action beyond arming for defense, the response to public venality and social unrest was twofold. In a direct reaction, they formed organizations such as the Civic Federation and the Municipal Voters League, in which they challenged the existing political leadership and, to a certain extent, the neighborhood structure of representation which supported it. They sought to return the city to the forces of good government. In their eyes, the forces of good government were largely

defined as the native-born elite whose leaders were predominantly businessmen.[27]

Franklin MacVeagh, a wholesale grocer and cultural
philanthropist, remained active in politics throughout his
life and was eventually rewarded when Taft appointed him
Secretary of the Treasury in 1909. He initially saw the
solution to the problem of municipal government admin-
istered "by unfit and unworthy men, in an undignified,
uncultured and demoralizing manner" in terms of remov-
ing national party labels from local contests. But by the
end of the nineteenth century he looked to an independent
mayor, a limited city council, municipal civil service, and
electoral reform as mechanisms that would purify city
government. What was more important than structure,
however, was "a change in the political habits of the
people—a change from habitual neglect of political duties
by the body of our so-called good citizens to habitual
attention to them." In the early twentieth century, certain
business leaders who similarly combined interests in culture
and politics held up the structure of the corporation as a
model for government. Frederic A. Delano, a railroad
executive who was a member of the Orchestral Association
and a trustee of the University of Chicago, felt that the
commission form of government based on the corporate
model linked authority with accountability, unlike the
divided government of mayor and city council.[28]

C. Norman Fay, the prime mover behind the Orchestral Association, was perhaps embarrassingly honest about
the class meaning of such a structural change. He took
it as an axiom that "no very high-grade, very able, very
successful man—the very man most needed in the momen-
tous concerns of the cities—will run for local office, cheap
and nasty, and limited, as it is bound to be, by reason of
machine power and ward lines." He cited a conversation
with the late Marshall Field who contrasted the possibilities
of serving as an alderman with "a working majority of

my own kind, elected . . . long enough to accomplish something" with the actualities: "sitting in that hog-pen every Monday night for two years, listening to Bath-House John pass special ordinances to stick bow-windows and electric-light signs out over the sidewalk."[29] By focusing reform concerns on the bribe-taker rather than on the bribe-giver and by devising structures to encourage control by businessmen, MacVeagh, Delano, and Fay were not proposing any necessary change in the content of decisions. It was their form, rather, that they were looking to alter: they wanted government to be run as efficiently and as predictably as business.

An alternative reaction to the urban situation taken by Chicago businessmen, including some of those active in political reform, was to build institutions outside the structure of government which, while serving the society, would remain in private control. Economic leaders in Chicago founded or reshaped churches, charities, schools, and museums, contributing to them their time and money. Within this general philanthropic movement were the great cultural institutions of the city—the Chicago Art Institute, the Field Columbian Museum, the Chicago Symphony Orchestra, the Newberry and the Crerar libraries, and the University of Chicago. Though these institutions rested to some extent on the enjoyment they engendered and on the model of the good life that they sustained, they also expressed the loyalty of a group whose special relationship to the city was threatened by national ties. Perhaps as important, these institutions were designed to change the nature of the city's life.

Cultural philanthropy was in keeping with the vital American tradition of voluntary associations. Moreover, it meshed with the laissez-faire ideology of these business-men, who would strictly limit the activities of government. Commitment to a sense of civic responsibility did not necessarily entail broad humanitarian sympathies. Indeed, as businessmen who had been successful in the accepted terms of the society, the men who became active in urban philanthropy were firmly wedded to the belief that they had won out fairly in a society that granted opportunity to all. An address on Lincoln gave George E. Adams, trustee of the Newberry and the Field Columbian Museum and former president of the Orchestral Association, a chance to dilate on the American system: "Millionaires we have in plenty. Nearly every one of them is the son of a poor man. Nearly every one of them has reason to believe that his grandson will lead a life of the same strenuous endeavor which to him has made life worth living. Three generations from shirtsleeves to shirtsleeves is an old American saying." Yet, even given the existence of an unequal distribution of wealth at any moment, there was no cause for concern: "The wealth of the wealthy is a pittance compared with the aggregate wealth of the poor." Harlow Higinbotham, long-time president of the Field Columbian Museum, surely agreed. As he gave to steelworkers examples of humble men who had become generals and presidents, he reminded the workers of their opportunities: "Each one of you to the extent of the ability with which you have been endowed by your Creator, is free to tread that upward path."[30]

There were some differences between the almost hysterical conservatism of Franklin H. Head, a wholesale grocer and Newberry trustee for whom the mild statement of Grover Cleveland about the increasing gulf between rich and poor seemed to endanger the basis of the republic, and the position of Charles Hutchinson, who supported Hull-House however controversial the activities of its residents; but the differences may have been of style and tone more than of content. However radical his contemporaries thought him, Hutchinson opposed labor unions and argued as late as 1905 that opportunities were there for anyone to make the most of. While he might sympathize with labor, it was the sympathy of Clarence Buckingham, a prominent supporter of the Art Institute, who established a milk fund for strikers' children while opposing their parents' strike. Even when A. C. Bartlett, a trustee of the Art Institute and the University of Chicago and a member of the Orchestral Association, accepted trade unionism in principle, it was only to reject labor militancy and to affirm a belief that the workingman's best hope lay in his trust in the natural order and in the goodness of employers who would pay fair wages.[31]

At its most generous, there was a paternalism here, a sense of noblesse oblige that could, when directed at another people, support either a vicious racism or an imperialistic benevolence. Franklin Head wrote of the American Indians that they were "treacherous, revengeful, jealous, suspicious . . . . in every way [they] are simply barbarians." The United States should not make treaties with them, for "they are nothing but little bands of bare-legged savages." Edward Ayer, however, became their champion and wrote a history of their treatment which contrasted Indian peaceableness with the broken promises of the government. But both Head and Ayer believed that the government's policy should try to turn the Indians to American culture. And both would have agreed with George Adams when he reflected that the beauty of the New Hampshire mountains had not been there two hundred years before, "because there was no eye to see, no soul to feel it. True, the Indians were there. . . . But the red Indian, being a primitive man, did not have that delicate sense of beauty, of form and color, which has been developed in the modern man, the heir of centuries of civilization."[32]

Edward Ayer was an indefatigable traveler and col-lector whose anthropological collections enriched the Field.

He firmly believed in the necessity and the value of imperialistic advance. When he was traveling through Tunisia, one of his constant refrains was to contrast the evidences of French technology with the native Arabs' primitivism. It is interesting that Ayer concentrated on preserving the traces of civilizations and nature that he was helping to destroy: as a lumberman specializing in railroad ties in the Southwest, he collected artifacts of southwestern Indians and supported the creation of forest preserves; and when the United States took the Philippines, he rushed to acquire historical and anthropological materials. Hutchinson, who treasured Egyptian antiquities, was quoted as remarking in 1898: "England is performing a great work for Egypt. The progress of the last sixteen years has been wonderful. The people of Egypt are like children. Some of them do not appreciate what is being accomplished. . . . they do not know what is best for themselves."[33]

It was this sense of superior wisdom that underlay cultural philanthropy in Chicago in the late nineteenth century. Perhaps it came naturally to this group of wealthy businessmen largely of British descent and with strong New England ties. These men modeled themselves after the image of the cultivated gentleman. They created cultural institutions as mediums for their own enjoyment and as ways of sustaining their sense of the good life. In an era when the economy was becoming an increasingly national one, these men were intensely loyal to the city where they had made their fortunes. They wanted for Chicago the recognition due a cultural capital. While powerful economically, these businessmen found themselves limited in their ability to control politics directly. Fearful of the violent potential of labor and disturbed by the atmosphere of corruption, they founded and supported institutions they could control in the hope of changing the nature of their city's life, though without alteration of the economic structure that had served them well. Through the establishment of museums, libraries, a symphony orchestra, and a university, they sought to redirect their city's values and preoccupations, to lift Chicago from materialism to the realm of spirit.

4

The Meaning of Culture

Whatever their interests and concerns, Chicago business-men would not have seen cultural institutions as avenues for civic reform had it not been for developments in their understanding of art and its social uses. Essential to their support of culture was the belief, shared with other Americans, in art's uplifting power. Further refinements in their conception would help to clarify the nature of the cultural enterprise and give to it enriched meaning.

In the years surrounding the Civil War, Chicago business and professional men had not held the idealistic understanding of culture assumed by Charles Eliot Norton and his genteel contemporaries in Boston and New York. This generation of civic leaders participated in cultural associations for personal enjoyment or because they had a sense that such involvement was appropriate for a respectable citizen. Even as they began to broaden their sense of civic responsibility to include culture as well as relief, it was initially with a limited sense of culture's role. Only in the 1880s, as a new generation emerged, would the broad powers easterners were giving to art come to shape Chicago thought and practice.

The earliest of the city-wide cultural institutions, the Newberry Library, demonstrates the initial constraints. Walter L. Newberry's will provided for the endowment of a library on the death of his wife if his daughters remained childless. His executors planned a reference library to be built on the North Side. Sometime before 1889, when the Ogden block was chosen as the site for the library building, a discussion of possible locations took place at E. W. Blatchford's house. It is clear that though not all the participants had been informed, at some prior point a decision about the nature of the library had been made. When various outsiders politely suggested that the library might have departments "attractive to a great number of persons," that it might display objects, or that it might be designed for general interest, they were definitively silenced: "The Trustees have settled that question." The library was to contain a noncirculating reference collection, the selection of which would reflect literary and historical standards, not public demand.[1]

The matter at issue in the meeting was more limited: given the predetermined nature of the library, should it be located in Lincoln Park? Dankmar Adler, the architect, and two professors at theological seminaries in Chicago had spoken in favor of this location as a handsome setting that would surround the structure with spacious grounds. E. B. McCagg, one of the older civic leaders who had been active in the Sanitary Commission, objected, using arguments that would have been supported by the designer of Central Park, Frederick Law Olmsted:

> I am wholly and entirely opposed to the library going to Lincoln Park. It is a public park for Public recreation . . . where people can get out of the city and into the country, and where there shall be grass and trees and blue sky and flowers, if you please, and nothing else. I do not think that Central Park in New York has been improved by the many constructions they have put in it. I do Know, I think, that

all of them have been quite outside of the idea of the
founders and the gentlemen who planned it. . . . I think
there is a kind of breach of faith in taking such an institution
as this into a public park.

"Such an institution as this": clearly then McCagg had
no thought that the Newberry Library would actually be
used by the wide public. Later in the discussion McCagg
clarified the distinction he was making. The park was
"established for a pleasure ground, for the use of the
people, not the class we belong to, but those who do not
get out of the city into the country." The park was for
the masses; the future library for an economic elite. There
was no intimation that the indirect benefits of the library
would be such as to justify the taking of park land. When
one of those favoring the Lincoln Park site rebutted that
the issue McCagg was raising was one to be considered
"by the proper parties" (presumably the park board),
McCagg retorted: "We are the proper parties. We are
asked to consider that question, not merely the moneyed,
beneficial aspect to ourselves for the moment, but what
is entirely right in reference to the fund, and in reference
to others and the public as well as to the fund." The
issue was not whether they had the right to make a
decision that affected the whole community, but what the
content of that decision should be. And to McCagg, a
member of the older generation, the limited usefulness
to the public of a reference library was clear.[2]

To one person at the meeting, not only did a private
group have the right to make a decision, but matters
concerning the library should be kept out of the hands
of the people. Robert Todd Lincoln, son of the Rail
Splitter, opposed building the library on park grounds
because it threatened trustee control: "A sentiment
[might] arise, if the location is in Lincoln Park, that its
future conduct should be determined by polular [sic]
election on the North Side." To prevent that danger the

library should be constructed on property owned by the Newberry.[3]

The Newberry was the oldest of Chicago's philanthropically endowed cultural institutions. E. W. Blatchford, who was to be president of the library until 1914, had been among those active in the Chicago Historical Society before the Civil War and had helped organize the northwestern branch of the Sanitary Commission. The size of Newberry's bequest allowed Blatchford to seek trustees within his circle, men like McCagg (who, however, refused to serve because of ill health) with a strong sense of public trust, but a limited conception of culture's role. Such men believed in the benefits of cultural association for themselves. And they were beginning to have a sense of the value of the arts and letters for the community. But this sense remained generalized and abstract. The Newberry Library was reticent about proclaiming its importance: it restricted its public statements to an occasional assertion of the library's contribution to Chicago as a literary center.[4] As we shall see, the programs of the Newberry would reflect this limited understanding of the institution's public role.

But through a variety of channels, eastern thinking about art flowed into Chicago and began to give a much broader role for art to play in the city. Some civic leaders had been educated in the East and, therefore, may have been exposed directly to the views of theorizers. For example, Martin A. Ryerson was at the Harvard Law School in the late 1870s at a time when Charles Eliot Norton was lecturing only a short distance away. Magazines such as the Boston-based *Atlantic Monthly*, which published the writings of genteel authors, were read appreciatively by men like Charles Hutchinson. The noted figures Matthew Arnold and James Russell Lowell came to Chicago. Beyond the playful furor they caused in the press were real encounters with Franklin MacVeagh and

and N. K. Fairbank. Chicago ministers, especially Frank W. Gunsaulus and David Swing, fused their personal approaches with the messages of such writers and preachers as Henry Ward Beecher to create an atmosphere in which —at least on Sunday—art and the life of the mind were highly valued. Other voices would be added to these: Theodore Thomas, the *Dial*, and Daniel Burnham would serve as conduits for eastern thought.[5]

Thus the most prominent member of the next generation of civic leaders saw the role of culture in the community in new terms. In 1888 when he was only the president of the fledgling Art Institute and a member of the committee of Fine Arts of the Inter-State Industrial Exposition, Charles Hutchinson delivered an address before the Art Institute entitled "Art: Its Influence and Excellence in Modern Times."[6] As he established his case, he was clearly influenced by what he had read and heard. He echoed Charles Eliot Norton when he asserted that art had been the chief expression of every age "of that which was deepest and the most sincere in the life of its people." He accepted the genteelists' position that art inspires man, giving him a sense of the grandeur and heroism of the past. Describing the reactions of Irish immigrants to a statue of Prescott on the Boston Common, Hutchinson intoned, "There before us stood the hero. Every attribute of manhood seemed personified. It spoke to them and it spoke to me. It bid us be brave and strong and noble. It urged us to stand for the right, and to die if need be for God and country." Hutchinson added the sense of the founders of the Boston Museum of Fine Arts that art also is an aid to industrial growth, for the example of carefully wrought works increases the skill of labor. And finally he drew on the arguments expressed in the early republic that art is the natural product of a mature civilization, one with wealth and leisure.

If subjected to analysis the elements of Hutchinson's

argument do not seem to build a logical structure. They have an additive quality, reflecting their origin in different periods of the nineteenth-century debate over culture. But beneath the seeming variety is a basic theme, linking Hutchinson to other Americans working to define art's role: art has the power to counter the dominant tendency of the age, materialism. From early in the nineteenth century the attainment of culture had distinguished the patrician from the *nouveau riche.* In addition, materialism had become identified with municipal corruption and with the unmitigated harshness of American cities. As the inheritor of wealth, Hutchinson was critical of his era and his city: "We live in a materialistic age under one of its most characteristic governments, and—I fear we must admit here in Chicago—in one of the most barren cities." The cause, he felt, was the single-minded absorption of businessmen in their private affairs. Hutchinson's condemnation of his contemporaries was a mild version of the usual critique of the newly rich: businessmen are caught in materialism, "a state of slavery where man shall exist for the state alone—a mere machine devoted to business." With "no time to devote to literature or art," "no time for self-culture," such men have no meaningful future ahead of them, only a "wretched existence . . . when wealth is gained and health is lost and with it all resources of enjoyment." Hutchinson asked rhetorically: "Are we not losing sight of the being created in the image of God, with heart and intellect and soul. Are we not losing sight of the human being in the business man?"

In Hutchinson's own life and in his public statements, he would find three routes out of the materialism that business enterprise threatened—religion, service, and art. While in his address it was only the last that concerned him explicitly, nevertheless for him the line between art and religion was one that joined, not separated. Like others who accepted the idealistic understanding of art, Hutchinson believed that art had the power to turn men away from their preoccupation with matter to focus on the world of spirit. "In the midst of this busy material life of our day, she [art] may call upon us to halt, and turn our thoughts away from so much that is of the earth earthy, and lead us to contemplate those eternal truths which after all most concern the children of God." Earlier in his talk Hutchinson had described how this could happen, how a young man "wandering largely about in a gallery of paintings, almost in the heart of the busy metropolis of the world" "in the midst of our modern Babylon" came upon a painting that portrayed a scene from a Keats poem and was led by the poem itself to study Milton and then "to contemplate all that is true and good and sublime in time and eternity." This man now "imbodies [sic] in his life that which is in his heart, put there by one of the greatest artists of all time."

For Hutchinson the value of spiritual development was not merely personal. Rather art could turn businessmen away from material pursuits to focus their energies on the community suffering from their neglect. A few years earlier in his capacity as superintendent of the Sunday school at Saint Paul's Unitarian Church, Hutchinson had voiced his disapproval of those absorbed by their private interests to the exclusion of concern for the commonweal. "Think of the great number of men and women living in Chicago today who never devote any of their time or energy or even money for the advancement of the public morals or characters,—who live unto themselves alone. Mere sponges, absorbing all and giving nothing. Sometimes it almost seems that we would be justified in considering such people no better than burglars. . . . Oh, business man, there is something in this life higher and better than business."[7] What disturbed Hutchinson about civic life was what disturbed Franklin MacVeagh about government—that the good people were apathetic, leaving the society to drift or to be led by the incompetent. The corruption that Hutchinson saw was not going to disappear or be spontaneously corrected by the people. Its removal was the responsibility of the elite: "The real work of this world is done by the minority." One could not justify one's selfishness by pleading goodness. Private benevolence was not enough. "The older I grow and the more experienced I become the more I believe in organized effort in working through the institution rather than the individual."[8]

In 1888 explicit moral or religious content seemed to be an important factor to Hutchinson in art's power to develop men spiritually: the scene from Keats, the statue of Prescott, or the Sistine Madonna in a Dresden gallery that makes one "seem to be in the presence of Divinity itself."[9] Yet even in this period it would be a mistake to read Hutchinson's examples too literally. Hutchinson had largely gone beyond the neoclassical commitment to art as offering lessons or models for emulation. What was more important was the creative role of the artist, the "power of art when the master is great."

Hutchinson was drawing here on the transcendental version of idealism: "It needs but little thought to lead us to say with Emerson, that truth, goodness, and beauty are but the different faces of the same all." Beauty is a manifestation of the ideal. Art is a mode of communication, by which the artist "can perpetuate in stone and bronze the lofty conceptions of his mind. . . . Ideas of grace, beauty, and power." These ideas, aspects of the universal Idea, the "all," have the power "to move . . . [men's] sensibilities and arouse the soul." Art takes men from the world of matter to that of spirit because it is the artist's attempt to express the beautiful and thereby represent the all.[10]

Hutchinson also accepted the argument that the more conservative thinkers like Henry Bellows were making at

mid-century. Art is a process: it raises men to a higher
level through refinement. Hutchinson accepted the definition of art as "the harmonious expression of human
emotion," and found that it applied "to all the fine arts,
music, dancing, poetry, sculpture, and painting." Art takes
the raw materials of man and makes of them something
purer, finer. "We need not to destroy our passions and
desires, but to master and refine them." Somehow the
appreciation of art is a direct agency in this process. "The
beautiful refines."

However refinement was to occur, it was clear to
Hutchinson that opportunities for contact with art in
Chicago were limited. From his travels and experiences
Hutchinson was familiar with the European city; and, like
a generation of Americans before him, he found values
there to admire. What struck Hutchinson, however, was
not the city as the model of order, but the city as the
setting of art to suggest and inspire. How different from
Chicago was England's Oxford whose "very air is rife with
suggestions of the literature of England. On every hand
quaint, beautiful and peaceful stand the homes of the
university." Or Florence or Rome where "art treasures of
many generations have been gathered together to delight,
instruct and inspire." Barren Chicago needed just such
accompaniments of civilization. It "would be richer, filled
with a higher intellectual life, had we more beautiful
surroundings, monuments of art, buildings, stored with
books and paintings and sculpture." Such a Chicago
would act as a moral force on its citizens, pointing the
way to more spiritual lives. "On every hand something
should suggest high and noble thoughts," causing one
occasionally to "pause and think upon something beyond
and above himself. I would that at every turn were a
statue or monument or building, rich in artistic design,
which would set forth ideas of beauty, grace or power."

Hutchinson knew that such a vision of the city

would call forth the image of Europe and the association of art with corruption and decline that had been made by thinkers of the early republic. "Devotion to art, they [critics] say, is sure to lead to luxury, and luxury to decay." But to Hutchinson it was clear that the important variable was not art, but the stages of a society's development. At one period the physical aspects of life are all-important, "health and strength of body are the first necessities." But later a society begins to accumulate wealth and its members have leisure and "amusements demand and receive attention. . . . Art is fostered, and properly so, for the fine arts are the truly intellectual amusements." The question was not whether society turns to the cultivation of leisure, but how, and in what proportion to material development. The arts "if rightly used . . . will bless. If abused, may curse."

Hutchinson hoped for the refinement not only of the individual but of the society, reshaped by the businessman-leader. He accepted, as did John Ruskin and Charles Eliot Norton, the belief that art expresses the "real character of a nation" and that "life shapes the art," but he also looked and hoped, as did other Americans who read Ruskin, for art to change the society: "There must in some degree be a counterinfluence of art over the life."

In the years that followed there would be no clearer single statement of the premises that underlay the development of Chicago's cultural institutions. There would, however, be clarifications, additions, and changes in tone and emphasis, stimulated in part by Theodore Thomas, the editors of *Dial*, and Daniel Burnham, who brought their own particular approaches to discussions of culture. And in the twentieth century there would be a major redirection of attention as the object of refinement shifted from the businessman to the masses.

Theodore Thomas, brought to Chicago to establish the Chicago Symphony Orchestra, would teach the Orchestral Association both the importance and the costs of standards. Thomas expressed an enthusiasm for cultural philanthropy in Chicago that must have been gratifying to his benefactors:

> One spirit seems to pervade the minds of those who are working together in this noble cause—it is the best Chicago spirit which has made realities of such vast undertakings as the Art Institute, the Chicago University, the World's Fair, and the Field Columbian Museum, and which thinks only of establishing something ennobling and refining in our great Western metropolis, to temper the influences of the daily struggle of life and to lighten its sordid cares.

Criticized because his programs emphasized symphonies at the expense of the more popular attractions that had delighted summer audiences, Thomas refused to bend to public wishes. Rather he would educate Chicago citizens to appreciate great music: "A SYMPHONY orchestra shows the culture of a community, not opera. . . . The master works of instrumental music are the language of the soul and express more than those of any other art. Light music, 'popular' so called, is the sensual side of the art and has more or less devil in it." This was the distinction Hutchinson had made between the art that would bless and that which would curse. And like Hutchinson, Thomas emphasized the ability of great art to touch and strengthen man's higher nature. Thomas felt his audience was learning the lesson he had to offer. The concert-going public "has discovered that there is a deeper joy and a nobler spirituality to be gained from familiarity with the higher art forms than it ever dreamed of seeking in the lower. It has discovered that while Strauss or Bizet will charm the ear, Beethoven and Wagner will warm and thrill the whole nature." The music of a light summer program "would be as wholly unsuited to our winter concerts as a chromo hung among the Dutch masterpieces at the Art Institute."[11]

More clearly implied in Thomas's arguments than in Hutchinson's was a belief in the dualism of nature and of man. Unique in creation, man linked the world of spirit and the world of matter. His body was matter and, as such, was subject to the flux of experience, change, decay, and death. His soul was spirit, eternal, and unchanging. Man was essentially at war with himself. His body had elemental needs—food, rest, warmth, and sexual outlets. It was impelled by drives that demanded gratification beyond the minimum level for self-preservation. The soul, in contrast, aspired to the realm of the ideal. It was the location of intellect, aesthetic longing, and virtue, striving toward truth, beauty, and goodness. Life was a battle between the body and the soul for control. Man's emotions were separate. They could strengthen either the impulses of the body or the influence of the soul. As the harmonic expressions of emotion the arts had the power to help man "master and refine" his emotions, to bring them into the service of the soul. In this way art could help man attain a higher spiritual existence. The *Dial*, Chicago's literary magazine, echoed this understanding in its appreciation of the contribution of the Chicago Symphony Orchestra to the community. The *Dial* spoke of the "ministry of every form of fine art." Music was the art "which contributes most immediately to the enrichment of life, to the enlargement of the spiritual part of man, to the strengthening of every worthy impulse and the deepening of every noble aspiration."[12]

Both Hutchinson and Thomas distinguished between the arts that blessed and those that abused, those that drew the emotions to the spirit and those with devil in them. This distinction is basic to an understanding of the development of the cultural institutions of Chicago in the late nineteenth century. It was not that Chicago residents were uninterested in the arts and letters. They supported a bustling life of clubs, choruses, and musical and dramatic productions. For those sons of native-born parents who were to become involved in culture, there were a natural science association and museum, a local historical society, a chorus, and a literary club. Chicago audiences saw performances of the important operatic and dramatic figures and enjoyed festivals and concerts of local and visiting musicians. The city boasted a large and popular public library. But from this welter of activity there was little that Thomas or Hutchinson would find that met their standards. Rather, most of what was going on seemed to reinforce the materialism of the age. The light music of the open-air concert or the technically accurate reproduction of daily life in the commercial gallery did nothing to draw men's emotions to the support of the soul.

The cause of this situation was the economics of art in the nineteenth century in combination with the state of public taste. The artist was a peddler, offering his wares to the public in the marketplace. The public wanted and supported what it enjoyed. This was the art that amused— and "abused"—not the art that refined. As the trustees of the orchestra wrote in answer to those critics who urged that the organization stand or fall by its box office receipts, the orchestra was "an art and educational institution, worthy of endowment. . . . Broadly speaking, there seems to be no possible union of pure art or pure education and commercial profit. There has probably not been in the history of the world a single self-supporting institution devoted to the higher forms of art or learning." For such an institution to exist it was necessary for those in the community who understood its value to underwrite its support. In this way its elevating influence could be maintained in the absence of public demand. Endowment would give the kind of freedom of selection that Norman Williams, the first president of the Crerar Library, enjoyed. As he wrote to a fellow trustee, Williams would "set a high standard in the selection of departments of the library and bring the people up to it." This was the proper approach: "It is a greater gain to society to bring one young man or woman in contact with an educating book, than to entertain five hundred with the popular literature of the day." It was in this spirit that men like Hutchinson assumed responsibility for the founding, endowment, and direction of the city-wide cultural institutions of Chicago.[13]

Strongly influenced by Matthew Arnold's vision, the *Dial* was to encourage this effort and give to Hutchinson's sense of the evolution of society a firmer structure. This literary review was founded in 1880 by Francis Fisher Browne, and its name reflected the eastern standards it hoped to bring to the Midwest. The *Dial* passionately defended the right of an institution like the orchestra to set standards in its selection of works. With an aesthetic snobbery that a man like Hutchinson would never have expressed publicly, the *Dial* retorted to critics of the Chicago Symphony Orchestra's programs, "The average Philistine resents being told that his own likings have nothing to do with the matter, that such and such works are the ones best for him to hear, and that if his self-sufficiency scorn the opportunity offered, he is not to be flattered by a descent to the level of his unformed tastes, but rather left to his own devices." The *Dial* suggested the proper way of dealing with such persons: " 'This masterpiece deserves your attention,' we should say, 'for it has the power to raise you to a higher spiritual level. If you do not like it now, pray that you may learn to like it, for the defect is yours.' "[14]

The *Dial* saw the setting of standards as a part of the critical process of development that Chicago was undergoing as it became a cultural center. A society was like a man, sharing his dual nature. Society had a body— geography, buildings, human groups, and institutions. And it also had a soul, as its members shared an intellectual, cultural, and religious life. Like men, societies grew: the city had a life span from birth to maturity. In its child-hood the city's physical life was all-important. It had to concentrate on economic development, construction, and population. As the *Dial* stated—in words that elaborated Hutchinson's earlier argument—"Chicago has put all the energy of this half-century of her adolescence into the development of a material body which is magnificent in its functional structure and health." This was necessary, but it was only one stage in the city's development. "We do not need evolution to tell us that the higher powers unfold later in all normal life—national and municipal as well as individual. . . . already the signs are clear that the season of mere physical life is over, and that the life of the soul calls for exercise and nourishment."[15]

The city would not only be equipped with institutions for cultural enrichment and enjoyment, but it would also become the home of artistic creation. The *Dial* saw creativity as the logical conclusion of the process of growth. Beyond what its associate editor, William Morton Payne, called the "period of clubs, and lecture organizations, and passive literary interests generally" was coming "its natural fruit," creative achievement. The city-wide cultural insti-tutions would form "centres of social activity . . . in which artists and scholars and educators will gather, at which ideas and ideals will prevail, and which, as an informal 'Academy,' will set standards that shall mitigate and transform the grossness of our hitherto material life." The eventual result will be that Chicago will become a creative cultural center, "an enricher of the treasury of human endowments."[16]

To men like Hutchinson, such a vision was attractive because it promised potential moral benefits and also because it could transform Chicago into a fitting object of their intense loyalty. These wealthy businessmen not only wanted their city to be a good place to live and work; they wanted it to be thought of as the very best.

As their horizons had expanded, they increasingly compared their city to other great cities of the world. It was no longer enough for Chicago to be economically powerful or even moral: the test it was forced to meet was the level of its culture. The city seemed determined to excel. Theodore Thomas once spelled this out in an article on cultural philanthropy in the *Chicago Tribune*: "It is this scorn of mediocrity and this indomitable determination to have the *best*, and maintain only the highest standard in all its enterprises, which makes the greatness of this city." Such loyalty was assumed in appeals for support. For example, the school of the Art Institute argued that, in contrast to the other institutions seeking funds, its quality would not be subordinate to the institutions of eastern cities: "There is no difficulty whatever in developing an art school so far superior to any other that it shall be above question."[17]

It was not enough that the city have excellent cultural institutions. It must also be the location of artistic creation. It was by its art that a society was ultimately judged. The writer, for example, lent to the city "the prestige of his presence and the distinction . . . [of] the literary products of his scholarship." Harlow Higinbotham, the president of the World's Columbian Exposition Directory, saw the "beautiful structures" of the fair as evidence that America had "not neglected these civilizing arts which minister to a people's refinement and become the chief glory of a nation."[18]

In contrast to his 1888 characterization of Chicago as barren, by 1907 Charles Hutchinson felt that Chicago had become "a center of art." It was a place "where people come for inspiration and education; a place from which an artistic influence radiates." Not only could an artist make a living in the city, but he could be supported by "a considerable number of persons who appreciate the good in painting, sculpture and architecture." In Hutch-

inson's view creativity flourished in such an atmosphere—
one of high standards, broadly disseminated.[19]

When Theodore Thomas set his standards, distin-
guishing between the "higher art forms" and the "lower,"
he was thinking of the lengthy, serious symphonic work
(perhaps by a German composer) as opposed to opera or
the waltz. Hutchinson put his choice within the terms of
his larger argument. Among contemporary painters it was
the pre-Raphaelites that Hutchinson admired. "They are
the great artists because they are the great idealists . . .
earnest consecrated men with high-minded thoughts,
which they endeavored to express in beauty." They stand
in contrast to the realists who excel technically but suffer
from "the lack of soul. Materialism, which so abounds
and poisons the life of to-day, has also permeated and
almost destroyed her art."[20] In time Hutchinson would
broaden his taste to include Impressionists among contemporaries and the Dutch Masters and El Greco among
artists of the past, but the basis of his choice would
remain the same—the expression not of the world of
matter but of the ideal.

Daniel Burnham, the Chicago architect and director
of works for the World's Columbian Exposition would
take the aesthetic idealism of Hutchinson and help turn
it to a specific cultural ideal—the Italian Renaissance. A
man such as Hutchinson was always conscious of eastern
standards: New England writers formed the staple of his
references. But through the fair, Burnham made contact
with a new group of eastern artistic leaders—the New
York-based architectural firm of McKim, Mead & White;
the sculptor Augustus St. Gaudens; and the painter John
La Farge—and brought them into Chicago's orbit. These
men were beginning to collaborate in the design and
decoration of buildings, the most famous of which was the
Boston Public Library. They brought to their work an
appreciation of the Italian Renaissance and a sense of

themselves as its heirs. The most vivid moment in Burnham's recollection of the planning of the fair came when St. Gaudens whispered at the close of the meeting that put the Court of Honor buildings in the mold of the Renaissance, "I never expected to see such a moment. It has been the greatest meeting of artists since the fifteenth century."[21] Burnham, who in his earlier partnership with John Wellborn Root had helped design many of Chicago's most imposing and pathbreaking early skyscrapers, was won over by the eastern group. He had fought to gain the commission for them against the opposition of Chicago promoters, loyal to local architects. As Burnham humbly told the writers and artists who gathered in New York in 1893 at the dinner to honor him: "You mould and direct the higher purposes of American life. You have called me here to stamp some acts of mine with approval." Burnham and the fair were to bring to Chicago the aesthetic preferences and philosophic approaches of this self-elected eastern academy.[22]

In Chicago, as elsewhere, the most obvious result was visual. The University of Chicago was planned in High Gothic, the Newberry Library and the first Art Institute building in a free adaptation of Romanesque. But the 1893 structure of the Art Institute would follow Renaissance models, as would the Field Columbian Museum (housed in the former Fine Arts building of the fair) and Orchestra Hall. The Renaissance impact would be most clearly seen in Burnham's Plan for Chicago proposed in 1909. The meaning of the shift to Renaissance modes involved more than visual preferences. It encouraged movement away from preoccupation with the explicit moral content of a work of art to an emphasis on the power of the aesthetic process itself; it reflected a sense of art less as a refinement on nature than as a counterworld to experience. Just as the Metropolitan Museum of Art in New York and the Museum of Fine Arts in Boston had shifted from reproductions to original masterpieces, so would Chicago's Art Institute.

The aesthetic idealism of the late nineteenth century, strengthened by Hegelian notions and the thought of Matthew Arnold, meshed with that of the fifteenth. Renaissance artists themselves had attempted to translate what they thought were eternal forms into buildings, sculpture, and paintings. In their works they sought to portray what was eternal and universal rather than what was fleeting, specific, or casual. Disregarding the sense of organic growth from nature of the Gothic, the Renaissance posited a formal world opposed to that of experience, a world to represent the eternal ideas that informed the world of matter. As the artist created a work, he attempted to get behind sensory data to the essence of his subject. It was this process, renewed by the observer, which ministered to morality, not any direct lesson that the work might teach.

Hutchinson could say in 1916: "It is not the sole mission of Art to amuse or to furnish moral instruction. The true mission of Art, as Hagel [sic] says, is to discover and present the ideal." The Renaissance understood that and therein lay its power: "The secret of the greatness of the Art of the Italian Renaissance is to be found in the fact that it was the ideal realization of Italian reality." This quality was not limited to a people or an age. "There is no one supreme master in painting. There are many. In every age of Art, painting has been a sufficient medium for the expression of men's minds." What defines artistic greatness in one age defines it in all—the effort to get behind the materialistic surface "to present the ideal." Thus the true work of art became eternal, its beauty unchanging (or as the *Dial* expressed it, "the beautiful remains the beautiful in all ages, its laws immutable and its strength sure").[23] Just as nature's beauty has spoken to all men in all times, so art will never "become commonplace or obsolete if it be grounded in universal fact and expressed in a universal language." Yet the ideal for Hutchinson never became simply a system of formal properties, as it did for Burnham. Rather, in keeping with his religious outlook, Hutchinson retained Ruskin's sense that the ideal encompassed the spiritual aspects of a civilization—its values and beliefs. "Man is still led by an inner light. The ideals, the moral convictions, and the vital principles of a people are the most important factors in its history." It was this inner quality of a culture that art was to express.[24]

The Renaissance was suggestive in social terms as well. For the artists it offered the model of aesthetic collaboration—painters, sculptors, and architects working together to harmonize their individual creations into a larger whole. Supporting their cooperation was a growing belief in the underlying unity of the arts. Daniel Burnham could write to Theodore Thomas after Thomas had been forced to resign as director of music at the fair: "The Park is desolate without you, and one of the four great arts is dethroned. . . . it was my hope that all the sisters should come out together." Almost a decade later when the principal artists of the fair were gathered in Washington to plan together the grounds and monuments of the Capitol, Burnham wrote to Thomas, recalling the fair: "Again has come the old joy of creating noble things and of dear associating together in the work. . . . And you have been with us, and we all think of how much of our power to dream truly we owe to you."[25]

Men like Hutchinson would share with Burnham this belief in the unity of the arts. It was an assumption that underlay the promotion of the various cultural enterprises in Chicago as parts of a common endeavor. The cultural philanthropists went a step further than Burnham: they would come to make no real distinction between the arts and scholarly or scientific pursuits. In 1888 Hutchinson had considered science and the scientific mentality as one of the sources of the materialism of the age. But a few years later his closest friend and cultural co-worker, Martin Ryerson, would endow a scientific laboratory at the University of Chicago and proclaim, "We are living in an age of marvels, and the marvels of the science of today outstrip the marvels of the imagination of yesterday." He shared the hope that the university would "be one of the leaders in the scientific progress of the world." Yet teaching and research would be "of little value unless they keep in view and tend to enlarge the higher ideals of life. It is even to this end that science should be cultivated." Science was not in conflict with art or religion. Rather, science would "correct our errors and elevate, not destroy, our ideals. . . . by doing its important part in the development of the human intellect, [it would] add to the capacity of the human race for a higher moral and intellectual life." Science was one more face of the all, and like the arts it was in conflict with materialism. Frederick J. V. Skiff, the director of the Field Columbian Museum, was said, on entering the museum, to lift his hat in respect.[26]

The Renaissance may have established its hold on men like Hutchinson because of the parallel between Renaissance patrons and themselves. Florence, like Chicago, was a commercial center where great fortunes were made and spent. Its ruthless leaders were new men who had grown rich in banking and trade, and they combined successful business careers with patronage of great art.[27]

George E. Adams, one-time president of the Chicago Symphony's Orchestral Association, spoke the most directly: "Painting, sculpture, architecture, and music were for centuries upheld by the mighty hands of the church—and when the influence of the church declined, and the Renaissance followed the age of faith, it was the splendid personal generosity of popes and Italian princes that gave Michael Angelo [sic] and Raphael for an eternal possession." Adams saw as their modern equivalent the Orchestral Association, and the broader public. "Disinterested patrons of art there must be whenever and wherever art is to find its highest expression. The difference between former times and now is that then the patron of art was a pope or a prince, while now and in this country the most effective patron of art is an association like this."[28]

But in the nineteenth century these men of wealth did not offer direct support to creative artists. Men such as Charles Hutchinson bought paintings, but they would not have considered putting an artist on hire for an extended period. Rather the "patronage" of creative art that they offered was largely indirect: they established institutions that would reshape public taste. In the late nineteenth and early twentieth centuries it seemed to these men that while the public now bought entertainment rather than art, this could be changed. Exposure to real art through cultural institutions would lead Chicago's citizens to appreciate true art, and they would begin to want it for themselves.[29] The refined individuals composing the public would no longer lend their support to what Hutchinson or Thomas regarded as second-class work but would back creative achievements of high quality.

Hutchinson felt that "the great artist must be an idealist." His hope was that "the skill of the present" would unite with "the inspiration of the past . . . and art . . . reach a state of perfection never yet attained." Cultural institutions could serve the artist by providing him with models for emulation. They would educate the artist, extending to him the "general culture" which was "as important . . . as technical skill."[30] As he contemplated the beautiful, the artist would strengthen his own spiritual nature. In exploring the great works of the past, he would become aware of those qualities that had made the masterpieces great and lasting, and he could use them as models for his own creative efforts. By inspiration and example, the art of the past would aid him in shaping an art of the present worthy of its city and its time.

Cultural institutions would educate and inspire the artist and shape the taste of his public so that the people would support the true works of art that he produced. Chicago would become a cultural center equal to the great cities of civilization. Businessmen would no longer be trapped by materialism in a barren and corrupt city. Inspired by a beautiful setting and by the finest creations of art, they would cultivate themselves and develop their spirits and thus be able to give to Chicago the civic leadership the community needed.

5

The City-Wide Cultural Institutions

What Charles Hutchinson or George Adams thought about culture mattered, because their notions shaped the direction and nature of their efforts to establish city-wide cultural institutions for Chicago. Confronting these men were myriad decisions. What forms of art or scholarship should be supported? What should a collection or a program contain and how should it be arranged? Where and how should it be housed? How should it be made attractive to the public?

Such matters were the province of men like Hutchinson: the nature of cultural institutions in the nineteenth century was such that the men who served them as trustees were, with certain exceptions, able to exert control over policy. The Art Committee of the board of trustees of the Art Institute decided on acquisitions—not only what the museum should buy, but what gifts it should accept and the nature of temporary exhibitions and loans. The trustees signed checks and authorized expenses. Though they consulted with the director and his staff, the trustees made the decisions about the building. Charles

Hutchinson's colleagues were probably less attentive than he in visiting the museum; but his daily presence meant that he was involved in the details of management, even to the extent of hanging pictures in the gallery and making corrections on the annual report.[1]

The internal relations of the Field Columbian Museum seem parallel. Certain issues, however, were drawn more clearly; unlike the Art Institute, the Field had a large staff of scientists who organized expeditions for materials and sought to publish results. Their proposals went before the president and the trustees for an approval that was not automatic. And more dramatically than at the Art Institute, trustees of the Field merged their own acquisitiveness and love of the chase with the desire of the museum to add to its collections. They frequently went along on the expeditions they supported. Edward E. Ayer seemed to scour continents in the Field's behalf. His overwhelming acquisitiveness, in fact, caused problems, as more conservative colleagues attempted to hold him to limits. The matter was obviously a delicate one, for Ayer had been an active contributor and promoter of the museum from the beginning.[2]

Ayer was to face a similar conflict at the Newberry, one which let to his resignation as a trustee and to the temporary withdrawal of the bequest of his library. Though on paper the power of the Newberry trustees was as great as that of their counterparts at the Art Institute or at the Field, in reality it was more limited, for, as we shall see, library trustees had to deal with an administrator who regarded himself as a professional. The librarian's craft was more highly developed than that of the museum director, and the librarian had a sense of the historical importance of his work and the support of contemporary professional fellowship. But though they were challenged, the trustees clearly determined the overall nature and limits of acquisitions, the basic policy regarding the relation of the institution to the public, and the design and plan of the building.[3]

The Orchestral Association, in order to persuade Theodore Thomas to come to Chicago, surrendered some of the usual power of trustees. As a part of the bargain association members struck, they promised the director complete freedom with regard to programs. The repertoire was to be his entirely, though after years of summer concerts and orchestral festivals the backers probably assumed they knew what they might expect. Because of scanty records it is unclear what exact authority remained in the Orchestral Association's hands. Certainly members had the responsibility for economic support, which probably meant that they made decisions relating to finances, such as the length of the season and the price of the tickets.[4] It also appears that the decision about the location of the building was ultimately theirs, though they did bend to Thomas's demand that a special hall be built for the orchestra. One senses that here, as at the Art Institute and the Field, strong personal ties developed between the trustees and the director; but in addition Thomas had a special influence from his role as cultural guide and spokesman.[5]

President William Rainey Harper's early creative role and his energy, prestige, and administrative ability gave him a commanding position over fellow members of the University of Chicago's board of trustees. The need for local financial and moral support, however, gave the other board members a strong voice in certain kinds of policy. In the early years of planning and building, Harper and the board worked closely together. The trustees shaped the physical design, from the overall plan and the style of buildings to the minutiae of heating equipment and desks.[6] Yet in other areas the trustees were limited. They had influence and they acted in the interests of the university, even to the recruitment of the initial faculty. But in deference to academic tradition and to Harper's obvious expertise, the trustees stayed out of curricular decisions and listened carefully to the president's views on institutional structure and programs.[7]

Just as the traditions of higher education had their effect on power relations within the University of Chicago, other, less well defined traditions may have had an effect on the other cultural institutions of Chicago. The city did not exist as an island isolated from national experience where each local institution was created anew. Chicago was a part of a national—even international—culture that offered models for emulation and rejection. Many of the men involved in cultural institutions in the late nineteenth century were born elsewhere, coming to Chicago in their early manhood. All traveled extensively on business or in pursuit of pleasure. Charles Hutchinson used his trips to visit museums and galleries, looking not only at the objects on display but also at the manner in which they were exhibited. For example, on visiting the Louvre, he commented in his diary: "It is a magnificent museum. . . . I wish they would re-arrange the Louvre Galleries. The collection would be so much more satisfactory if one-half of it was removed." Hutchinson and the director of the Art Institute, William M. R. French, in their memoranda to each other would note programs of eastern museums and evaluate the Chicago institution by Boston and New York standards.[8] Yet beyond these specific, conscious references were the set of requirements and plans that came to mind when trustees thought of a museum. The model they followed may not have defined jurisdictions as carefully as the academic tradition did, but it gave the outline of what the collection ought to be, how it should be housed, and how it should be offered to the public.[9]

Yet the fact that such models were available and that comparable institutions existed elsewhere did not mean that museums and libraries and universities would be created in Chicago out of any inherent necessity. If so, one could hardly explain the lag of more than twenty years between New York's American Museum of Natural History and the Field Columbian Museum; it would be equally difficult to see why, in cities comparable to Chicago, it was to be well into the twentieth century before art museums or symphony orchestras were established. Moreover, once created, the institutions did not fit into any exact mold. Rather they varied in plan and emphasis from their counterparts in Boston or New York. While models served to shape conceptions and inform about specifics, those who created Chicago institutions selected the elements that fit their local circumstances. The basic model itself was acceptable because the cultural philanthropists in Chicago shared with those in New York and Boston an idealistic understanding of art and its potential social uses. But just as that conception came to have peculiar meanings in the Chicago context, so, too, the specific institutional arrangements took on distinctive shapes.

The most basic decision to be made was about the kinds of institutions that the city needed. It is not probable that cultural philanthropists surveyed the urban scene to determine by a rational process what institutions were desirable. Yet the sum of the separate decisions to support specific institutions had the same result. Certain forms were endowed and others neglected, and a pattern of decisions was clearly discernible. As the *Dial* concluded in an overview in 1893, endowment was still lacking for a theater, a newspaper, and a symphony orchestra.[10] The symphony did find support, though no thought was given to free admission, a common policy for museums and libraries. But in the nineteenth century none of the businessmen involved in culture would have thought of endowing a theater or a newspaper, as they would never have considered supporting opera, an industrial museum, or the novel. By their very nature, all these forms were like the light music that Thomas rejected: they appealed to man's baser nature and served to support materialism. Painting and music and pure science, on the other hand, were forms that had the potential of capturing the ideal and helping man strengthen his spiritual nature. Such forms were worthy of endowment.

One can see how this understanding shaped the major outlines of a collection. When Walter Newberry and John Crerar left bequests to establish libraries in the city, they had in mind circulating libraries of general literature. Crerar even set guidelines for the selection of literature for this kind of library. "I desire that the books and periodicals be selected with a view to create and sustain a healthy moral and Christian sentiment in the community and that all nastiness and immorality be excluded. I do not mean by this that there shall be nothing but hymn books and sermons, but I mean that dirty French novels and all skeptical trash and works of questionable moral tone shall never be found in this library."[11]

But Newberry had died in 1868, when leaders in the cultural institutions of the native-born elite had a different understanding of culture (his bequest only became effective two decades later on the death of his widow). Crerar, though living until 1889, had never been involved in Chicago's cultural life and hence was isolated from the currents of thought of the city's active cultural participants. Both men left their funds in trust to boards of friends and business associates who, by the late 1880s, had rather different ideas.[12] Though somewhat limited in their conceptions of the uses of culture, these civic-minded members of Chicago's native-born elite wanted institutions that would contain refining influences. The circulating library of general interest must have seemed too much like the Chicago Public Library, which supplied the people of the city with the literature that they desired—largely the novels and romances of the day. Excluding such popular works from its shelves, the Newberry became a reference library housing a collection of selected literary and scholarly works, as well as the rare books and manuscripts for which it is now known. The legacy of John Crerar, who had conceived of a circulating library to serve the South Side of the city, was used by his trustees for another city-wide reference library, designed to focus on areas of the life of the spirit not covered by the Newberry. After some reshuffling of collections, the Newberry became the library of the arts; the Crerar, of the sciences. The critical distinction for these men was between cultural enrichment and entertainment, not between art and science.[13]

A decision that on its face seems to be in opposition to the understanding of culture held by Chicago philanthropists actually brings out its essential nature even more clearly. This was the establishment at the World's Columbian Exposition of 1893 of the Midway, the strip of land devoted to amusement and recreation. The Midway was created because the central area of the fair devoted to culture, the Court of Honor, made it necessary. As the head of the Directory of the fair remarked, "The eye and the mind need relief after the contemplation of vast exhibits of the results of human activity and the triumphs of art." The Midway was designed to be separate from the Court of Honor, a means by which the real fair could be kept pure. It gave the "opportunity for isolating these special features, thus preventing jarring contrasts between the beautiful buildings and grounds and the illimitable exhibits on the one hand, and the amusing, distracting, ludicrous, and noisy attractions of the 'Midway.' "[14]

Yet in the Court of Honor and the immediately surrounding ground, "the illimitable exhibits" were not under the control of the Chicago Directory and did not represent its understanding of art or science. Contrasting with the buildings, largely in Renaissance dress, were massive displays of technological progress: streetcars, railroad engines, the telephone and phonograph, a moving sidewalk. At night the whiteness of the fair came from alternating current, making the White City itself an electricity exhibit. There were divisions of manufacture and of mines and mining as well as of fine arts. Chicago sources did finance scientific explorations to gather material for anthropological exhibits.[15]

When the Field Columbian Museum was organized as the repository of the exhibits of the fair, the vast industrial and historical collections came with the contents of the Anthropological Building. This was only a temporary arrangement: by the turn of the century the museum abandoned the industrial and historical fields—with the exception of transportation—returning material to donors, distributing it to schools, museums, or libraries. Even a newly acquired collection given by the president of the Field's board of trustees, Harlow Higinbotham, was returned to him to be "presented to a museum devoted to commercial ends." The Field Columbian Museum was to be a repository of science, not of industrial achievements.[16]

Thus the main outlines of the content of a cultural institution—what for simplicity's sake we shall call its collection—were clear. Designed to present works of art and intellect rather than to provide entertainment or economic gain, the institutions were limited to certain forms and to certain fields within them that could represent the ideal. Yet beyond this general definition, the understanding of art held by the cultural philanthropists guided the range of the collection and its arrangement and classification.[17]

Such men as Martin Ryerson and Charles Hutchinson viewed works of the mind and of art as representations of the eternal ideal. Yet these same works were also products of human history, expressions of the values of a society in a historical moment. This dual nature—both timeless and yet within time—provided a structure for the museum or library collection or for the symphony program. A collection was to consist of the great works which successfully represented the ideal. Because each society and each period expressed itself in its own way, the collection should consist of examples of art throughout the range of history. Similarly, in its representation of natural reality or of human societies, a scientific collection was to offer examples of the phenomena of natural history; scientific research was to be pursued in all areas.

Chicago's city-wide cultural institutions took comprehensiveness as their goal. In the nineteenth century the Art Institute lacked the money for extensive acquisitions and was thus dependent on loans from private collectors and on their gifts. There was never any thought of limiting the collection to one art form or period, however. Rather than restrict its scope, the Art Institute filled out its holdings with reproductions. But these approaches were hardly ideal; they were strategies until there were sufficient funds to allow a more systematic development of a permanent collection. Hutchinson and his associates kept watch over movements in the art markets and demonstrated a willingness to purchase within a generous range of periods and styles. Their acquisition in 1894 of the Dermidoff Collection of Dutch Masters set a high standard. Their more daring selection of an El Greco demonstrated their independent judgment.[18]

As a museum of natural science, the Field Columbian Museum held an even greater mandate to cover everything. It could boast that "today from one end of the museum to the other can be traced almost without a break, the living and instructive story of man and his work." A curator expressed the sense of urgency with which the desire for comprehensiveness could be held. "It is recog-

nized that there are vast regions of America, and even
one entire great continent and many regions of other
continents, which are but poorly represented or not
represented at all." The very existence of these regions
was a call for acquisitions: "To these regions must be
directed the energies of the future, if the high educational
objects of the Museum are to be adequately fulfilled." The
desire to include examples of all kinds extended even to
the symphony orchestra. In his plans for music at the
fair, Theodore Thomas explicitly sought "to give an
exhibition of every school, period, and nationality."[19]

It was not a question of comprehensiveness alone.
For full understanding and appreciation, the works of art
or examples from nature should be organized according
to their historical development or their natural sequence.
Within the Art Institute, the Elbridge G. Hall collection
of casts of sculpture was designed to give "comprehensive
illustration of the whole history of sculpture." In keeping
with this end it was arranged chronologically. The museum
collection as a whole was first broken down into the various
media: oils, pastels and watercolors, prints, and sculpture.
Within each division, the works were separated by country
and period and placed in separate rooms. In arranging
these rooms it seems that some effort was made to have
them follow in chronological sequence. The Art Institute
was a museum of the history of art.[20]

The Field Columbian Museum had an even greater
appreciation of order and system. A contemporary described the arrangement of artifacts in the museum. In
each area, corresponding to a scientific field, the order
"of the specimens . . . follows that of some standard
textbook on the subject, so that each section may be
considered as illustrative of such textbooks." The museum
itself characterized its own collection as "a sequential and
systematic exposition of the wonderful and instructive
things of the world we live in."[21]

At the World's Columbian Exposition, Theodore Thomas's musical programs were to be a systematic survey of the world's great music. Chicago's most astute musical critic, W. S. B. Mathews, realized the problems of this approach when it involved musical performances rather than a display of manufactures. In contrast to the brief time it took to walk through a hall, the observer could only compare musical works over an extended period of performance. While Thomas's efforts at the fair were cut short by financial pressures and by hostility to his control, his arrangement with the Orchestral Association gave him both the time he needed and a free hand with the Chicago Symphony Orchestra programs. There, after an extended period of education in which he brought his Chicago audience up to the "symphonic standard," Thomas ventured his ultimate attempt to treat music systematically. In a set of six rather ponderous programs, he highlighted the entire history of orchestral music.[22] Thus the Art Institute, the Field Columbian Museum, and the Chicago Symphony Orchestra had the same goals: they were to be like visual or auditory representations of a written text which would be both comprehensive and systematic.[23]

Not only was there to be system and order within an institution, there must also be order among the city-wide cultural institutions as a group. Certain cultural philanthropists supported a range of institutions, extending their perspective to the cultural needs of the whole city. Consequently they were willing to have their institutions divide a field and specialize, even when that meant a loss of part of their collection. The point of decision came with the Crerar bequest. A survey was made of libraries in Chicago to determine existing strengths. The report confirmed the belief of the trustees that what was needed was not a circulating library to duplicate the work of the Chicago Public, but rather a reference library that focused on areas not covered by the Newberry. The decision was

made that the Crerar take "the special field . . . of the
natural, physical, and social sciences, and their applica-
tions," over the objection of a friend of John Crerar that
the benefactor had really had a literary library in mind.[24]
In the next few years materials at the Newberry relating
to the sciences, including a valuable medical collection,
were transferred to the Crerar. The Art Institute and the
Field Columbian Museum achieved a similar working
understanding.[25]

Cooperation did not mean loss of independence,
however. Though the institutions shared many members
of their boards of trustees, they generally saw themselves
as separate bodies. The University of Chicago differed in
this respect. It had a more diverse staff, having imported
a faculty distinguished in many disciplines. Its energetic
first president clearly saw the university as a center around
which to organize cultural life in Chicago. He attempted
to bring the Art Institute, the Field Columbian Museum,
and the Chicago Symphony Orchestra into the structure
of the university as departments. The city-wide cultural
institutions resisted and maintained their autonomy.[26]

While comprehensiveness and system established di-
mensions and form appropriate to collections of works
of art or scholarship, the two standards also related to
what the cultural philanthropists understood to be the
needs of the public. The viewer could see objects in proper
perspective if the collection were complete and if the
objects were organized in an orderly, systematic survey.
But these goals assumed the public had gone so far as to
enter the building. By definition, the cultural institution
housed art or science rather than entertainment. The
basis on which it was founded excluded those areas popular
with the public: by design, these institutions were offering
to Chicago's citizenry what it did not choose to have.

Faced with the strong possibility of unpopularity, the
city-wide cultural enterprises had several options. They

might compromise their standards, but to do this would go against the fundamental premise on which they were founded—the nature and function of art as the representation of the ideal. The second possibility—to ignore the public—was equally untenable. The museums and libraries had not been built merely to satisfy the aesthetic interests of the elite. Rather they had been designed for the whole city, to lift it out of the throes of materialism and to lead it to a higher spiritual life. In the years after the institutions' founding, this commitment did not fade. The responsiveness of the public remained the issue of greatest continuous interest to the businessmen involved in culture. The annual reports contain quite careful records of attendance. The measure of success seems to have been growth in numbers. It was said that Charles Hutchinson reviewed the attendance figures of the Art Institute daily. Hence only one choice was open: to make an earnest attempt to get the public to experience the culture gathered in museum or library collections or in the symphony's repertoire.[27]

But in the late nineteenth century the public for whom the cultural institutions were designed was made up of the relatively privileged classes—those businessmen in danger of losing their souls; those men and women who took from the city without serving it in return. Hence the means chosen to attract visitors were limited in scope. The institutions were designed to appeal to the literate, the relatively leisured, and those who traveled freely between their residential neighborhoods and downtown.

The institutions differed somewhat in the degree of their commitment to the public and in their choice of means to attract patronage. The range of their efforts included routine administrative practices, hucksterism, educational programs, and the designs of the buildings themselves.

At the end of the nineteenth century many now-routine practices of museum administration were regarded as innovative techniques to attract the public. For example, after registering pleasure at the orderly and attentive visitors to the museum, the Art Institute described its intention of having labels provided for all the objects in the collection. This was seen as a vital bridge to the public: "It is upon these points of contact with the public that much of the usefulness of the museum depends." The Field Columbian Museum gave this aspect greater emphasis. Its director, Frederick Skiff, saw a fundamental distinction between an institution such as a university, whose primary task was research and the discovery of truth, and the museum, whose function was the diffusion of existing knowledge. Hence he underscored the central importance to the museum of "those principles of Museum work that appeal to the public and concern the great mass of people to whose betterment and uplifting institutions of this character are dedicated." What Skiff was talking about was the arrangement of display cases, exhibits, and the labeling of objects. With such a focus, a technique such as the use of black cards with aluminum lettering was able to be seen as an important innovation designed for the public.[28]

At the other extreme were those efforts to sell a collection through obvious hucksterism. Only once in the nineteenth century did this approach become an issue in Chicago. The World's Columbian Exposition, which had opened in an atmosphere in which "the matter of 'dignity' was . . . so jealously guarded as to become at times almost a bugbear," took on a quite different tone halfway through the summer. Sensing the need for diversion "to instill life into the vast and beautiful expanse of grounds and buildings" which was the Court of Honor, the artist Frank D. Millet was engaged for the effort of promotion. His program of processions, sports, and music included mock battles and a parade honoring the imaginary Prince of

Joho. While these events undoubtedly enlivened the fair, the effort went against the understanding of art held by the cultural philanthropists. The *Dial* saw Millet's program as one of several examples of a turn toward commercialism and heaped scorn on the directors.

> Amusement, of cheap and even vulgar sorts, is being substituted for education, because most people prefer being amused to being instructed. The popular devices of the country fair are being resorted to, and the greased pole figured in a recently published list of attractions for a particular day. Such pleasing novelties, announced in great variety from day to day, are converting the Exposition, as far as it is possible, into a huge circus . . . and mark a process of degradation aptly described by its sponsors as that of "barnumising the Fair."[29]

The fair was a unique episode in Chicago's life. While to a large extent it can be seen as a local cultural institution, its public was a national one and its economic base combined philanthropy with the hope of some reimbursement. For financial reasons it needed to draw the masses. More characteristic of Chicago's cultural enterprises than the fair's promotional efforts were the educational programs that became integral parts of their institutions.

Perhaps the most familiar medium of education in the late nineteenth century was the lecture. The Art Institute maintained a regular series, staffed by Chicago's best-known artists, on painting, sculpture, and architecture. It also held special talks as a regular part of its enterprise. One of the most important additions to its building was its large assembly room, Fullerton Hall. From its beginning the Field Columbian Museum also held lecture series. When its own hall was judged a fire hazard, the Field was made welcome at the Art Institute's facilities.[30]

The Field also had its publications. Beyond the annual reports that were common to most of the institutions, it had a set of scientific reports by which members of its staff could communicate their findings. On a much larger scale, the University of Chicago's range of scholarly publications was part of the grand design of William Rainey Harper. An object of endowment rather than a source of profit, this endeavor initially met resistance on the part of the Chicago board of trustees. But convinced of the standing the enterprise would confer on the university, the board eventually lent its support. On a different plane, the symphony orchestra's notes that accompanied each concert were designed to bring the audience to an appreciation of the works performed.[31]

Among art museums throughout the country, the Art Institute was unique in its relation to other local organizations and in its series of temporary exhibitions. The museum building served as headquarters for a variety of Chicago associations of artists and those interested in fine arts. The associations conducted annual exhibitions held in the museum. Thus the Art Institute directly encouraged local artists by providing them with a prominent place for displaying their works of art and offering them for sale. On its own the Art Institute arranged temporary shows as well. In so doing the museum seemed to go beyond the limits that the commitment to attracting a middle-class public assumed. While in the twentieth century the relation between the exhibitions and the permanent collection was to change, in the nineteenth century it was a little like that between the Midway and the Court of Honor at the fair. Without compromising the standards of its permanent collection, the museum allowed a more popular attraction to build up clientele. Whatever the cause, the result was success in the terms that the businessmen involved in culture knew best. By 1899 the Art Institute was attracting more than a half million people a year, almost three thousand on an average Sunday afternoon. The Field Columbian Museum also had impressive statistics. During the same year more than a quarter of a million people had visited its collections.[32]

Perhaps because their boards of trustees drew on an earlier generation of civic leaders, the Newberry and the Crerar libraries were at the other extreme in their relation to the public. Though the Newberry served as the location of lecture series promoted by its librarian, neither library was active in devising programs to bring the public into the building. Quite the contrary: the Newberry, open during the usual working week but closed in the evenings and on Sunday, seemed to have devised its hours to exclude those who were neither scholars nor persons of leisure.[33]

The class nature of the efforts to attract a public can be seen most clearly in the case of the Chicago Symphony Orchestra. In some respects the orchestra designed its structure to keep the people out. The extent of musical interest in Chicago in the nineteenth century was a matter of wide comment. The enthusiasm for the summer concerts and the range of choral groups testified to the special role that music played in the lives of large numbers of its residents. The Chicago Symphony Orchestra, however, ran a continuing deficit. To the critic W. S. B. Mathews the causes were obvious. The programs were uninteresting to the average concert-goer, providing no relief from the strenuous symphony, and at the same time the prices were too high for the people to attend. Whatever the supposed aim of the Orchestral Association, "the educational intention has been balked by the absence of material to educate." After a decade in which the financial problem remained unresolved, Mathews thought he saw the solution. He hoped that the Chicago Symphony Orchestra would alter its programs or broaden its base of endowment to allow regular concerts at a low admission charge. This would have brought the symphony in line with the other city-wide cultural institutions which had no expectation of full support by patrons. But the Orchestral Association saw things differently. They assumed that, except for occasional special nights explicitly designated as "People's Concerts," the public would pay, possibly because, unlike a museum or library, the symphony orchestra performed and thus was, to some extent, entertainment.[34]

Thomas and his associates thought the problem was one of place. The concerts were held in the Auditorium, a hall so large that it could accommodate all who desired to attend. There was thus little reason for the public to buy subscription tickets for a season, the source of predictable revenue. The solution was obvious—to build a smaller hall that would force those who could pay to buy season tickets. It was a curious reversal of the cultural philanthropists' relation to the public that the fund-raising drive to build the smaller Orchestra Hall for a limited audience attracted contributions from 8,000 Chicagoans.[35]

Certain concerts were both less expensive and more popular: the Friday afternoon series constantly attracted a large audience. But, though cheaper in price, these concerts were hardly accessible to those for whom Friday was a work day. Rather on Friday afternoons the orchestra played to the well-dressed women of the city. Sunday, when a broader attendance was possible, was a day of rest for the orchestra. When special guest concerts were held on Sunday, the price was invariably higher. Arrangements for Sunday concerts were not in the hands of the Orchestral Association, even in the twentieth century when they were held in Orchestra Hall: the trustees' only decision was the negative one that the orchestra not play. The effect on the Chicago audience, however, was discrimination against those for whom a two-dollar ticket was a sizable sum.[36]

Given the strong musical interest of many immigrants and their children, particularly the Germans, it seems reasonable to assume that they composed a large proportion of the mass audience that the price of symphony tickets kept home. The lack of encouragement went beyond price, for the Chicago Symphony Orchestra did not advertise in, or send complimentary tickets to, the German language newspapers. When the business manager of the *Freie Presse* questioned Charles Norman Fay about this, Fay responded that the policy seemed justified for while there have been "Germans who have contributed to the support of the Orchestra, either in the purchase of tickets or by direct donation . . . they are . . . few in number, and their donations have been . . . small in amount." This was when the official language of rehearsals was German to accommodate the majority of the members of the orchestra.[37]

A major debate of the World's Columbian Exposition, whether or not to close on Sunday, also involved Chicago's ethnic groups. Initially the Chicago directors had vied to keep the gates of the fair open on Sunday, although they encountered widespread hostility that the United States Congress wrote into law. The subscription of souvenir coins was made contingent on the Sunday closing. As a court case pended, the fair was at first kept open. But while people came, they did not buy; for they were the local population "of small means," the immigrants and their families who enjoyed the continental Sunday. Despite the pleasure that the experience of the buildings and the design obviously afforded, the head of the Directory, Harlow Higinbotham, ordered the gates closed on his own initiative: "The management was by this time thoroughly tired of the agitation, and was anxious to close the grounds."[38]

Decisions about the nature and location of the building were other factors in the institution's relation to the public. The building was not merely a shelter to house a collection. It was also an opportunity for businessmen interested in culture to serve as direct patrons of the arts. And it was meant to provide a controlled setting that established the proper relation between the public and a collection.

Chicago in the 1890s was the scene of creative developments in architecture, the further articulation of the style that has become known as the Chicago School. In their private capacities as businessmen and homeowners, cultural philanthropists supported these innovations, so important in the development of the modern aesthetic.[39] In the 1880s they had chosen these same architects to design the buildings of their cultural institutions. Daniel Burnham and John Wellborn Root designed a structure for the Art Institute in 1882, a building with a Romanesque motif later sold to the Chicago Club. The Auditorium was planned and decorated by Dankmar Adler and Louis Sullivan in a way that united bold Romanesque design to delicate stenciling. But by the 1890s a change had taken place. The great Chicago architects were still being asked to design skyscrapers, but plans for the cultural institutions were of a different style and contracts were frequently going to different men. Henry Ives Cobb, who had produced an understated Romanesque library for the Newberry, designed a Late Gothic cathedral for the University of Chicago. The Art Institute went outside the city and hired the Boston firm of Shepley, Rutan, and Coolidge to decorate the classical palace in which the museum is housed today.

While it is generally agreed that aesthetically the work of Root, Adler, Sullivan, and other contemporary Chicago architects was more innovative than that of their eastern counterparts, one must not confuse such judgment with historical understanding. The choice of Shepley, Rutan, and Coolidge was not simply a lapse of taste. Rather it came out of an identification with the Italian Renaissance and an understanding of what the building housing a cultural institution was designed to do.

A museum or library was to be, first of all, functional.

A great importance was placed, at least verbally, on the technical efficiency of the building. A typical statement was made in reference to the Art Institute: "It is planned with great care for exhibition purposes, and there are few better buildings in existence for the exhibition of pictures and fine art objects, as regards lighting, accessibility, simplicity of arrangement and convenience of classification." Proponents of a functional aesthetic would have had the building visually express its structure and technical processes. But supporters of Chicago's cultural institutions would not have agreed. To them a building was to express its use in a different sense, its relation to human lives. A structure that housed a cultural institution was to say so by its obvious importance, its dignity. Moreover, a building was a work of art, capable of performing the offices that this implied. The architect W. A. Otis, for decades the lecturer on architecture at the Art Institute, considered the nature of the library building. Since books had always been housed in the "best and fairest" buildings, it was generally accepted that "the home of books should be not merely a store-house for books, but should be also a beautiful building and an artistic center in its broadest sense." The result was the uplifting of a community. The library "is seen and felt by more people who need it and should be raised by art, than almost any other place."[40]

Consistent with the idealistic approach to art, the building was to be no trivial or fleeting expression. Rather it was to express one of the great moments of art, generally Greek antiquity, the Gothic Middle Ages, or, increasingly, the Renaissance. It was to be lasting: those individuals who gave buildings (or parts of them) could expect their contribution to be an enduring one, giving to them a measure of immortality.[41] The building was to work on the spirit of the observer both in itself and as the appropriate setting for other works of the spirit.

For the many who came to the institutions from

modest homes, the experience was memorable. One art student recalled her first evening lecture "in the most exquisite room—doors all hung with plush and satin, stained glass on windows, Persian rugs on the floor. Paintings, busts, and mirrors filled the walls." A reader in the Crerar Library remembered its "dark wood tables and shaded lamps, where the chairs just seemed to fit . . . [and] the atmosphere was a comforting one of quiet erudition and culture."[42] It may have been that such elegant structures solved a problem that had been the bane of the popular Chicago Public Library, "the foulness arising from the large number of unwashed and unkempt persons." It was difficult to set standards for admission. The solution that some eastern libraries had found was to introduce "such elegance and refinement of taste in the furniture and appointments of their reading rooms that unclean persons will not frequent them." The design of a building and its furnishings could insure a middle-class clientele.[43]

Yet beyond the luxury of the furnishings and the attention to decorative detail were the vast enclosed spaces spanned by arches or topped by domes, suggestive of European grandeur. The Art Institute was finished as parts of the collection grew in size and as funds for building were donated. The monumental staircase, sought for many years, was completed in the twentieth century. "Nothing since the original erection of the museum has done so much as the construction of this grand staircase to dignify and ennoble the building. Immediately upon entering the visitor is aware that he is in a great public building devoted to art."[44] Such an interior space defined a cultural institution: the enclosure of a significant area created a world within which one might breathe a refining atmosphere.

The exterior of the building was intended to impress. Solid and balanced, in a historical mode that commanded respect, it invoked the great names of the field for which it was the repository. The Art Institute called forth such figures as Donatello, Botticelli, Leonardo da Vinci, Raphael, Titian, Holbein; Orchestra Hall emblazoned the names of Bach, Mozart, Beethoven, Schubert, Wagner. The very names themselves lent the dignity of association. To further separate the museum from the city street, the Art Institute followed the London model and installed lions at its entrance on Michigan Avenue.

The World's Columbian Exposition captured the essence of the cultural philanthropists' understanding of the meaning of the building. A local endeavor projected onto an international exposition, the fair spotlighted tendencies that before had been only partially expressed. Here could be created not just an isolated structure, but—for the moment at least—a total environment. The Renaissance buildings of plaster of Paris and straw were arranged in a horseshoe around a lagoon, their related design emphasized by a uniform cornice line. The approach at the open end was marked by Daniel Chester French's immense statue *The Republic*; directly opposite, closing off the line of vision, was Richard Morris Hunt's Administration Building capped by a monumental dome. For all the fair's variety and amusement, what struck visitors most profoundly was the White City itself. The dramatic landscape was an overwhelming experience to those used to the multiplicity, even chaos, of the American city street. The Court of Honor had been consciously designed to be beautiful, the product "of a desire for structures more noble and landscape effects more beautiful than any the world had hitherto seen."[45]

Both to local artists and to those from outside the city, the White City was the apotheosis of culture. The Chicagoan Harriet Monroe, in an early, quite traditional poem, played on the contrast between the fair's fleeting quality and the eternal values it represented. The fair was "a water-lily . . . White, wondrous," a dream "that ere the falling of a summer sun . . . must pass."

> Yet knew I well her beauty could not die.
> When she hath gone her power is but begun:
> Death sends the soul to God's eternal day.

The influential editor of the *Century*, Richard Watson Gilder, a New Yorker, returned again and again to assertions of the eternal nature of the fair. "Thou shalt of all the cities of the world/. . . ever more endure. . . . In the world's living thought." The fair was the ultimate expression of art.

> O never as here in the eternal years
> Hath burst to bloom man's free and soaring spirit,
> Joyous, untrammelled, all untouched by tears.

The fair was "Art's citadel and crown," "ecstasy envisioned."[46]

Early in planning, Chicago leaders had hoped that the World's Columbian Exposition could be held at a site on the shore of Lake Michigan at the eastern edge of the business district. To provide a large enough area it would have been necessary to fill, requiring permission from the War Department (which held authority over the harbor). This permission was refused, and the fair site was moved south of downtown to Jackson Park. However, the one fully permanent structure of the fair, the building housing the World's Congresses, raised by the combined resources of the fair and the Art Institute, was built downtown on Michigan Avenue at the Lake Front. When the fair closed, this building became the permanent home of the Art Institute. The Auditorium and the Crerar Library had, from the beginning, a downtown location near the Chicago Public Library. They were to be joined in the twentieth century by the Field Columbian Museum and the Chicago Symphony's Orchestra Hall.[47]

Edifices of beauty, they were not to be located in the neighborhoods of wealth where they might have found fitting complements, as in other cities where "art has . . . set itself apart." Rather, in keeping with the prevailing sense of art's function in a materialistic society, "proximity to the heart of the city is an overwhelming recommendation in the eyes of the Trustees, for no object is more distinctly entertained by them than the benefit of the great masses of people, to whom convenience of access is essential." Given the limited extent of public programs, the restricted hours of certain institutions, the prohibitive costs of others, and the intimidating elegance of the buildings, the "masses" were probably understood to be the middle classes who did go downtown to shop and to transact business.[48]

Moreover, the central location served a symbolic function important in the Chicago context. Downtown was the real heart of city, the place where decisions were made, where businessmen endangered by their absorption in materialism had their offices. To set the buildings there would underscore their importance and give them opportunity to act as countervailing spiritual forces. At the focal point of Chicago would stand buildings designed to be beautiful, representing in steel and stone the idea of art that would transform the city's life.

On a quite different plane, the buildings expressed another aspect of the cultural philanthropists: their business sense and their urge to speculate. Active in the commercial life of their city, these men were willing to employ their expertise and skill in their cultural institutions.

In planning a building, or (in the case of the University of Chicago) a campus, the elite thought in terms of the total design. Where the institution was at an early stage of growth or where resources were insufficient, the structure was built in stages. In 1891 Thomas Wakefield Goodspeed, secretary of the board of trustees of the University of

Chicago, explained to President Harper, "Mr. Ryerson has sketched a complete plan for the buildings. . . . The idea of Mr. Ryerson and Mr. Hutchinson is to draw out on paper the entire plan at the start, with the locations of buildings indicated, and then go forward, building by building, as we are able." Within a single structure this was the procedure of the Art Institute as well. By this, the trustees retained control over architecture at the same time that they stimulated and guided gifts. These businessmen were agreed on the importance of the building from the standpoint of the giver as well as the observer. The building could "appeal to the average imagination. Men wish something to show for their money." By executing a master plan in stages, the trustees could give potential donors a quite concrete idea beforehand about how their money would be used, attracting them, while channeling their gifts to meet specific needs.[49]

The Art Institute managed this quite adeptly in adding to its collection as well as its building. The most important early acquisition, the Dermidoff Collection, fourteen paintings by Dutch Masters, was bought as a lot with money borrowed by several trustees. The Art Institute then asked the public to buy individual paintings from the collection as gifts to the museum. By 1901 the system reached a kind of maturity. The museum listed its greatest needs with their approximate costs, ranging from books for the museum library to a $100,000 hall for architectural casts. One of the most important functions that the annual reports of all the institutions served was to thank donors and to stimulate further gifts.[50]

Behind this approach was a basic assumption that it was the nature of an institution to grow. "The Trustees call attention to the fact that it is the necessary growth of the institution which constantly taxes our resources. If we could stand still, the income would very soon equal the expense. But the work constantly expands, and no

friend of the Institute would have it otherwise." There
was no thought that once a collection had been developed
or a structure built, the institution would remain static.
Possibly because its area of concern lent itself to exploration, the Field Columbian Museum was the most aggressive. It not only encouraged gifts and made purchases, it
supported scientific expeditions for natural specimens or
anthropological artifacts. The most extensive venture in
the period was the three-year trip to Tibet undertaken by
Dr. Bernard Laufer, resulting in an extraordinary collection
of art, artifacts, and books shared by several of the city-
wide cultural institutions.[51]

So strong was their commitment to growth that the
cultural institutions were willing to expand beyond available resources. The most notorious in this respect was the
University of Chicago. Harper constantly overreached his
budget. A building that was intended to cost $150,000,
for example, was built at a cost of more than $200,000.
Faculty were hired not on the basis of existing funds,
but on Harper's hope for future endowments. Harper's
speculative bent went far beyond the level of the university's trustees, who tried to limit university programs. Their
pressure on Harper may have come out of a fear of angering
John D. Rockefeller, who had to be called on constantly
to bail the university out (his endowment eventually totaled
35 million dollars), for the Chicago institutions supported
only by these local trustees took risks also.[52] When it appeared that the Chicago site of the World's Columbian
Exposition was endangered by New York's higher pledge
of funds for the enterprise, the Chicagoans bidding raised
their promise from five to ten million dollars. Like the
University of Chicago, the fair continually exceeded its
budget: beginning with an estimated expenditure of 17.5
million dollars, the final cost has been estimated at 46
million. The Art Institute trustees handled the situation
in a more controlled way. Technically staying within their

means, they were willing to build only a foundation when they lacked resources to complete a wing of the building.[53]

What emerges from this is the willingness of trustees, in some instances, to use their speculative drive when they were planning for culture. They not only believed in growth—they were betting on it. They were also willing to use their business sense to further their institutions' development. Both the Art Institute and the Field Columbian Museum, and later the Chicago Symphony Orchestra as well, developed categories of membership designed to tap the various levels of wealth and interest. A governing membership in the Art Institute cost $100 upon election by the board, followed by $25 each year or $400 for life. From there one might move down the scale to a regular membership purchasable for $10.[54]

This business sense affected the nature of the institutions in some degree. Success, which in reality had to do with the quality of the cultural experience, was translated by the philanthropists into numbers. From the standpoint of the collection and the building, the relevant statistics were endowments and additions. In terms of a relationship with the public, they were the number of visitors. Yet except in the case of the fair, this perspective was limited in the nineteenth century by the definition of the desirable public as the middle class. Looking ahead to the directions in which some of the institutions would move in the twentieth century, one might hypothesize that the business sense of the cultural philanthropists contributed to their willingness to change their institutions' approaches once their own interest in culture shifted from the businessman to the urban masses.

To point up the distinctive nature of the institutions supported by cultural philanthropy and to understand something of their impact on the city, it seems useful to examine a cultural institution of a different nature, the Chicago Public Library. Sharing to some degree the functions of the privately supported institutions and their understanding of culture, the public library, nonetheless, had a distinctive commitment to serving the city that called for a different kind of collection and a different relation to the public. Yet the conceptions of culture held by the philanthropists became more and more influential. Increasingly, the public library appeared on the defensive and tried to justify itself in idealistic terms, to see its role as inspiring rather than as serving Chicago's citizens. Its supreme attempt in this direction was its building, erected at the end of the century. The next years would reveal the costs of this mistake.

The Chicago Public Library was founded as the repository for books donated after the Great Fire of 1871. Its board, chosen by the mayor, reflected the different political constituencies of the city, including prominent members of the city's ethnic groups. These men saw their work as contributing to Chicago's glory and as serving the less fortunate who sought opportunities for advancement through education. The library was a public one and was actually meant for all the people. To those who would have limited the collection to only certain kinds of books, the board answered:

> This is a Public library, supported by public taxation, and every person in the community, however humble, or lacking in literary culture, has a right to be supplied with books adapted to his taste and mental capacity. The masses of readers are not scholars, and have little of what passes in the world as literary culture; hence they read largely works of the imagination and the lighter class of literature, and are benefited thereby. To deprive them of such books is to exclude them from the use of the library.[55]

By the late 1880s it seemed important to differentiate the function of the public library from the new reference library, the Newberry. While "private or reference libraries . . . are of great and most important and continuous benefit to the student and the dilettante—treasure houses for the storing of the unattainable and the curious in letters . . . they are not for the people directly." It was service to the people that defined the Chicago Public Library.[56]

This assertion was made in the face of some rethinking of the public library's function. From the beginning, the library board had experienced doubts about its purposes, for it also saw a responsibility to shape the taste of the community. Increasingly, the library was seen as the repository of culture: "Here the soul of the past is ready to impart intelligence and experience to the living." Yet stronger than this interest in culture was the commitment to satisfy the public demand for books. Requests in the late nineteenth century were largely for American and English fiction. As these forms were held in rather low regard by proponents of culture, meeting popular demand seemed to conflict with the promotion of culture. Efforts in the period to deny any conflict indicate the degree of tension. Supporters of the library argued that no matter how low a book, it was always of a higher spirituality than its reader. Hence whatever books were read, the individual was raised by exposure to them. Those books of gravest concern, the light novels, "are not vicious books; they are simply thin, feeble, and sensational; but they are above the standard of the people who read them."[57]

The library's books, meeting the demands of the population, were to reflect the city's heterogeneity. The collection was to be open to all schools of thought. "Free to every reader, it will also be free to their books. Neither nationality, party, or creed can take offense, because the shelves are ready to receive the books of all creeds and schools." The initial collection had included books from the Continent, as well as from England and other parts of the United States. The library remained willing to meet the demands of immigrant groups for books in their native language, granting, for example, the request by a group of Hungarians to purchase 100 Hungarian books.[58]

The Chicago Public Library was a genuinely popular enterprise. In 1897–1898 a total of 1,346,131 books were borrowed. Consequently the library did not have to think of programs designed to get people into its building. It did seek to facilitate access through hours that enabled people from all walks of life to use the collection and through a partial decentralization that brought books into neighborhoods. Delivery stations were established throughout the city where books could be picked up and returned. The library also cooperated with the public schools, allowing teachers greater borrowing privileges and accommodating class visits, even gathering reference collections on specific topics for projects.[59]

For years the Chicago Public Library, like the Crerar, used rented quarters. Its first librarian had moved slowly on acquiring a building because he saw the difficulties of planning for unpredictable growth. He had also been a major proponent of library buildings designed for efficient use rather than for visual effect. The library's desire for a central location further delayed the building until the 1890s, when permission was granted for the use of Dearborn Park. By then new cultural values had their weight. The nature of the collection remained invulnerable, although its character could be distorted. While the list of holdings makes it clear that the library's strength was in literature, the aspect that the board chose to emphasize was its reference collection of Americana and fine arts. The building provided an opportunity to redefine the institution. The library that had begun so humbly in the watertower now acquired a dazzling building. Designed by the architects of the Art Institute, the Chicago Public Library building coupled internal efficiency with lavish decoration. Inside its classical exterior were more mosaics

of fine glass and marble than had been used since the
thirteenth century. Within their patterns were the names
of great authors, mottoes on the value of books, and the
symbols of famous printers. Like the Art Institute, the
Chicago Public Library building was to act on its visitors
as a stimulus to the higher life. The supply of desired
books took second place to the splendor of a house of
culture.[60]

Consequences for the institution were severe. For the
next decade the city, feeling that its responsibility had
been fully met, cut back library funds, necessitating, at
times, evening and Sunday closing, the curtailment of
delivery stations, and a halt on acquisitions. Perhaps the
library was hoping to limit the public to the middle class.
In any case, its policies must have done so. In the nineteenth century no lesson about priorities was learned.
Without questioning the purposes for which the gift was
intended, the library board accepted a quarter of a million
dollars for the erection of a branch library modeled after
the Erechtheum in Athens to be "a centre of culture and
progress, . . . its influence to be felt throughout the
community." For the time being, at least in this respect,
the Chicago Public Library was willing to emulate those
institutions established by the cultural philanthropists,
looking to refine Chicago's population rather than to serve
their personal convenience and their tastes in reading.[61]

Despite its capitulation to culture in its magnificent
building, the Chicago Public Library remained different
from its philanthropically endowed counterparts. Popular
because its collection was meeting public demands, the
library saw little need in the nineteenth century to devise
special programs to attract a larger clientele. By contrast,
the city-wide cultural institution based its collection not
on public demand but on an abstract understanding of
what constituted the arts and letters. Because it dealt
with culture that was timeless yet expressed within time,

the collection was to be comprehensive, with examples from all the important moments of creativity; to aid the observer, objects were to be arranged systematically. While the city-wide cultural institution was not founded to meet the felt needs of Chicago citizens, it was designed for them: only by reaching the public could the city be lifted above materialism. To bring the people into their buildings, some of the institutions felt an obligation to develop special programs, such as lectures, publications, and temporary exhibitions, and to house the collection in magnificent buildings. However, given the identification of the public with the middle class, efforts to popularize were balanced against or were defeated by measures that excluded large segments of the population.

Chicago's city-wide cultural institutions were not static. In the next decades they were subjected to scrutiny and criticism, both direct and indirect, that took issue with their definition of the public, their idealistic understanding of art, their conception of the building, and their notions of the creative process. In the twentieth century a new spirit would infuse cultural philanthropy. Innovative efforts, both within existing institutions and without, would go far to meet the objections of critics. Yet the heritage of the nineteenth century would continue as a compelling force.

6

The Settlement House Reformers' Critiques

On April 10, 1901, Charles Hutchinson dined at Hull-House with Jane Addams, John Dewey, and Henry Blake Fuller. Their conversation may have been merely a genial, good-natured one. This would have been in keeping with Hutchinson's personal style and with a recognition of the many social bonds which united the four. Hutchinson was a contributor to Hull-House (he later would become a trustee), and he was the treasurer of the board of trustees that theoretically employed the University of Chicago faculty, of which Dewey was a distinguished member. Dewey was a close friend and intellectual co-worker of Miss Addams, as well as a trustee of Hull-House. His ties to Hutchinson were deepened by the support given to the Laboratory School by friends of Hutchinson who were parents and benefactors. Fuller's links with the other three were purely personal—forged through his friendship with members of the University of Chicago faculty, with Harriet Monroe (who had lived at Hull-House and continued to be a contributor), and with Hutchinson himself. Had the four allowed themselves, they could have engaged in a fascinating discussion about the nature of art and its relation to the city. For however they may have been linked by personal and institutional ties, Jane Addams and John Dewey had come by 1901 to differ deeply from such cultural philanthropists as Charles Hutchinson in their conception of culture. It was Henry Blake Fuller's tragedy to agree with them both.[1]

As a young woman Jane Addams had accepted the dictates of aesthetic idealism and had attempted to live, like her contemporaries, that combination of society, charity, and pursuit of culture that defined the leisured woman's role.[2] The results had been crippling. Rather than feeling herself growing spiritually, she had been plagued by a loss of vitality and a sense of futility: "I am filled with shame that with all my apparent leisure I do nothing at all. . . . my faculties, memory receptive faculties and all, perfectly inaccessible locked up away from me." Travel in Europe with its full-time pursuit of culture only intensified Miss Addams's distress. Yet it also provided a way out. On her second trip Jane Addams visited Toynbee Hall, an outpost of Oxford graduates in the slums of the West End of London. There, through educational and cultural programs, young men were attempting to live out John Ruskin's injunctions and to infuse an impoverished urban neighborhood with the fruits of their cultivation. Through the medium of Toynbee Hall, Miss Addams was able to locate her problem—isolation from the currents of real life and feeling and self-indulgent pursuit of her own sensibilities. Through the West End outpost, she was also able to approach the realities of the city, its overwhelming poverty and brutality. With her friend Ellen Gates Starr, she decided to return to America and to establish in a Chicago lower-class neighborhood her own residence.[3]

The move scarcely implied a rejection of the claims

of culture. Although the two women got support and settled on Halsted Street with no clear, conscious plan, they were too deeply influenced by Toynbee Hall and by Ruskin not to conceive of themselves as bringing the insights and pleasures of the arts to their new neighbors. When they invited them in for the first time, it was to a reading of George Eliot's *Romola*. "The first furnishings were . . . pictures. They were hung upon all the wall spaces and were largely selected from photographs which the two original residents had the previous year together purchased in Europe." But what her own life and Toynbee Hall had taught Jane Addams was that the personal appreciation of a work of art in isolation had little value or meaning. Only when shared by all was art satisfying: "The blessings which we associate with a life of refinement and cultivation can be made universal and must be made universal if they are to be permanent."[4]

As the goals and approaches of Miss Addams in taking up residence on Halsted Street began to take shape in the 1890s, she came to understand the problem of the city as fragmentation. It seemed to her as though the social organism had broken down. On the one hand, the poor were totally absorbed in the struggle to gain subsistence. They lived apart from institutions, traditions, or social organizations as she had known them. On the other hand, those in a position to aid the poor and to link them up to the broader society, the wealthy with "the social tact and training, the large houses, and the traditions and customs of hospitality, live in other parts of the city." It was not only private contact with culture that the poor lacked; it was equally "the clubhouses, libraries, galleries, and semi-public conveniences of social life . . . [that were] blocks away."[5]

Implicitly Miss Addams indicted the businessmen involved in culture. It was they who had the resources and the cultivation to share with the poor. These men might answer that the institutions they promoted could serve residents of Halsted Street as well as those from other parts of the city. Their downtown location theoretically made the institutions available to all. Yet, as we have seen, in the late nineteenth century the major cultural institutions of Chicago were designed to counter the materialism of businessmen and their families more than to meet the needs of the masses. The nature of the attending public could be obscured by the philanthropists' perspective. These businessmen looked at the city from downtown. When they read the attendance figures of their institutions, these men were concerned with the total numbers who came; not where they were coming from. Miss Addams worked from the other end. The essence of her effort was involvement in a neighborhood to assess and change the quality of its life. She saw not Chicagoans but immigrants and their families struggling to survive in the Halsted Street area. These people lived their lives on a block; they did not venture downtown. The city-wide cultural institutions were not serving the ethnic groups of the city.

Jane Addams established her residence in 1889 in the rather generous quarters of what had been the middle-class home of the Hull family, which had remained from a day before immigrants inhabited the neighborhood. The rooms were warm and comfortable, in the decor of a contemporary residence. In the house lived and worked the settlement staff, which grew as the institution flourished. Its rooms were also meant for the neighborhood. It was to be that large, hospitable residence open to all, in which immigrants and the poor would find ties to the broader society.[6]

Initially Hull-House attempted to act as a link between the existing civic institutions and the residents of the neighborhood. Jane Addams described the settlement house in the early years as a "commission merchant. Without endowment and without capital itself, it constantly acts between the various institutions of the city and the people for whose benefit these institutions were erected. The hospital, the county agencies, and state asylums are often but vague rumors to the people who need them most." While each institution had been established to serve the people, it had forgotten them in its ongoing administration. An institution was "apt to lace itself up in certain formulas"; it was "in danger of forgetting the mystery and complexity of life."[7]

Increasingly, however, Hull-House sought to include within itself what the neighborhood needed, expanding its physical structure from the single house to a complex of buildings to serve the varied needs of the 9,000 who came each week for classes, meetings, recreation, and aid. While Miss Addams generally spoke of the city as a whole rather than of the neighborhood, other settlement house reformers found in the neighborhood a key concept. Graham Taylor, the head of the Chicago Commons, saw the neighborhood as the crucial link between the family and the wider society. He sought to decentralize agencies such as the public library so that they would serve and strengthen the smaller units. His influence would be important as Chicago's cultural institutions responded to the changes of the twentieth century.[8]

The communal rooms of Hull-House were devoted to varied activities, including health and housekeeping care. But as important as these practical concerns was the attention given to culture. Areas were set aside for reading, the exhibition of pictures, choral practice, and musical concerts. In the nursery were reproductions of Raphael Madonnas and Donatello and Della Robbia statues. Delighted at the response of the children who kissed these works, a Hull-House spokesman commented, "Surely much is gained if one can begin in a very little child to make a truly beautiful thing truly beloved." It seemed an important change that immigrants in the neighborhood replaced their cheap chromos with reproductions of great works. The first addition to the house was an art gallery donated by Edward B. Butler, a prominent Chicago cultural philanthropist.[9]

The economic contrast between Hull-House and the neighborhood was not to be minimized. The setting was to provide the "particular amount of luxury that shall tend to 'free' the social expression of its neighbors, and not cumber that expression. The residents at Hull House find that the better in quality and taste their surroundings are, the more they contribute to the general enjoyment."[10]

In the early years of her work, Jane Addams had a sense of her role that shared an elitism with Ruskin, the men of Toynbee Hall, and Chicago contemporaries involved in cultural philanthropy. In 1893 she described her understanding of the ideal society in terms of listening to "a thousand voices singing the Hallelujah Chorus in Handel's Messiah": "You have found that the leading voices could still be distinguished, but that the differences of training and cultivation between them and the voices of the chorus were lost in the unity of purpose and the fact that they were all human voices lifted by a high motive." What the settlement house attempted was to create that kind of wholeness. It would give to the neighborhood "the results of cultivation and training," while it received in return "the volume and strength of the chorus." The example that Miss Addams selected, the musical composition of a great master, was significant. The art objects chosen to adorn the settlement house reflected an attitude similar to that of the Art Institute: respect for the masterpieces of the Western tradition.[11]

While in her view of society and in her sense of what comprised a work of art Jane Addams was like Charles Hutchinson and his colleagues, she differed from these businessmen, even in this early period, in her emphasis on the purposes art could serve. Rather than a means to lift the select few out of their material concerns, art was a resource that should be available to all. Art was a cement to bind the individual to his society. It was the relationship of members of the chorus to each other, rather than to the work of art itself, that was most significant. Art could be a means of shared experience that would link all together in the society. It could also bind the individual to his past. For the immigrants who had been severed from the culture of their homeland, art could "preserve and keep for them whatever of value their past life contained." It would be a way to heal the divisions between the generations, as the sons discovered values in the lives of their fathers. And it could connect the immigrant to American society as he learned that some Americans shared his respect for the life of the spirit. The value of a work of art was not in its ability to uplift, but in its force as a medium of human thought, crossing the barriers of culture and time to speak to men about what was human.[12]

This sense of art had a broader application that suggests the kind of goals John Dewey had for the school. As Miss Addams expressed it, "freeing the individual from a sense of separation and isolation in his emotional experience," usually the function of art, was to be the goal of the settlement house. While the artist selected images from the real world and shaped them to reveal their eternal essence, the settlement house would achieve this "in terms of life itself." A goal of its programs would be "the putting forward of the essential so that the trivial will appear unimportant, as it is." It would "select the more typical and enduring forms of social life," eliminating the "irrelevant things which crowd into actual living."[13]

Miss Addams's understanding was a growing one. Her own frustration and the Ruskinian example of Toynbee Hall led her away from the search for personal fulfillment in aesthetic appreciation to a plan for sharing culture.

But it was her experiences at Hull-House and her contact with John Dewey that developed her awareness. Initially she and her co-workers had seen that the existing civic institutions were not meeting the immigrant community's needs. They established a homelike environment in the neighborhood to make possible a close contact with the population. Their cultural programs were designed to encourage people to go to existing institutions or to place in a more accessible location the same collections or programs as the city-wide museums, libraries, university, or orchestra. In time Hull-House residents came to place value in the settlement house experience for its selective reconstruction of life. And broader experience, contact with their clients, and the stimulation of new modes of thought led them to question whether or not the cultural standards they had shared with the major cultural institutions of the city any longer had meaning.

One can see this in the rethinking of settlement house programs. Hull-House was one of the early sites for the University of Chicago's extension program, which it welcomed eagerly. Yet by 1899 Hull-House was questioning the value of extension. Just because the settlement residents had gone to college, it did not follow that college classes were what the laborers around Halsted Street needed. That was to take a "priggish attitude" that treated members of the community as children. Rather the extension classes seemed too detailed, too academic. "A course of lectures in astronomy, illustrated by 'stereoptican slides,' will attract a large audience the first week who hope to hear of the wonders of the heavens, and the relation of our earth thereto, but instead of that they are treated to spectrum analyses of star dust." Such an approach was "bookish and remote." It was academic, reflecting "an idle thirst for knowledge which lacks any relation to human life." What the settlement house audience wanted were "great things, simply told." W. S.

B. Mathews reported a discussion that reached a similar conclusion. Musicians and those with musical interests met to consider what would be the best offerings for Hull-House concerts. The discussants were obviously still concerned about whether they should seek to entertain or to educate their audience, but the focus of their conversation was an interest in what they thought the people wanted to hear, program music and operatic selections.[14]

Chicago's cultural philanthropists had seen art as the representation of the ideal, meeting standards that had no relation to any given society. The individual through the experience of art gradually came to appreciate what was worthy in and of itself. While the creative art of a society would reflect that society's unique values, it would nevertheless capture the essence of the ideal. An implicit corollary was that great art was possible whatever the conditions under which a society lived. Miss Starr and, for a time at least, Miss Addams began to question these assumptions. While they agreed with Chicago's cultural philanthropists that the absence of great art in contemporary America was the fault of a lack of taste, they disagreed on the cause and cure. Their experience on Halsted Street led the two women to appreciate and make their own that aspect of John Ruskin's thought that carried a harsh critique of the industrial order.

The Ruskinian inheritance was a complex one that could be appropriated in a variety of ways. Ruskin moved some Americans to study nature and to view art with heightened respect; others he inspired through his call for an elite leadership to uplift the masses by bringing them culture. In his later years Ruskin had become one of industrial society's severest judges. By focusing on the experience of the worker in creating the object of art or industry Ruskin indicted the modern world. Jane Addams and, with greater resonance, Ellen Gates Starr, would echo his words.

One could not create taste by introducing people to great works of art, for it was impossible to "put the fringe of art on the end of a day" spent as those in Chicago were forced to spend it. Art was an expression of the life of a society and was only healthy when the society creating it was healthy. Nineteenth-century American society, dominated by the machine, afforded to its citizens misery and hence was incapable of a rich, vital art. Only labor done in joy could create works of beauty. In the face of this understanding, the settlement might serve two functions. It could work toward a better society, "toward the rescue of those bound under the slavery of commerce and the wage-law." And it could extend the experience of works of art more broadly.[15]

In the existing state of society, art had only a limited function. It could not save—it could only keep up man's spirits. "The soul of man in the commercial and industrial struggle is in a state of siege. He is fighting for his life. It is merciful and necessary to pass on to him the things which sustain his courage and keep him alive, but the effectual thing is to raise the siege." The value of the effort to extend art was exceedingly limited, and its results were almost cruel. "It is a feeble and narrow imagination which holds out to chained hands fair things which they cannot grasp,—things which they could fashion for themselves were they but free." In the long run it was the reformation of the society, not the extension of culture, which was to determine the future of art. Only a society in which all worked in joy could sustain art. "If gladness ceases upon the earth, and we turn the fair earth into a prison-house for men with hard and loveless labor, art will die."[16]

This Ruskinian vision led Miss Addams and Miss Starr to work on two levels: to attempt to restore the right relation of men to their crafts; and to struggle to create a humane industrial order. Responding as had many English followers of Ruskin, Miss Starr founded an arts and crafts society at Hull-House to promote handicrafts. She returned to England to learn the art of fine bookbinding and taught it at the settlement, aware, however, of the deep incongruity of practicing a craft whose products could be afforded only by the rich.[17]

As she became aware of the life and needs of her neighborhood, Jane Addams found a different alternative, one that signaled a redefinition of culture. She established the Hull-House Labor Museum, which not only displayed the collection of textiles of the Field Columbian Museum, but, more important, housed a room of spindles and looms where the immigrant women of the neighborhood demonstrated to each other and to their children the techniques of spinning and weaving they had employed before coming to America. On a social level the museum restored, if only momentarily, the proper relationships between parents and children as mothers instructed their sons and daughters in the practices that had once been such meaningful personal accomplishments. But it also provided an illustration of industrial history that Miss Addams was coming to see as a critical element in education. In contrast to the early programs of Hull-House, what seemed to be needed was not adult education added to a day of meaningless labor or education designed for social mobility. Rather contemporary society called for some form of industrial education that would give social value to the workers' experience. If the individual's separate tasks were put in the context of the whole product and the total economy and into the perspective of history and the evolution of technological process, he could understand his contribution to the general good. This learning was not an alternative to "culture," but its essential element. For culture was not isolated in fine arts but was that "understanding of the long-established occupations and thoughts of men, of the arts with which they have solaced their toil." While one might argue that to the slaughterhouse worker or the factory operative who repeated a process every minute such education could offer little, it was Miss Addams's hope that it would help to change the nature of work so that labor would "cease to be senseless drudgery with no self-expression on the part of the worker." Moreover, educational programs at Hull-House were joined to a receptivity to the labor movement. Not only did Hull-House sponsor lectures on trade unionism and special gatherings to consider problems such as Sunday closing, but it provided space for regular union meetings.[18]

Miss Addams's hopes for industrial education sound much like the redefinition that John Dewey was giving to education in the same period. Both were concerned with the split between beauty and life, art and work. And both hoped to use their institutions as controlled social settings that would "reconstruct," as Dewey said, the experience of the immigrant or child. As a frequent visitor and speaker at Hull-House, Dewey had an important effect on Miss Addams: he served to crystallize and give theoretical formulation to the settlement house experience. But it would be a mistake to read Miss Addams in Deweyan terms, for the influence, while significant, was only partial.[19]

This is clear in their different approaches to art. At the turn of the century Dewey questioned the fundamental assumption behind cultural idealism. Art was not "set off in a little sphere" different from everyday life "so that we pass from the things we call material to the things which we call spiritual as many people pass from week days to Sunday and back again." This was to treat art as an end in itself rather than as a means to experience. The past became "an ornament and solace; a refuge and an asylum," not an aid to change contemporary life. Such a separation of art from life arose out of the division of labor in society that separated leisure from work. Art should unite work and play as the "occupation which fills the imagination and the emotions as well as the hands." It should be "industry unusually conscious of its own meaning." As such it is capable of revealing in experience "a depth and range of meaning" through "the concentration and consummation of elements of good which are otherwise scattered and incomplete."[20]

Such a reevaluation of culture struck at the heart of the assumption behind cultural philanthropy. Like Ruskin, though in different words, Dewey was putting the issue back into social and economic terms. But Dewey went beyond Ruskin to question the value of transmitting the whole cultural apparatus of Western civilization. Art's emotional dimension had small worth in itself if it did not grow from experience, the social environment emerging from cooperative labor. As a result, in the classroom there seemed to be little place for traditional culture and then it was useful merely as an adjunct to the core concern, the economic and social process. Penelope in the *Odyssey* was "a classic in literature only because the character is an adequate embodiment of a certain industrial phase of social life," more particularly, weaving. Jane Addams was more firmly tied to the creative fruits of the Western tradition than Dewey and found the emotional level of art of deeper meaning.[21]

Her approach related, in part, to her audience. Unlike Chicago's cultural philanthropists or John Dewey, she saw herself, realistically or not, as working with immigrants whose experience included the art, literature, and music of Europe. Art at the settlement house would be for its neighbors not indoctrination, but rather a way to "preserve and keep for them whatever of value their past life contained." And as she came to consider the young people around her and many of their encounters with the society, she arrived at an understanding of youth that led to a new appreciation of art's power. Young men and women had an emotional and sexual nature that sought expression in play. Criminal behavior that appeared pathological on the surface was really a distortion of the capacity of the young for adventure, commitment, and love. With no legitimate outlets in the city, adolescents leading cramped lives in factories turned to the commercial exploitation of vice and to pranks, robbery, and drugs. What they needed was play to tap their energy and imagination and direct it to a heightened expression. The Greeks understood these needs. To them "the world of fact was also the world of the ideal, . . . the realization of what ought to be, [which] involved not the destruction of what was, but merely its perfecting upon its own lines."[22]

Jane Addams came to a renewed appreciation of art, returning in a new spirit to its powers of refinement. The fine arts, particularly music and drama, were emotional outlets with the power to loosen sex "from the things of sense and to link it to the affairs of the imagination." A great work by Schiller or Shakespeare could command the involvement of adolescents. The drama's difficulty only "dignified and enhanced" its pleasure. Yet the art of the past must be linked to the vigor of the present. Miss Addams's conception of art included folk customs as expressed in festivals; it recognized sports as a legitimate form of expression drawing together all classes of the community into common endeavor. Moreover, Miss Addams brought to her renewed interest in traditional culture a new spirit. The community should provide opportunity for expression not so much to ward off the threat of social disorganization as to help conserve the contribution the young had to make. To leave drama to the commercial theater would be "to deprive the real world of that warmth and reassurance which it so sorely needs and to which it is justly entitled; furthermore, we are left outside with a sense of dreariness, in company with that shadow which already lurks only around the corner for most of us—a skepticism of life's value."[23]

The changes in the definition of culture are reflected in the purposes posed for public parks. From the early decades of the city, land had been set aside for recreational purposes. Out of the political conflicts of the late nineteenth century a structure was worked out that divided the city into separate park districts and reserved generous amounts of land for public parks. As idealistic notions gained increasing acceptance, these areas were seen as preserves of beauty, where nature both free and cultivated would refresh the spirit. Settlement house workers living in impoverished areas of the city were first struck by the absence of park areas near these districts. Demanding more land, the reformers shifted the terms of argument: they sought land for their constituencies less for beauty than for use. What they wanted were playground areas for children in the neighborhoods where the children lived. Given land by a reform politician, Hull-House established in 1893 the first public playground in the city. In the twentieth century parks came to be seen as important centers of communal life, providing opportunities for aesthetic endeavor and common play through festivals and pageants and the organization of sports and culture on the grounds.[24]

By offering an alternative, the settlement house may have caused the cultural philanthropists to rethink the relation of such institutions as the Art Institute to the city. The basic shift in the conception of the public to be reached by these institutions may well have come from the ideas and programs of Miss Addams and her co-workers. In the twentieth century it would no longer be businessmen and the middle class who were the primary target for culture but rather the masses, including the immigrant poor. These people did not venture downtown. They lived in neighborhoods, not the city at large, and they seemed to appreciate the homelike settlement buildings nearby. And as the settlement house opened its cultural programs to satisfy popular taste and to include tools and processes outside traditional definitions, its neighbors responded with interest and enthusiasm. The success of Hull-House was there for Charles Hutchinson and his friends to see.

However, given the understanding of the arts and letters held by the cultural philanthropists, given their economic and social position and their politics, there were clear limits on the effects that the changing approaches of settlement house reformers could have. There could be no real rethinking of the role of culture. Dewey understood this when he opposed the plan for a State Commission of Vocational Education supported by the Commercial Club. Dewey argued against the division between industrial education and humanistic studies that the commission reinforced. Though "manufacturers anxious to secure the aid of the state in providing them with a somewhat better grade of laborers for them to exploit" might approve, the educator must object. To separate manual training from liberal arts would allow general education to remain with "all its academic vices and its remoteness from the urgent realities of contemporary life untouched." Rather than serving as a lever for radical change in education and society, industrial education would come to support the existing order. And manual training's other side, involving a thorough rethinking of the relation of art to society, would thus be avoided.[25] A basic questioning of idealism could not be attempted by businessmen whose goal was to bring discipline and creativity to Chicago, rather than to lay the basis for a new society.

Moreover, the businessmen involved in culture could hardly follow the settlement house reformers as they began to consider the limits of philanthropy. For Jane Addams and Ellen Gates Starr, Ruskin's vision demanded not only providing man with what he required to "sustain his courage and keep him alive," but it called for efforts "to raise the siege." Increasingly Miss Addams turned to political and economic reform. She sought to improve sanitary conditions, to protect workers from the insecurities of injury and from the miseries of inadequate pay and long hours. She sought fairer treatment of women and guarantees of their political rights. But culture and politics were not exclusive spheres. It was in the same period that Miss Addams was redefining culture to include industrial labor. Ellen Gates Starr, committed as she was to traditional handicrafts, lent her support to labor organization and picketed with unions during strikes.[26] These reformers were reassessing the nature of social responsibility. They were shifting away from the clean government campaigns and the philanthropy Miss Addams shared with the businessmen involved in culture and turning to a demand for government regulation of industrial life.

In settlement house work and in her campaigns to unseat Johnny Powers, the political boss of the Nineteenth Ward, Jane Addams had not shirked broader responsibility. But as she became aware of the scope of urban problems through Hull-House investigations and the proddings of the more radical settlement house workers and as she saw the limitations of her own efforts, Miss Addams came to understand philanthropy as operating at a lower stage of social evolution than the mutual efforts of workingmen to better their own lives. Responsibility for what is for the people should be placed in their own hands. "Public parks and improvements, intended for the common use, are after all only safe in the hands of the public itself." Businessmen could not best direct public enterprises, since they were cut off from the new mutuality of workers—"the great moral life springing from our common experiences." Philanthropy was useful only to initiate experimental programs as demonstrations to convince the public of their value. Then projects should come under municipal management.[27]

When she opened an exhibit on Chicago children and the agencies to aid their nurture, Jane Addams pointed out that on one side of the exhibit were the activities of philanthropy while on the other were the activities of the city. To her this was not only natural but pointed the direction of the future. She told her audience: "You will see that the city with its schools, its libraries, its health department, its playgrounds, is taking over and absorbing into itself the manifold activities which were formerly under philanthropic management. . . . just as soon as the votes are ready, the philanthropists will be only too eager to hand over to the city all the rest of the things which they are now carrying on." For those in Chicago who still saw culture as a critical means of reform, Miss Addams might have seemed to suggest that the goals of the city-wide cultural institutions could now be achieved in the political arena, that municipal government could take over the function previously limited to voluntary associations.[28]

In looking to philanthropy as an innovative force, Miss Addams recognized that its possibilities were limited to a certain level of welfare—"churches, educational institutions, libraries, and art galleries, . . . model dwellings, recreation halls, and athletic fields." For the more difficult problems of regulating industrial conditions, private endeavors were inadequate. On these issues there was no possibility of winning the support of cultural philanthropists. Beyond a new involvement with the municipality in cultural affairs, such businessmen were engaged in efforts to change the structure and personnel of municipal government, an endeavor that Miss Addams came to see as merely negative, designed to remove corruption but hardly able to gain the loyalties or improve significantly the lives of immigrants for whom the political boss provided jobs and funerals. To bankers who opposed silver and to industrialists and merchants who were fighting labor organizations, Jane Addams and other settlement house workers could merit personal respect only, not sympathy with their politics.[29]

Julius Rosenwald would have his chauffeur drive one of the settlement women to join a picket line of workers striking against him, but he did not allow her to influence his negotiations. Charles Hutchinson could reassure Jane Addams of the appropriateness of her involvement in the Progressive campaign of 1912 at the same time that he himself was "not in sympathy with the new Third party." His wife could write Miss Addams to express appreciation for her record *Twenty Years at Hull House*—"one cannot help being thankful for the gift to the world of this delicate, sensitive yet powerful spirit"—and yet remain aloof from politics. As Jane Addams knew so well, her own conceptions of social responsibility—and of culture—were, in the twentieth century, on quite a different level from those of Chicago's cultural philanthropists.[30]

7

The Administrators' Alternatives

In their seeking and questioning, reformers such as Jane Addams were joined by others who shared an interest in culture but who also had an immediate stake in the city-wide cultural institutions. Among the museum curators, librarians, orchestra conductors, and university presidents were those who, in varying degrees, were moving toward professional status and developing their own sets of standards. In the process they were groping, if only in a tentative and fragmentary way, toward a definition of the nature of the institutions different from the one held by their employers, the members of their boards of trustees.

The commanding position of the trustees was modified by two seemingly opposite tendencies—their friendship with the men who staffed the institutions as administrators and the conflict fostered by the administrators' emerging sense of professional community. Relationships could never be wholly characterized by either harmony or discord, for even the most accommodating directors had perspectives and goals that differed from those of their boards; and even in the most strained relationships, recognition of the trustees' power forced administrators to work at influencing their boards and preventing open breaks.

The first professional heads of the Art Institute, the University of Chicago, and the Chicago Symphony Orchestra had played key roles in the creation of their institutions. William Rainey Harper's ideas dominated the planning for the university even when he was a member of the faculty at Yale. W. M. R. French, trained as a landscape architect, had been the secretary of the Academy of Design, a position he retained with the academy's reorganization into what was to be the Art Institute. The Orchestral Association was specifically designed to support a permanent organization for Theodore Thomas. But when no administrator was on hand at the initial establishment of an institution, the qualifications desired of such a man became explicit. He should, first of all, be a gentleman, of a background and breeding that would insure behavior acceptable to civic-minded businessmen engaged in culture. He should be well trained and have experience of a technical and administrative nature. It would seem only natural that an administrator with such attributes or one who had participated in the creation of the institution that employed him would be a person with an independent cast of mind and a willingness to take on wider responsibility.[1]

As "gentlemen," administrators generally did not differ significantly in ethnic or social background from their trustees. Theodore Thomas was German-born, but for a musician this was to be expected. More typical was William Frederick Poole, the librarian of the Newberry. Brought to the Newberry from the Chicago Public Library, Poole shared with many Chicago cultural philanthropists a New England heritage, having immigrated to Chicago in the 1870s. Like some of the Newberry trustees, Poole belonged to the Literary Club, and he brought to his membership prestige from his respected historical studies of New England antiquities. What distinguished Poole from his board of trustees was not his social origins but his professional identification: his primary link was with the community of librarians and not with the city of Chicago.[2]

To a greater degree than other administrators, the librarian could feel himself part of such a professional community. While other administrators shared elements of the librarian's position and were beginning to seek a professional identification, at the turn of the century the librarians were serving as a professional vanguard.[3]

Most of the administrators came to Chicago to take positions in the cultural institutions. Many of them in subordinate capacities would not stay. To a significant degree, national professional organizations, such as the American Library Association, perpetuated the strong tie to profession rather than city. These organizations brought together members of the same occupations, sifting them out from the cities their institutions served. Members corresponded with each other, seeking advice or help from colleagues. For example, Poole kept in touch with Justin Winsor of the Harvard University Library and with Melvil Dewey of Albany, New York, seeking and extending advice about library arrangements, career, and personal matters. When a president of the American Library Association tried to combine the separate libraries of the country into a "world" and to define its essence, she was only extending logically the thrust of a professionalism that separated the librarian from his city and joined him to his professional peers.[4]

Librarians in Chicago organized the Chicago Library Club. Initiated largely by the Newberry librarians to promote their interests, the club brought together all librarians in the city. By linking the professionals in the philanthropically endowed libraries with those in the public institution, the club set aside the distinction that

the early trustees of the Newberry and Crerar had emphasized.

Given their strong sense of identification, librarians in
Chicago came to voice openly their desire for a greater
degree of power. While the trustees defined the administrators' role as that of implementation, certain librarians
were seeking a formal voice in decision-making. At the
initial meeting, the keynote speaker considered the purposes
of association. A club to him suggested "a weapon to
enforce your aims. A club to me is aggression, a power
to clear a way, make itself felt, lay low opposition. . . . As
librarians we must make ourselves a factor in this city's
work, a power in the community. As a member of a
library club we are each of us clothed with a mysterious
majesty which belongs to our corporate professional capacity." Later in the speech he was somewhat more
specific. Among the purposes of the club was agitation
to gain the respect, not only of the wider community,
but more specifically of the trustees, so that they would
"no longer dub us 'impractical persons with bees in our
bonnets,'" and of architects, so that they would "respect
our opinions."[5] Yet even among librarians, the reality of
their role within their institutions dominated actual decisions. Whatever the administrators' hopes, their power
was limited to their ability to influence their boards of
trustees. Poole recommended that the first two trustees
of the Newberry—E. W. Blatchford and William H.
Bradley—be invited to join the Library Club.[6]

This understanding of institutional power would have
been appreciated by the museum directors and to a lesser
degree by Harper and Thomas. But so would have been
the impulses that led to the formation of the club.
Embedded within institutional correspondence are clear
signs that, friendship and amicability notwithstanding,
there was a sense of separate interests as well as differences
in approach between administrators and their boards of

trustees. Frederick J. V. Skiff, the director of the Field Columbian Museum, served on his own board of trustees and was not only respected by his businessmen-colleagues, but seems to have enjoyed warm relations with them in contrast to the formality between himself and his subordinates on the staff. Yet, when a trustees' meeting was called at a time when Skiff was out of town, the director's second-in-command ignored the president's request that Skiff not be bothered and wrote him immediately, feeling it best that Skiff be kept informed.[7]

It is not this sense of tension or the struggle for power between administrators and trustees per se that is important for our purposes, but rather the differences in approach to the problems of their institutions. In a significant number of cases administrators expressed a different set of aesthetic and social values from that of their trustees. At least in a fragmentary way, there lay within the professional spirit an alternative to the understanding of Chicago's cultural philanthropists.

Implicit in the argument for the independence of administrators from their boards of trustees on the basis of training and knowledge was a belief in the authority of the expert. As we have seen, those involved in cultural philanthropy had elitist notions of art, based on an understanding of artistic standards as absolutes. But any person could become a true appreciator if sufficiently exposed to art and in this way refined. The professional ethic did not include that possibility. To be a professional, one needed special training in which one was taught the skills and knowledge necessary to make decisions. Without such skills one was essentially an amateur, who despite his love for the subject was not necessarily equipped to make judgments about it. Appreciation and refinement were not enough: decisions required professional training and experience. In this respect Chicago's literary magazine the *Dial* shared the professionals' point of view. It argued that until the whole society reached the level of culture of Matthew Arnold's "remnant," experts, "agents specially chosen with regard to fitness for special work," should be entrusted with power. It praised William Rainey Harper of the University of Chicago for establishing a precedent that policy be set by the professionals (in this case the faculty), relegating the area of trustees' concern solely to the endowment.[8]

One can see this emphasis on expertise in the directors' sections of annual reports. Here in sober tones the administrators gave an accounting of their responsibilities, which, in the case of a library, meant primarily the acquisition and cataloging of books and the keeping of attendance records. The precision of these reports is striking. To give the extreme example, the Crerar librarian not only counted the number of requests for books and the number of visitors to the library, he also tried to compute the number of books actually used, however casually, in the course of a year. He calculated to the second decimal place the waiting time for delivery of a requested book: in 1898, for example, it was 1.65 minutes. One can see a similar dwelling on administrative detail in communications from the Field Columbian Museum emphasizing installation, display, and labeling of natural science materials. Among the primary concerns of administrators who were reaching toward professionalization, these technical matters were elements of the body of knowledge and technique that formed the basis of the professionals' craft.[9]

The emphasis on expertise is significant for our purposes because the basis on which decisions governing the institutions were to be made was not beauty but utility. While the professional would probably have agreed with the elite that any refined man could determine the beautiful, some of them would have insisted that only the trained and experienced could know what was useful.

Poole, who had written a manual for librarians, campaigned for more functional library structures. He criticized the monumental library buildings of other cities. For example, while still head of the Chicago Public Library, Poole found the Baltimore Peabody Institute to be "certainly a stately and imposing structure; and if we will banish from the mind all considerations of convenience, utility and economy, and regard its architecture simply as an aesthetic recreation, we may pronounce the picture before us beautiful." While a businessman involved in culture might find in such a statement a compliment, to Poole, aesthetic judgment was simply irrelevant. A library was a building designed to do something—to house books and to accommodate readers—and it was on these terms that it was to be judged. Poole complained that the Baltimore building was appropriate for a Gothic church of the Middle Ages, not for a library structure. With its plan of nave and aisles, over half of the space was wasted, "a solid block of vacuity." The building was difficult to heat, and yet, at the upper levels, the temperature was so high as to destroy the books. It was an enormous fire hazard. The noise that carried through the room made it as difficult to study there as in a city thoroughfare. Poole's most pointed comments came as he discussed the possibilities of expansion:

> Shall it be extended heavenward, and more galleries be piled on these, with more wasted space in the nave, greater difficulty of access to the books, and more extravagance in the heating. Shall transepts and a chancel be built, so that the plan will represent the true ecclesiastical cross? However pious these improvements and gratifying to the taste of the refined architect, they are expensive, they involve demolishing much that has already been constructed, and they will give but little additional room. Why library architecture should have been yoked to ecclesiastical architecture . . . is not obvious, unless it be that librarians in the past needed the stimulus to their religious emotions.

When he considered an alternative, Poole struck a new note: "The same secular common sense and the same adaptation of means to ends which have built the modern grain elevator and reaper are needed for the reform of library construction."[10]

When Poole criticized in similarly harsh tones that ultimate example of civic architecture, the Boston Public Library, he won the praise of Chicago's gadfly Henry Demarest Lloyd. Lloyd was delighted with Poole's terse conclusion that "when they get through with their building they will have a façade, but they will not have a library," and equated it with his own efforts at social reform. "There is too much façade, also, about many other things than libraries, in this mock world of ours. If all of us devoted ourselves, each in his sphere, to the abolition of façadism. . . ." Yet, Lloyd may have partially misinterpreted Poole's effort, for his essential concern was not with the outward appearance of the building. In planning the Newberry Library's structure Poole did not recommend an exterior in the unadorned style of the office buildings coming to dominate Chicago's downtown. The outside simply did not matter to Poole. It was the interior he was willing to fight for, tilting swords with the Newberry board of trustees and the architect they had hired, Henry Ives Cobb. While Cobb had designed a large, dramatic reading room to be serviced by a stack, Poole sought a series of smaller reading rooms, each to convey the ambience of a gentleman's library. So adamant was he that he hired another architect to draw up the plans he was promoting. His successful campaign ended with their acceptance and publication. After determining the structure and the interior, Poole was willing to trust an architect to give the design "artistic dress." It mattered little whether the outside was to be a Renaissance palace or a Gothic cathedral, for the important element, the interior arrangement, was set.[11]

The Field Columbian Museum, artfully designed by Charles Atwood as the Fine Arts Building for the World's Columbian Exposition, offered a fitting contrast to the Newberry. While the exterior reflected the ideal of beauty appropriate for cultural institutions, the building was unserviceable both for museum work and for the collection. The exterior of plaster of Paris and straw was gradually replaced, and the foundation and floors strengthened; but the building was plagued by heating problems and fire hazards. The museum's head, Frederick J. V. Skiff, lacked the independence of Poole. After a decade of patchwork repairs on the structure, rather than demanding a new building, he cautiously stated, "I do feel compelled to direct the attention of the Board of Trustees to the necessity which exists, in my opinion, for seriously considering at an early date the welfare of the material whose intrinsic value must be over $3,000,000.00 and whose educational value is incomputable."[12]

The librarian of the Crerar did not agree with Poole that the exterior was unimportant. Clement W. Andrews saw the need to avoid a style that was too costly or too difficult to maintain, but he did not want "an absolutely plain-building in the modern factory style." He felt that such an architectural design would "almost certainly cost the institution the respect and perhaps the good will of all who see it and use it," which would be detrimental to its endowment and to the cooperation of staff and public. The pragmatic grounds on which Andrews's argument rested are interesting. He did not see the building as a refining influence on Chicago's citizenry as had the board of the Chicago Public Library in 1898. Rather, he merely found it expedient for the library to try to meet people's expectations about what the building of a cultural institution ought to look like.[13]

This concern with utility was not limited to the design of the building but extended to the critical areas for the cultural institution, the nature of its collection. The Newberry made a decision in the twentieth century to use its resources for the books necessary for scholarship rather than for rare and costly incunabula. The Crerar probed the question even further. Clement W. Andrews had an unusual and refreshing sense of the limitation of books— their impersonality and the inadequacy of sheer book knowledge ("If I ever have an automobile I shall not employ a chauffeur who has to consult a book to find what to do in an emergency"). He seemed to lack that reverence for the rare and the fine that often shaped decisions about collections. He also lacked the drive for comprehensiveness that characterized the cultural philanthropists. A library was of value because of its usefulness. Since it could aid its readers through interlibrary loans, it need not have books that other libraries contained. Nor should it build up whole collections when another library was recognized as the leader: "Why, for instance, should the John Crerar Library have 14,000 volumes of Orientalia, even if they are on subjects within its scope, if the Library of Congress is making a collection which must in the nature of the case be far more complete and be the first resort of Oriental scholars. . . ?"[14]

Moreover, an object within the collection should be truthful, even if that meant destroying some of its beauty. A case in point, important because of the explicit goals of the institution it served, was the decision to remove restoration materials from the Greek vases at the Art Institute. Perhaps responding to criticism, the annual report asserted, "The resulting unsightliness of exposed repairs is quite outweighed by the fact that the ancient work is now visible." Even at the Art Institute the professional regarded it as more important that an object tell the truth about itself than that it fulfill the idealistic goal of inspiring through beauty. With a similar sense of priorities Theodore Thomas refused to conduct a second performance for a soloist after he found her work insincere. He explained to Charles Norman Fay why it was necessary to break the contract: "Expression in music comes from the soul—and in the interpretation of a masterwork the honesty of purpose is easily detected: whether a thing is done for effect—for the market—or whether it is honest."[15]

It is clear that Thomas's commitment to truth was quite distinct from a business sense. In the nineteenth century there were several points of conflict in which administrators asserted a professional ethic that ran counter to business practice. For instance, forced by the head of his board to bargain with a colleague for a set of books, Poole subverted the demand by a personal postscript: "I made the inquiry about discount, at the request of one of the Trustees who is a *business* man. I am sometimes happy that I have not been trained as a *business* man." While Theodore Thomas worked in harmony with a symphony board that accepted his decisions, he faced continuing abuse from the World's Columbian Exposition Commission because he refused to limit performance instruments to those placed on exhibit. He demanded his right to stand by his initial guarantee to the performing artists that they could have full freedom of choice. Stated in general terms, decisions about the nature of a collection were not to be made primarily on economic grounds.[16]

Consistent with their utilitarianism, concern for efficiency, and interest in truth was the value the administrators placed on discipline. The need to oversee a staff explained part of the emphasis. But the feeling about discipline transcended expediency to express a moral dimension of the professionals' concerns. Daniel Burnham, whose task was to oversee the construction of the entire world's fair, was moved to speak about the way the architects for the fair undertook their work. He emphasized that he had entrusted the work to experts. In dealing with them he had urged that they feel a spirit of crisis so that they would willingly work together and submit to the demands of "self-sacrifice." "The success of this undertaking depends upon team work: if you work for the Exposition as a whole, it will be a great success." When the head of the Chicago Directory of the fair, Harlow Higinbotham, distributed praise for what he felt was a job well done, he picked up Burnham's connection between professional status and the spirit with which the work was undertaken: "The discipline and efficiency of the force was greater than that of a veteran army, for it was largely composed of intelligent, well educated, professional men, each one eminent and respected in his particular line of work." It was a judgment that any administrator would have been pleased to receive from the president of his board of trustees.[17]

Extending logically this emphasis on authenticity and discipline, a few administrators saw their role as scholars. Dr. George A. Dorsey of the Field Columbian Museum regarded the true function of the museum as the discovery, not the diffusion, of knowledge. The museum was not to uplift the city, but rather to promote the "advancement of science": the museum "must not go to the public; it must lead." Certain other administrators shared Dorsey's concern with scholarship: their role would be to engage in and to encourage research. At the University of Chicago a significant portion of the faculty would find this a congenial position.[18]

The primary impact of administrators on Chicago's cultural institutions was in a different direction, however. They pushed their institutions to become more public. In the eulogies of W. M. R. French after his death, his associates attributed to him the crucial role in opening the Art Institute to the community. While this may have overstated the case, it is clear from French's correspondence with Charles L. Hutchinson, the president of his board, that French exerted pressure to increase the public's exposure to the resources of the museum. His reaction to the proposition that the photographs of all children in the Chicago public schools be deposited at the Art Institute seems characteristic, "At first it struck me as a ridiculous idea; then it occurred to me that it might advertise the institution among the whole population." A year later French relayed to Hutchinson the suggestion found in the *Nation* that museums lend out exhibitions of paintings not being used in its galleries. Within a few years the Art Institute was sending its paintings to recreation buildings in Chicago parks.[19]

In proposing this outward thrust of the Art Institute, French was following the lead of other administrators who had been advocating extension since the 1890s. William Frederick Poole actively promoted university extension in Chicago. The Newberry Library was one of the first locations of the lecture series conducted by college professors under the auspices of the Chicago Society for University Extension. The University of Chicago would take this approach and turn it into a major instrument of public education.[20]

The relation of the University of Chicago to the public was unique among Chicago's city-wide cultural institutions. It was not open to all, but rather served a relatively small number of persons, largely young people, who could meet its academic and financial standards. Yet the school was of great significance in the city's cultural life. Not only did it increasingly serve as a focus for artistic and scholarly activity, but its extension program had an important impact on other cultural institutions in the city. William Rainey Harper came to the presidency from a Yale professorship and from teaching and administrative service at Chautauqua, that vast camp-meeting of public education in New York. Thus he was a man deeply concerned about the relation of scholarship to democracy or, more concretely, of the university to the society. He found a variety of ways to resolve intellectually the very obvious conflict in his mind between the elitism of the university and the egalitarian demands of a democratic society. Through the extension system he found an institutional means of resolution. Faculty would engage in scholarly research to advance the world of knowledge. The university proper was to be confined to regular students who were largely engaged in the traditional disciplines of the university. But there was also to be a special program designed to serve the needs of the broader population. This was university extension—a combination of lectures in Chicago and outside, classes held downtown, and correspondence courses. Neither the idea nor its implementation in the Chicago area was new, but the scale was; in the first decade, for example, there were 368 lecture centers in twenty-one states offering 1,326 courses.[21]

The ideas guiding the effort were familiar to Chicago's cultural philanthropists, but Harper carried them a step further. University extension was for everyone, "rich and poor, men and women alike"; moreover, like the American church, it was "essentially missionary in character." Its goal was similar to that of the other city-wide cultural institutions: to create "in the community at large that demand for the best of everything in the intellectual, aesthetic and moral world which is at once the evidence of, and the surest means toward, the higher civic life." But the technique developed by the University of Chicago to reach this goal was different; accepting the task of making people "desire the things it can offer," the university thrust itself out beyond its walls to reach the people where they were.[22]

Martin Ryerson and Charles Hutchinson, president and treasurer of the board of trustees, were co-workers with Harper in the early years of the University of Chicago. The three worked together not only in decisions about finances and in the planning of buildings but also in the recruitment of faculty. Harper came to rely on the two businessmen to the point that he found himself depressed when they left Chicago to travel abroad. Moreover, as Harper became involved in other cultural institutions in Chicago, he was accepted by the cultural philanthropists on their boards.[23] But as Harper's ideas about the University crystallized into programs, he and his two most active trustees came into conflict over budgets. Harper's plans always exceeded university resources. And concerned as they were about retaining John D. Rockefeller's good will, Hutchinson and Ryerson became the "bugbears" on the board of trustees who assumed the responsibility of trying to hold Harper down. What they seemed to object to was Harper's more experimental designs. Ryerson wrote to Harper cautioning him about his "tendency toward elaborate 'organization.'" Apparently Hutchinson was an important force in limiting the affiliated academy in Morgan Park to boys and in the plan to introduce partial sexual segregation into the university in 1903. From Harper's remark that he was going to compose a letter in the hope of countering Hutchinson's "lack of interest in University Extension," it would seem that Hutchinson was unenthusiastic about this venture also.[24]

In the years that followed, this indifference or hostility to extension on the part of men like Hutchinson would vanish. The redefinition of the public to include all Chicago citizens required a reexamination of the meaning of location. The Art Institute and the Field would find in the extension idea a practical approach for bringing their collections to the people. Initially "extension" was used to mean merely the responsibility of the institution to educate the public. But by the twentieth century, extension had a specific institutional meaning—the projection of materials and programs outside the central building to reach new groups in the population.

Prominent administrators—Poole, French, and Harper

—played innovative roles in promoting extension in the late nineteenth century. In the twentieth century their effort to make their institutions accessible to a wider public would attract greater support and expand in a variety of directions. Younger administrators, perhaps less tied to their institutions, sought to join forces to generate change. They were the cultural contingent of that larger body of professionals in the Progressive era who, finding themselves at odds with cities so casually run, where their organizational skills and expertise mattered all too little, proved to be a creative force. For Chicago's cultural institutions these administrators served as an important source of innovation.[25]

One can see an early impact of this newer professional spirit in library journalism. The national association had the *Library Journal*, which combined inspirational messages and professional news. Under the sponsorship of the Library Bureau, a commercial distributor of equipment, those interested in library matters in Chicago established *Public Libraries*. As the first issue announced, *Public Libraries* would focus on new developments in the library field: "The opening of a new library; the erection of a library building; the adoption of modern library methods by an old library; the change in attitude on the part of any librarian, from thinking of it as a storehouse to thinking of it as a workshop, a laboratory, a people's school."[26]

Of possibly greater significance to Chicago librarians was the Chicago Library Club, which was, as we have seen, designed to promote the professional interests of its members. Its early projects included the compilation of a manual of libraries in the Chicago area and of a combined list of their serials—both geared to increase the efficiency of the city's library system. As the club moved into the twentieth century, however, its concern shifted to broadening the services of the library beyond its walls. The club discussed jail libraries, traveling libraries for schools, and home libraries. The club began to reach out into the community. On the one hand, it tried to cultivate greater civic interest in the library. For example, in April 1902, it sponsored (rather unsuccessfully) a public meeting to arouse the support of business and professional men. On the other hand, the club brought in people to speak on the library needs of the city. On December 10, 1902, Jane Addams spoke on branch libraries and their relation to the community. She emphasized the immigrants' need for books in foreign tongues. In the first decade of the twentieth century, the Chicago Library Club meetings convey a sense of exploration and discovery, as librarians throughout the city came to an awareness of Chicago's social problems and the possibilities their own profession provided for meeting them.[27]

In their concern for the city the professionals listened to the settlement house reformers and singled out two groups as needing special consideration—the immigrants and children. In contrast to the cultural philanthropists who supported the downtown building, designed for the middle class, the professionals began to experience something of the reformers' concern for the other Chicago. The immigrant needed a neighborhood location where he might feel comfortable and books in the language he knew best. Neighborhood locations were also important for children as alternatives to traveling downtown, but of greater significance were the special rooms appropriate to their age and interests, staffed by special librarians. While the trustees may have seen increased usage of the library by all citizens, the professional was aware of "restless, eager children waiting in long lines, kept in order by a policeman." The professional sought to change this situation within the existing library system, unlike the settlement house reformer who created alternatives outside. Coupled with the nineteenth-century administrator's contribution of extension, this twentieth-century emphasis on specific needs would serve as a major innovative force in Chicago's cultural institutions as they sought a wider public after 1900.[28]

The professional spirit hardly existed in whole cloth: in the nineteenth and early twentieth centuries it was fragmentary, at least among the administrators staffing the city-wide cultural institutions. But in Chicago one man gathered together and articulated the gropings of his fellows. The thought of Thorstein Veblen provided an eccentric version of the new understanding of the professionals.[29]

In his *Theory of the Leisure Class*, Veblen criticized the explicit goals of cultural enthusiasts and settlement house reformers alike. His understanding was so different from that of others in the city that he could not serve as a direct influence for change. The administrators of Chicago's cultural institutions, however, could have found in his argument a biting defense of their position.

Throughout his writings Veblen asserted the distinction between the businessman and the engineer. The businessman, a latter-day barbarian, lived off the labor of the truly productive members of the society, the engineers. These professionals, trained and experienced, made the constructive decisions. The businessmen sabotaged production for their own gain and sought the emulation of others through conspicuous consumption and conspicuous waste. Culture was merely one form that the struggle for emulation took. In contrast, the engineer was motivated by the instinct of workmanship and was not caught up in this contest for esteem. He used his abilities constructively in organizing the processes of work.[30]

Though Veblen was thinking of the economic system as a whole, his thought was adaptable to cultural institutions. The creative force in a museum or library would then be the administrator who was trained for the task and who was closely engaged in the actual work. He would make decisions, such as that about the design of the building, on the basis of the work needs of his organization and according to the standards of efficiency and truth. The actions of the board of businessmen would only disrupt the work patterns and sabotage the goals of those with a special competence.

In terms of Chicago's cultural movement Veblen may be less important for his defense of the professional and his critique of institutions and reformers than as a promoter and an exemplar of a whole new way of thinking. Veblen dealt savagely with culture as a form of conspicuous waste. Its acquisition was a "voucher for a life of leisure," testifying that the possessor had engaged in a "non-productive employment of time and effort." Cultural philanthropy was merely an extension of waste on a larger scale. The increasing impersonality, size, and mobility of society generated a need to impress others with one's taste quickly and in a striking manner. Thus businessmen were moved to endow hospitals, colleges, and museums. Veblen moderated the rigors of this critique by introducing the possibility that the class position of sons of wealth could protect them from the predatory struggle, allowing them to revert to peaceable ways. When all the status considerations of philanthropy were accounted for—the enhanced reputation from "large and conspicuous expenditure," the participation in upper-class organizations that "serve to authenticate the pecuniary reputability of their members" and to remind them of the "contrast between themselves and the lower-lying humanity in whom the work of amelioration is to be wrought"— "there is left some remainder of motives of a non-emulative kind."[31]

Veblen also indicted contemporary taste as a form of conspicuous consumption. Here the professional could hear echoes of his own position. The product of workmanship was to be true to its use. Function should determine its design, rather than extraneous considerations of beauty. The machine-made object was aesthetically preferable to the handmade. What passed for beauty was often the "gratification of our sense of costliness" in disguise. Real beauty had nothing to do with cost: it was the intrinsic beauty that inhered in the truthful object. An effective aesthetic test reversed the collector's measure: the truly beautiful excited no desire for possession, for its qualities could be enjoyed without ownership. Even here Veblen saw a hopeful change, as, for example, in landscape gardening. As the leisure class grew in numbers, expensive landscape displays no longer served to distinguish the individual man of wealth. Thus his sons were reverting to a love of the natural rustic setting. One could assume that Veblen would have approved the complementary developments in architecture, particularly the structures of Frank Lloyd Wright and his campaign for acceptance of the machine.[32]

Finally, Veblen raised the question of the conflicting claims of science and the humanities. While the concern of science was efficiency, that of the humanities was culture. Veblen conceded that if one accepted the values of its proponents, culture was "higher" and "nobler." But those words lost their meaning if one focused on economic and social efficiency; they became only the signs that the user was working within an archaic system of thought. Ideas about culture were not "wrong." They were merely irrelevant, because they were part of a system of thought that was wrong.[33]

Despite his eccentricity, Veblen's rejection of the vocabulary of cultural idealism was not unique. Rather he was one of a large contingent of critics who were seeking a new way to understand social and intellectual phenomena in the early twentieth century. The answers they found contradicted the basic conceptions of the nineteenth century—including the understanding of cul-

ture held by Chicago's philanthropists.[34] One might think
that to the degree the new approaches became accepted
they endangered the city-wide cultural institutions. But
this would be to misunderstand the nature of institutions,
which, once established, have an ability to withstand
changes of purpose and technique.

The cultural institutions of Chicago sought in varying
degrees to adapt to the twentieth century in their collections and programs. In a few instances there were attempts
to modify the theoretical basis on which the institutions
rested. Among the professionals could be found those
who faced the issues of modernity head on in a spirit and
vocabulary that struck a new note. Here again professionals
and reformers met on common ground. Henry E. Legler,
the librarian of the Chicago Public Library, was a case in
point. Personally dynamic, he promoted plans for the
reorganization of the library system with arguments that
Veblen and Jane Addams would have understood. As he
spoke to his professional colleagues, Legler called for
monuments "of iron and of concrete which are the
expression of this age." He saw as the task of the library
not to refine, but rather to contribute to lives shaped by
the monotony of industrial labor and the new leisure that
the economy offered. As we shall see, Legler's innovative
policies creatively adapted the Chicago Public Library to
the twentieth century, bringing to the cultural institutions
of the city new alternatives.[35]

In their passage to the twentieth century, the professionals shifted their major concern from efficiency to
service. The cultural philanthropists had emphasized
service too, but while the elite had established institutions
to meet the needs of the business community and the
middle class, the professionals were developing a growing
commitment to immigrants and children. In so doing
they listened to the settlement house workers and were
influenced by them. Open to the new intellectual develop-

ments of the twentieth century, certain administrators began to think in ways outside the old cultural framework, paralleling the movement of certain reformers away from cultural concerns to the social and economic sector. While the reformers worked, for the most part, outside cultural institutions, the job of the administrators was, by definition, within. As the twentieth century progressed, the administrators helped to channel reform and the newer understandings into the city-wide cultural institutions, reshaping them directly and also affecting the thought of their governing boards.

8

The Appraisals of Artists & Writers

When reformers in the settlement house movement and administrators of cultural institutions considered the relation of culture to the city, they posed two kinds of challenges: they pointed to aspects of the museums and libraries that could be changed through innovative programs, and they presented political and philosophical alternatives to the cultural philanthropists' conceptions that no internal adjustments could really answer. Jane Addams raised questions about the relation of art to the nature of work and communal life and looked to the people themselves for leadership within a democratic society. The professional ethic was at odds with reverence for beauty, pushing administrators, especially librarians, to value truthfulness, discipline, efficiency, and service.

Artists also raised questions at two different levels. Chicago's artistic establishment agreed with the cultural philanthropists on basic principles, but criticized the lack of patronage for their own work. More disquieting, two Chicago novelists, Henry Blake Fuller and Robert Herrick, turned their private doubts about the value of art and the motives of culture-seeking into material for their novels.

As writers who were personally close to leading cultural philanthropists, Fuller and Herrick may have shaken the idealistic faith of some of these men at least enough to have opened them to the currents of modernism which were beginning to swell around the young artists and writers in Floyd Dell's circle.

Certain members of Chicago's artist community were very close to the cultural philanthropists. Adolphus Clay Bartlett's son Frederick Clay Bartlett, like several other children of prominent members of the cultural elite, followed his father's interest in arts and letters to its professional conclusion. Edward B. Butler made the jump from philanthropist to artist within his own lifetime: a successful merchant, he served on the board of the Art Institute and was a guarantor of the World's Columbian Exposition, a member of the Orchestral Association, a trustee of Hull-House, and an active participant in the innovative cultural projects of the early twentieth century. After loosening the reins of his business enterprises, Butler took up painting and produced some creditable work that was exhibited in Chicago.[1]

The movement between philanthropy and creative activity sometimes worked the other way. Just as a professional, such as University of Chicago President William Rainey Harper, could become involved in a variety of city-wide cultural institutions, so could an artist with the necessary interest, energy, and resources. Daniel Burnham, who in his early partnership with John Wellborn Root had helped create some of Chicago's finest skyscrapers, turned after Root's death to a different kind of practice. As director of works of the World's Columbian Exposition he organized and supervised the mammoth stage setting of the fair, accepting as the guiding style the classicism of the prominent New York firm of McKim, Mead and White. Chicago's cultural elite drew Burnham into their enterprises, and he came to serve on the boards of both the Chicago Symphony Orchestra and the Art Institute. There is every indication that Burnham came to be accepted by the businessmen on the boards as one of their own. He and his wife traveled with the Hutchinsons and Ryersons in Europe and with Edward E. Ayer in the Philippines. Perhaps as the head of a firm whose staff of over a hundred executed commissions in major cities across the country, Burnham felt comfortable in the presence of wealthy businessmen. Increasingly he influenced their conceptions of art. He became their official architect, designing not only office buildings but also the Chicago Symphony's Orchestra Hall. His Plan for Chicago was to shape the city's physical development in the early decades of the twentieth century.[2]

When Kenyon Cox, a New York painter and spokesman for traditional artistic values, shared his observations of the Chicago cultural scene with the readers of the *Nation* in 1911, he dwelt on "the friendly and familiar cooperation of artist and layman," something he found unique. It was not merely of a purposive nature, "efforts for the betterment of artistic conditions"; it occurred on the social level as well. Cox described the Cliff Dwellers, a private club that met in the penthouse of Orchestra Hall. The composition of the society was unique: "There come the painters, the sculptors, and the architects, the writers and the musicians, and there come also the bankers and the officials of the Institute." Yet Cox did not have in mind Bartlett, Butler, or Burnham, these three unusual men who bridged the worlds of artists and philanthropists. Nor seemingly was he aware of those iconoclasts such as Theodore Dreiser, whose writings shocked the public's morality even if they failed to stir its conscience, or of the newspapermen whose humorous jibes and blatant criticisms of culture-seeking matched their ethnic and class separation from the cultural promoters. Rather the artists to whom Cox was referring were of a limited coterie: they were members, in a loose way, of Chicago's artistic establishment.[3]

At the center of this group was Lorado Taft, a handsome and thoroughly agreeable sculptor in the Beaux-Arts tradition. With him were his two brothers-in-law, the author Hamlin Garland and the painter Charles Francis Browne. They were joined by Ralph Clarkson, another painter, the writers Henry Blake Fuller and Hobart C. Chatfield-Taylor, and the drama teacher Anna Morgan, among others. In winter these friends met at Taft's Midway Studio and at the Fine Arts Building on Michigan Avenue. During the summer many of them gathered at the Eagle's Nest Camp where they lived in a semicommunal fashion what seems a light-hearted existence, faintly tinged with Bohemianism.[4]

The group had crystallized in the 1890s with the formation of the Little Room, a regular gathering after Friday afternoon symphony concerts. As prospective members were informed, the Little Room was designed to create in Chicago a necessary "atmosphere" in the belief that "association and conversation had largely to do with inspiration." It was to be "very personal and restricted for very obvious reasons," though by 1903 its members had reached out to include, along with a broad spectrum of artists, John Vance Cheney (the librarian at the Newberry), Jane Addams, and a limited number of philanthropists who perhaps saw themselves as artists as well as business and professional men.[5]

Leadership, however, remained in its initiators' hands, and the Little Room continued to promote its founders' spirited playfulness. In 1899 Harriet Monroe described to her sister the annual Twelfth Night production of the Little Room, expressing her delight in the antics of the evening. Escorted by a little king "very meek and lamblike in his royal robes and gilt crown" was Chatfield-Taylor as queen "with all his amplitude of height and girth set forth in the most resplendent costume. . . . He was a master-piece, and the way he achieved a decollectic [sic] feminine effect was a caution." The editor of the *Dial*, William Morton Payne, was Folly "wearing striped satin and a five-pointed cap with dangling bells." Henry Blake Fuller was Crime "with a black mask and a knife and gore." The characters sang and then each read a poem "generally very clever ones, with all sorts of gags and puns. . . . It was really very funny. . . . In the supper room there were cold meats and chafing-dishes and raw materials and people cooked what they wanted."[6]

Wishing to link up the men in this clique of artists with the art appreciators and philanthropists of the city in "a union of the aesthetic elements of Chicago and the West," Hamlin Garland proposed a new club in the early twentieth century, modeled after the Players and Century clubs of New York City. He invited all the men of the Little Room to join, as well as other artists and scholars; and he added to them a list of laymen that could have served as a directory of the city's cultural elite. More sedate than its uninhibited progenitor, the Cliff Dwellers attempted to offer to its members the solid comfort and good food of a men's club as a base for conversation and as a snare for visiting artists. In a newspaper interview Charles Hutchinson was reported to have called the Cliff Dwellers "the most enjoyable club in the city."[7]

It is not surprising that Chicago's artistic establishment shared the values of the cultural philanthropists, at least in their public statements. Trained in Paris, Taft saw his works as successive attempts to capture the ideal. His brother-in-law Charles Francis Browne described one of the sculptor's more monumental efforts, the "Fountain of the Great Lakes": the composition would be "the first large and purely ideal group erected in America . . . a sculptural ornament whose excuse for being resides in its realization of beauty without personal or memorial suggestion." Taft, "brought up on a western prairie," had made a "difficult and discouraging journey." After mastering the technical aspects of his art, he had undergone "a slow psychological change from extreme materialism, literalism, and objective reasoning, to an awakening realization of the significance of art" and hence to idealized conceptions.[8]

A touchstone of Taft's sympathies was his reaction to the World's Columbian Exposition. The fair was his first major commission, surely a factor in coloring his comments; but his enthusiasm went beyond. Taft compared his experience to that of the sculptors of the Parthenon or of those living in Florence during the Renaissance. Fuller joined enthusiastically the ranks of those among the artists who regarded the fair as beginning a new era for the city. He shared in what he would later ironically remember as "the universal expectation that the spirit of the White City was but just transferred to the body of the Great Black City close at hand, over which it was to hover as an enlightenment—through which it might permeate as an informing force." Hamlin Garland, then a self-proclaimed realist, saw Chicago as the future cultural center of the United States and decided to make the city his home.[9]

The core of the artistic establishment—Taft, Garland, and Browne—shared much of the cultural philanthropists' commitment to educating the public. A word often used in reference to their efforts is "missionary." Taft and Browne regularly gave lectures at the Art Institute. Taft was said to have given his most famous lecture, "Clay Talk," several thousand times and in every state but Florida. Perhaps closest to the conception and method of Chicago's cultural elite was Taft's dream museum which was to cover the whole history of sculpture.[10]

In the 1890s this artistic coterie founded the Central

Art Association. Thinking more of Chicago's hinterland than of the city itself, they were concerned that while each town had a library and a theater, most lacked galleries for painting and sculpture, and thus the development of taste was being held back. The association sent a traveling art exhibit to midwestern towns, along with a program of study. It published *Arts for America*—"For the Promotion and Dispersion of Good Art Among the People"— which printed courses of study material along with news of art matters in the Midwest and provided its promoters with a forum for expressing their own concerns. Initially, the organization's support was not particularly fashionable, though it included Ellen Gates Starr and the liberal ministers David Swing and Jenkin Lloyd Jones; but increasingly the Central Art Association turned to the Chicago businessmen involved in culture to serve first as counselors and then as patrons.[11]

Yet *Arts for America* was dissatisfied with the indirect approach of cultural promoters in these years. While editorials and articles by Ralph Clarkson and Charles F. Browne might not have agreed with Mr. Dooley's opinion that institutions such as libraries never encouraged art "anny more thin tombstones encourage livin'," they would have seconded his conclusion "What lithrachoor needs is fillin' food." The primary way to make Chicago an art center was to *"Buy pictures."*

> Buy them for the parlor, the sitting room, the dining room. . . .
> *Buy Pictures.*
> Buy them at the Art Institute. . . .
> *Buy pictures.*
> Buy them of the art dealer.
> *Buy pictures.*
> Buy them of the local artist. You cannot expect artists to remain in the city when they are dependent upon Eastern exhibitions for their sales; and you cannot create an art center without artists.[12]

Ralph Clarkson, hardly a rebel, complained bitterly of those "who have traveled abroad, who own works of art, who know the studios of Paris and who do not know the *name of an artist* in their own city." He himself knew others "who love Chicago and who will not admit that it is second in anything; yet they spend much time away from here, and money on works of art no better and ofttimes not as good as what they might find here." The only way for Chicago to become "anything but a gigantic commercial center . . . a home of the arts where those who have aesthetic taste can find enjoyment and companionship" was to "show encouragement to the artists who seek to make it their home"; and this, too, meant "buy the work of the artist." The twentieth century would blunt this criticism as Taft was virtually endowed to create monumental sculpture for the city and as Clarkson became the almost official portraitist of Chicago's cultural elite.[13]

A member of the Little Room and a lifelong friend of the leaders of the artistic establishment, Henry Blake Fuller was to take their assumptions about culture and the city and, in his novels, turn them into problems for exploration. As he did so, he probed the lives and the motives of businessmen and cultural leaders in Chicago. His works must have been a source of discomfort to the cultural philanthropists who were linked to him by friendship and social background.

Fuller was an unusual phenomenon in the nineteenth century, a third-generation Chicagoan. Born in 1857, he was the grandson of a New Englander who had come to Chicago and established the family's wealth in the city's early growth. Fuller became an adult at a time of declining family fortunes. High school graduation ended his education, and he took up work first in a crockery store and then in a bank. His interest was culture, however, rather than business, and he immediately began saving from his salary to finance a trip to Europe. Since he was without great means, Charles Hutchinson's alternative was not open to him; but through his observation and his writing Fuller began to shape his own resolution: he would become a writer in the business world that was Chicago.[14]

One of the opportunities for an artist in Chicago, particularly during the exposition decade, was to serve as a cultural observer and reporter to outsiders. Fuller took up this role in a major contemporary statement about Chicago's life—"The Upward Movement in Chicago," an article published in the *Atlantic Monthly*. In a straightforward, though slightly condescending, way (after all, a sophisticated man could not show pride in Chicago too openly to Boston), Fuller chronicled the movements toward political reform and the establishment of cultural institutions in the city of the fair. Clear throughout is an unstated assumption that these developments were by their very nature good. Though not essentially a political person, Fuller sympathetically accepted the municipal reform efforts of his friends. He met socially with the businessmen involved in culture, dining with Charles Hutchinson at the banker's home and at Hull-House. Such a cultural philanthropist could read Fuller's article with his faith in the value of art and of the city's cultural institutions unquestioned.[15]

Yet when Fuller turned from exposition to fiction, the assumptions of his essay became questions to explore, questions whose very posing challenged the beliefs behind the city-wide cultural institutions. Fuller was essentially a novelist, not a cultural promoter. As such, he could not simply rely on the rhetoric of cultural idealism, but was forced to face, in a very personal way, the meaning of art and the enthusiasm its pursuit and promotion generated among Chicago's moneyed elite. Moreover, as a writer who had been moved by the works of Henry James and William Dean Howells, he was attracted by the realist's aesthetic. And as a novelist in the nineteenth century, he wrote for a broad public and therefore worked outside the network of patronage by the wealthy. This may have contributed to his sense of distance, freeing him to look at his contemporaries in the city with a more critical eye.[16]

In its combination of culture and business, Fuller's initial foray into fiction was symbolic of Chicago's cultural life. In his business office Fuller is said to have written on a discarded envelope what were to be the first lines of his first published book: "It was the Chevalier of Pensieri-Vani who halted his traveling carriage upon the brow of the Ciminian Forest to look down over the widespread Campagna di Roma." In *The Chevalier of Pensieri-Vani* Fuller sought to give voice to his interest in the cultivated life. Unconsciously perhaps, he also gave voice to some of his doubts.[17]

This first exercise of his literary gifts has been rightly seen as a juxtaposition of the new, materialistic America against old, cultured Europe in terms that would remain part of Fuller's essential vocabulary. The heir of a large American fortune has ventured to Europe in search of an environment more satisfying than his homeland. His experiences leave him bewildered rather than inspired. Troubled by much of what he has seen, he realizes that Europe should not be his home. He would not be happy in America: "Every day, every hour of his life . . . would bring its own peculiar discomfort." Yet caught in an unresolvable dilemma, he had to return. "Birth and habit drew him in one direction; culture and aspiration, in another; but he had never been a good American, and he feared he should never make a good European. He was between two fires, both of which scorched him."[18]

The decision to return to America is in keeping with the central movement of the book. On the surface it celebrates the pleasures of the cultured life in Europe led by a charming dilettante, the Chevalier of Pensieri-Vani;

unwittingly perhaps, Fuller exposes that life in a series of essentially destructive confrontations. The Chevalier opens an Etruscan tomb only to have its remains disintegrate upon exposure to the air. He improvises on an organ, building up to a deafening climax, only to have the instrument break at the height of the music. The Italian landscape and its history, a collective work of art, provides a means of escape, soothing the Chevalier as a kind of narcotic, shielding him as Fuller's language lulls the reader, from the frustrations and aggressive nature of the pursuit of culture.

In *The Chevalier of Pensieri-Vani* Fuller probed and withdrew from an inquiry into the nature of art. The questions he raised were largely hidden. His work was accepted by the leading upholders of culture in Boston: Charles Eliot Norton's praise moved Fuller to dedicate to him the revised edition. Yet Fuller felt a need to put the artistic enterprise in the Chicago context. In two novels, we encounter a similar, but more explicitly fruitless, pursuit of art, now juxtaposed against Fuller's deliberate consideration of the nature and meaning of cultural philanthropy.

Fuller's first novel of Chicago, *The Cliff-Dwellers* (whence the name of Garland's club), is concerned primarily with the power of a ruthless banker whose tentacles hold fast the lives of his family and business associates. Culture as a theme exists only in the background. Chicago is a city not of artistic creation or aesthetic enjoyment, but of money making, "a great checker-board over whose squares of 'section' and 'township' keenness and rapacity played their daring and wary game." Art is an ornament for such a person as Jessie Ogden, a charming native daughter who becomes an exploiter as she enters the race for social prominence. It is the crushed dream of the banker's son, driven to drunkenness and violence by his father's rejection. Most important, the development of

Chicago's cultural institutions is the fragile mainstay of the older Chicagoan Fairchild, giving him objects upon which he lavishes his pride in the city: " 'You have seen the foundations. . . . It has taken fifty years to put them in, but the work is finally done and well done. And now we are beginning to build on these foundations.' " Agreeing that "the present intellectual situation in Chicago is precisely that of Florence . . . of the Medici after the dispersal of the Greek scholars from Constantinople," Fairchild boasts, " 'We know what there is to learn, and we are determined to master it. Our Constantinoples are Berlin and London and the rest—yes, Boston, too; and all their learned exiles are flocking here to instruct us.' " As Chicago would be the financial and political center of the country, so its libraries would make it the literary center: " 'Chicago is Chicago. . . . It is the belief of all of us. It is inevitable; nothing can stop us now.' " But Fairchild's faith is of no value in helping him withstand the force of the banker, for whom Fairchild comes to serve merely as a useful decoration, a name giving respectability to shady dealings.[19]

Fuller followed *The Cliff-Dwellers* with a closer look at Chicago's cultural impulse. *With the Procession* centers on the struggle of a family of old settlers whose social standing has failed to keep pace with their economic power. The book chronicles the efforts of Jane Marshall to apprise her family of their situation and to lead them into the social prominence that their wealth and social background deserve. Modeling her approach after that of her friend Mrs. Granger Bates, she pushes her family into a new house and her father into philanthropy. In Mrs. Bates's case, both furnishings and philanthropy are meant to convey an interest in culture. In an important moment of the book, Jane is guided by Mrs. Bates through her richly decorated but tasteless house, where the prominence of cultural objects and symbols—the grand piano, the books, and the paintings—is crucial. But when Mrs. Bates opens up, she reveals that the rooms are merely for show, the piano is never used, the bookcases are locked.[20]

But this is more than the familiar exposé of the shallowness of wealth's pretensions to culture. For Mrs. Granger Bates is also, at age fifty-five, taking piano lessons, determined to play Chopin and Tchaikovsky. Furthermore, despite her awareness that to work for cultural endeavors is negotiable social currency, she is scornful of women who do nothing for the city. But the real story of Mrs. Bates is neither her pretentious house nor her genuine social and civic interests. It is rather that moment in which she reveals herself to Jane as living essentially in the days of her pioneer beginnings. At the end of the tour, Mrs. Bates takes Jane to her own private quarters, a replica of the room of her childhood. There she plays on her old piano not the concert pieces she was determined to master, but "Old Dan Tucker" and the "Java March"— songs from her simpler past. This moment is the very heart of the book. The two women stand revealed to each other, and whatever action they take from this point on is balanced by the integrity of the encounter.

Fuller's cultural attitudes are clearly revealed by the novel. He was sympathetic toward Jane and her friend Mrs. Bates not because of their cultural strivings but because of their ability to remember and enjoy their folk origins. This is in keeping with the rest of the book. While one's sympathy is drawn to Jane's brother in his struggle with his father over the right to pursue his artistic inclinations, basically the young man is a caricature of the pretentious and irresponsible dilettante, complete with an orchid in his lapel. Furthermore, a central concern of the book—will Jane's father begin to use his money, as have his associates, to endow cultural institutions?—is linked with the story of his pathetic last days. Lying in delirium, he is harassed by anxiety about which of the many enterprises should receive his money. While his illness is precipitated by many family and business worries, Jane judges her efforts to bring her family into the establishment, to join the procession, as the root cause. One need not accept this as Fuller's final position, but it does suggest that he had deep doubts about the cultural enterprise. From the novel emerges the sense that what is real and true is neither aestheticism nor cultural philanthropy, but rather the earthy integrity and folk patterns of the pioneer.

Fuller himself would never lose this essential insight. Yet it was a painful one. Much as he might respect the pioneer past, support intellectually realism's preference for the natural over the contrived, or enjoy singing "Old Dan Tucker," he was a man of cosmopolitan tastes. In fact, Truesdale Marshall, the dilettante son in the novel, is a spokesman for Fuller's reactions to Chicago: " 'So little taste,' sighed Truesdale; 'so little training, so little education, so total an absence of any collective sense of the fit and proper! Who could believe, here, that there *are* cities elsewhere which fashioned themselves rightly almost by intuition.' " Fuller loved Europe—its atmosphere, its scenery, and its art. It was the "pierian Spring," the fountain sacred to the Muses, while the Midwest was "the dry belt." He advised a friend traveling in Europe to do as he must have done: "drink . . . be a camel; fill up your stummick." Yet torn as he was between America and Europe, Fuller fashioned characters who had taken their fill as small, insignificant figures, living a marginal, unproductive life in the city.[21]

In *Under the Skylights* Fuller would appear as Adrian Bond, a writer on the fence, uncertain whether to remain a Dilettante or become a Veritist. The book chronicles the transition of Abner Joyce—Fuller's friend Hamlin Garland—from the radical realist who wrote with "the fist" to the stolid clubman, cultural promoter, and literary romancer that Garland became. Admiring realism as more serious and more solid than the "slight, flimsy, exotic, factitious" writing he was doing, Bond expresses the difficulty Fuller faced. Joyce's early realism could be Bond's "if to know and to like were one with me." The problem was that "the things I know are the things I don't like, and the things I like are not always the things I know—oftener the things I feel."[22]

Fuller loved art in its traditional European terms; in this he shared the enthusiasm of Charles Hutchinson. Yet, unlike the philanthropist, Fuller felt art could play no vital role in the Chicago to which he was bound. Though he could occasionally be found in the ranks of aesthetic promoters, Fuller never shared the idealistic assumptions of their faith or their belief that the creation of cultural institutions led to civic and artistic progress. Art had no power as a refining force. Worse, it could be misused as a weapon in the social struggle. Fuller understood, as had Jane Addams, that what was vital was the communal experience rooted in the real life of the society. Chicago's pioneer world, with its integrity, stood in contrast to the assumption of culture.

Robert Herrick shared with Fuller both a close relationship with certain cultural philanthropists in Chicago and a deep skepticism about art and its relation to society. In the twentieth century Herrick would shift his tone, suggesting in one of his works that creativity flowed beyond society's conventions. By the expression of this idea, he established kinship with the younger artists and writers gathering in the city.

In 1900 the Little Room put on a spoof of Fuller's *The Last Refuge* as its Twelfth Night extravaganza. Herrick, though a member and a fellow novelist, probably did not watch, for such high jinks were not his style. The Cliff Dwellers must have been more to his liking, not only for its manly decorum, but also because it linked him formally to the cultural philanthropists with whom he enjoyed private friendships. He and his wife traveled with the Ryersons in Europe. Their relationship with the Hutchinsons was such that a personal tragedy in the Herricks' life, the death of their child, brought these friends from their Lake Geneva home to the Herricks' side immediately. Yet Robert Herrick kept his emotional distance. A transplanted New Englander, a native of Cambridge, Massachusetts, and a graduate of Harvard College, he come to Chicago to teach English in the new university. But he kept the way cleared to return to the East, and after World War I and the dissolution of his marriage he did move back to make his home in York, Maine.[23]

Yet perhaps more important than his eastern ties was his novelist's eye, which attempted to penetrate the appearances of things. In 1895 his diary records a meeting in Paris with Frances Hutchinson, Charles's wife. With only a few words he cuts through the veil of face powder that hides her in official portraits. She shook hands with Herrick "giving this convention a little nervous shiver that accorded with the flash of her eyes, as if this old greeting were really an original method found by her to express warmth and interest." Herrick wonders about her seeming youth. "She has never had children, and so I fancy her flesh and form have retained an indian summer kind of spring perfection—a sort of steal from nature that must be found out at last, and crumble. Has she begun to crumble? . . . She is a cautious woman, as I have never found another, so cautious not to 'make trouble' as to make herself ridiculous."[24]

Herrick's life was not a happy one. In his works he would return compulsively to the troubled home of his childhood, dominated by an aggressive mother whose sense of the social status lost because of her marriage was only confirmed by her husband's unsuccessful career and early

death. College opened to Herrick ideas, lifelong friendships, and the benevolent gaze of George Herbert Palmer,
a distant cousin. After a brief term at Massachusetts
Institute of Technology, Herrick was invited to teach at
the new University of Chicago as one of the corps of
easterners who would bring their expertise and their more
traditional notions of university life to Harper's circus.
His way into Chicago eased by Palmer's wife, Alice Freeman Palmer, dean of women at the new university, and
by his own marriage to a vivacious and social-minded
cousin, Herrick quickly established himself in university
and Chicago circles. He had begun writing at Harvard and
had attempted a novel (never published) before coming
to Chicago. His new setting was to stimulate his pen by
clarifying his perspective and by providing new matter for
the working of his essentially moral vision.

Herrick, like Fuller, found open the role of observer
and interpreter of Chicago life to the outside. In 1895
he published a rather extensive article on the University
of Chicago in *Scribner's Magazine*. The article is not
uncritical: Herrick gives an indication of his harsh view of
the urban landscape when he wishes for a park or suburb
to grow around the campus to protect the university "from
the roar and smoke of the city." But when he considers
the activities and interests of Chicago the tone of Herrick's
remarks is indistinguishable from that of the cultural
promoters:

> Anyone who takes an intelligent interest in American life
> must perceive the energies of the middle West—of Chicago.
> These energies are not solely commercial; the enthusiasm for
> the Columbian Exposition, the two large libraries already
> existing, with a third planned and started, the nucleus of a
> great museum provided by Mr. Field—all these and more
> indefinite signs indicate that Chicago is ready for a further
> expression of intellectual life than the pressures of the past
> quarter century has made possible. The people of Chicago
> are eager, in a sense that is true nowhere else in our country,

for art, literature, education, the accompaniments of a complex civilization.[25]

Within the University of Chicago setting Herrick shared the trustees' doubts about Harper's innovations. Coeducation, the extension program, and the addition of professional schools struck Herrick in the same way it struck Hutchinson—as a deviation from eastern models. Yet Herrick also shared the more innovative approaches to culture of some of his business friends, actively supporting the establishment of an endowed art theater, for example.[26]

Yet privately Herrick did not altogether accept the idealistic assumptions that underlay aesthetic uplift. The pursuit of culture, however pleasurable, did not necessarily improve the pursuer. In an 1897 trip to Europe, Herrick observed one of the products of forced culture, Mrs. Kinsley, Charles Hutchinson's mother-in-law: "She had travelled, and towards the close of her life was industriously, even laboriously reading and observing." Her newfound culture did not help her conversation: "At every chance she put in something as apropos of Mark Twain that on the steamer to Australia everyone was talking of his book. . . . A study in opportune propriety. Painfully proper in speech." Herrick was then delighting in a year of travel, enjoying the renewal offered by the older, aesthetically richer culture. Yet Europe had no moral advantages. Herrick reestablished his acquaintance with Bernard Berenson who had been a Harvard contemporary. Fascinated by him, Herrick was at the same time repelled and highly critical.[27]

Herrick came to use his meetings with Berenson in his novel *The Gospel of Freedom*, which took culture as a major theme. Rather than playing upon the ambiguities of a complex character, as Fuller might have done, Herrick subjected culture and culture-seeking to the rigors of moral judgment. The central figure, Adela Anthon, is a new woman who seeks personal fulfillment for herself in her

marriage and, when that disappoints her, in the pursuit
of aesthetic satisfaction. As her entrepreneur husband
becomes increasingly absorbed in business, Adela seeks the
usual social and cultural round of the wealthy matron,
leisure activities that symbolize her husband's success.
She learns of his involvement in an illegal traction deal,
and she reencounters her old acquaintance the aesthete
Simeon Erhard (modeled after Berenson). Erhard seems
to offer her a life of personal freedom and aesthetic fulfillment. Europe with its treasures would be open to her.
Leaving husband and city, Adela seizes experience and
art with enthusiastic abandon: Florence at first seems the
realization of her dreams. But Erhard, the spokesman for
art, is a manipulative, snakelike figure who has substituted
aesthetic responses for feelings, and instead of a full life
Adela experiences the emptiness and frustration of an
existence as his patroness and researcher. A young man
committed to Chicago's reform brings Adela to realize
that her pursuit has been a self-indulgent exercise. He
offers the alternative of a return to her home and to a life
dedicated to service.[28]

In *The Gospel of Freedom* culture was for Herrick
only the window dressing for wealth or a channel for
egotism and self-indulgence. What mattered was the life
of service. Other heroes and heroines would be chastened
in the manner of Adela Anthon: at some moment of
crisis they would be forced to choose between selfishness—
whether expressed in art collecting, sexual indulgence, or
even ill-health—and altruism. Lacking great imaginative
powers, Herrick repeatedly traces his own past and leads
his characters on a pilgrim's progress from temptation to
renunciation. This movement was one that Herrick's
University of Chicago colleague Thorstein Veblen would
have understood, for it translated into moral terms the
distinction Veblen was making between the pursuit of
conspicuous consumption or conspicuous waste and pro-

ductive labor. Its austerity fit well the new professional spirit of the late nineteenth and early twentieth centuries.

After *The Gospel of Freedom*, Herrick never elevated art to a central theme, but twice he used artists as characters, enabling us to probe more fully his sense of the relation of art to society. *The Common Lot*, published in 1904, takes its title from the crushed hopes of Jackson Hart. The nephew of a wealthy Chicago industrialist, Hart thought he would be set apart from the struggling masses by a bequest from his uncle; but when a school for workers is endowed instead, Hart is forced out on his own to gain from the practice of architecture the wealth and stature he craves. Step by step he begins to compromise his standards in return for favors offered by a ruthless contractor who squeezes extra profits by substituting shoddy materials under elegant facades. Their chicanery is first discovered in the monumental edifice Hart has designed for his uncle's school; but it is not until one of his apartment buildings (appropriately named the Graveland) burns and Hart watches as people die in the firetrap, that he begins to understand what he has done and is ready to begin a life committed to honest work for others.

Herrick makes a particular point about the effect of Hart's dishonesty on his art. His school building is wooden imitation: Hart is drawing on his European training in a sterile way. In contrast, Hart's former employer, a professional of unimpeachable integrity, designs distinguished buildings that are original, yet restrained. Honesty is equated with American design based on native needs.

Hart's wife recognizes that he is not an evil man, only weak and hence vulnerable to the drive to success and the questionable ethics that characterize Chicago. As an old-timer laments, "It's money every time. The professions have been commercialized." In the world that is Chicago, nothing is safe from business values. Only a man of special spirit can keep his standards. In the end Hart must submit himself and become a subordinate member of a firm in order to stay honest and be capable of good work. To friends who were cultural philanthropists—and businessmen—Herrick's sense of the relation between commerce and ethics must have been a source of unease.[29]

Only once, at least in the years before the war, did Herrick want more of his artist than discipline. In 1913 he published *One Woman's Life*, whose egotistical heroine seems to have much in common with Harriet Herrick. After successfully propelling herself from lower-middle-class dreariness to the fashionable world of the Near North Side, Milly Ridge dashes her chances by breaking her engagement to a successful banker and marrying Bragdon, a young unproven artist. The delightful "life of art" that she anticipated, "meeting a lot of interesting people, endless clever talk over delightful meals in queer little French restaurants or in picturesque and fascinating studios" is hardly hers, and she finds herself with the care of house and child while her husband spends the day at his studio as regularly as a banker at his office. And yet in Europe when a new possibility emerges—when Bragdon, in painting the portrait of a Russian baroness, captures on canvas her inner spirit—Milly is terrified. Whether Bragdon's knowledge of his subject is sexual or merely a deep emotional understanding is immaterial: it takes Bragdon beyond the pale of safe convention and outside Milly's capacity or control. Milly forces her husband to come to Paris, and from there family and economic pressures return him to America and to the tedious life of an illustrator and art editor. Years later, after a seeming acceptance of his lot, Bragdon dies. Called home by his death, Milly only realizes the destruction she has caused when she sees a roomful of half-finished canvases, executed in a frenzy of painting during her husband's last days. In the midst of these is the baroness's portrait which she had returned to remind Bragdon of his gifts.[30]

Though Herrick would have denied it totally, *One Woman's Life* linked him to the new artistic forces surfacing in Chicago. In the novel he suggested the relation between sexual and artistic energies and the need for freedom beyond bourgeois conventions for the creative life. At the time Herrick was writing, Floyd Dell was gathering around him a coterie of artists who would seek in Chicago personal and aesthetic liberation.

Coming out of Davenport, Springfield, and Elyria, Floyd Dell, Vachel Lindsay, and Sherwood Anderson moved to Chicago. They were attracted to the city partly because of the galleries of the Art Institute and the Chicago Symphony Orchestra's concerts. They also came for jobs, for anonymity, and for the magic hold the city had on the midwestern imagination. In *Moon-Calf*, Floyd Dell's fictionalized autobiography, Felix Fay

> saw again in his mind's eye, as he tramped the road, a picture of the map on the wall of the railway station—the map with a picture of iron roads from all over the Middle West centering in a dark blotch in the corner. . . .
> "Chicago!" he said to himself. . . . But his tramping steps went to the rhythm of a word that said itself over and over in his mind: "Chicago! Chicago!"[31]

In 1909 Dell himself came to Chicago where he joined the staff of the *Chicago Evening Post* as a writer for the *Friday Literary Review*. Edited by Francis Hackett, an Irish Fabian socialist, the literary supplement brought new critical approaches to Chicago readers. In contrast to the *Dial's* support of the genteel tradition, Hackett and Dell opened their pages to appreciations of realism, the newest European trends, and literary treatment of social problems. They were interested in the interrelationship between art and society and in the personal reactions of their reviewers. In their hospitality to new work they gave many unknown writers a hearing.[32]

Professional and personal styles merged. In their apartment in Rogers Park and then in their separate studios on the South Side, Dell and his wife, Margery Currey, opened their doors to an influx of those like themselves coming to Chicago to make their way. Their friends from Davenport, Iowa, George Cram Cook, Susan Glaspell, and Arthur Gordon Ficke, formed a nucleus. But as reputation of the Dell-Currey receptivity grew, strangers such as Sherwood Anderson would come by with manuscripts and hopes. The couple would not let them down. Margery Currey, sensing Anderson's anxiety (he had gone away on the first try without knocking), would walk with him around Jackson Park and help him regain his confidence and composure. After reading Anderson's manuscript, Dell would announce to his readers in the pages of the *Friday Literary Review* that Anderson was an important writer. Seeing the review, Anderson recalled, made him feel as if he "had of a sudden been chosen, elected as it were, given a kind of passport into some strange new and exclusive world." Eunice Tietjens came to the Dells' one evening for dinner and found poetry: as she walked home she danced in the streets. Margaret Anderson rejoiced in the good conversation and recalled fondly that "Sherwood and Floyd would talk to chairs if they had no other audience."[33]

It was "a time of excitement, something seemingly new and fresh in the air we breathed." Outside the web of family and hometown, the young writers lived in the heady atmosphere of creative friends seeking new personal and aesthetic definitions. Sexual liaisons and friendly separations were accepted; open collars, scarves, and capes took the place of neckties and jackets; socialist economics were the norm. Margaret Anderson lived with only a piano for furniture and then left her apartment behind as the need for economy gave her the excuse to move into a tent on the shore of Lake Michigan. Such liberties

with social convention accompanied and seemed to encourage aesthetic freedom. Loosening the bonds from life
seemed one with loosening them from art, a point of view
seemingly supported by the critical shapers of modern
consciousness, Freud, Nietzsche, and Marx.[34]

These were years of true creativity: Sherwood Anderson's *Winesburg, Ohio*, Carl Sandburg's *Chicago Poems*,
Edgar Lee Masters's *Spoon River Anthology*, Vachel
Lindsay's "Captain Booth." Introducing new forms and
injecting a heightened sensibility into words, each writer
in his own way was attempting to express what was in
the heart, not what social, political, or aesthetic conventions prescribed. Their works revealed the hidden agonies
and joys of common people—of the small town and of the
urban working masses—and thereby elevated them to a
new dignity and power.[35]

As creativity flowed, hope surged. George Cram Cook,
then associate editor of the *Friday Literary Review*,
expressed it best in his letter to Susan Glaspell:

> Nietzsche maintains that a hundred men bore the task of
> the Italian Renaissance. If conditions happen to be ready a
> movement may be started by the dropping of a pebble. From
> the cool solitude of this day of mine I drop this page as
> possible pebble.
>
> An American Renaissance of the Twentieth Century is
> not the task of ninety million people, but of one hundred.
> Does that not stir the blood of those who know they may
> be of that hundred? Does it not make them feel like reach-
> ing out to find each other—for strengthening of heart, for
> the generation of intercommunicating power, the kindling
> of communal intellectual passion?

This was also the hope of Charles Hutchinson and of
the businessmen involved in culture.[36]

Yet critical differences divided the two groups. The
young rebels enjoyed the city-wide institutions of culture:
the concerts, the galleries, the collections of books were

part of the excitement of Chicago. But these writers did not seek culture as a means of escaping from materialism, for they did not reject Chicago's industrial and commercial life. They took the city as they found it, stockyards and smokestacks, concerts and lake front. They exulted in Chicago's scale and power. The Black City was to them triumphantly "hog butcher of the world." They loved Chicago uncritically as only those can who have come to it from the constraints and isolation of a Davenport, Iowa. The cultural institutions were not alternatives to the city but were an integral part of its pleasure and wonder. The city, both an economic and a cultural entity, was there to be used, a medium in which to seek personal freedom.[37]

Nor were the Art Institute and the Chicago Symphony Orchestra to set standards based on the great tradition. Such academic approaches were among the restrictions the younger artists were seeking to escape. Institutions were to provide means of putting new works before the public; they would thus both support creativity and establish suitable settings for good talk. When Harriet Monroe set up the offices of *Poetry* magazine and when Maurice Browne organized his Little Theater, the two attracted the creations and the presences of the Floyd Dell circle. Margaret Anderson set out to commandeer both with her *Little Review*.[38]

Thus these younger artists did not pose a critique of the movement for cultural uplift but rather an implicit rephrasing of it, based on certain different assumptions. The fact that the new generation did not separate the arts and letters from life as a means of refinement did not mean that they devalued culture. Rather with romantic belief in its power they linked culture to the world of experience and vitality as its heightened expression. The importance of institutions remained. While they had no business setting standards of taste according to traditional

values, institutions served as the means of rewarding work
and broadcasting new forms to a new age. With such an
approach this generation of artists and writers would
infuse into the cultural life of Chicago a new spirit: they
would bring to the city the enthusiasm, vitality, and innovative spirit of early modernism. And they would find
Chicago receptive.[39]

Lorado Taft, Ralph Clarkson, and Charles Francis
Browne had emphasized the need for the patronage of
artists working in Chicago. Fuller and Herrick had raised
more profound and troubling questions. As a third-
generation Chicagoan, Fuller knew the strivings that underlay the drive for cultural uplift. Committed both to
realism and to the glories of the European tradition, he
was stuck in an unresolvable contradiction. There was
no true bridge he could erect between the authentic folk
spirit of Chicago's pioneers and the monuments of Italy.
Art could not serve as a refining force. Culture could not
elevate the individual or the city. Herrick, the transplanted
New Englander, could see no positive relation between art
and morality. The pursuit of art was often tied to self-
indulgence and sexuality that ran counter to the self-denial
and service needed for the worthwhile life and decent
society. Only once did Herrick suggest a possible alternative: that art must make its own standards and that
egotism buttressed the demands of conventional life.
While a more acceptable position to the younger artists
of the twentieth century, it was no closer to the idealism
of Lorado Taft or Charles Hutchinson.

Fuller and Herrick accepted, even welcomed, the
libraries, museums, orchestra, and university supported by
their friends and associates. But the two novelists could
not join the movement for cultural uplift: the assumptions
that called the city-wide cultural institutions into being
and shaped their structure and programs the two novelists,
perhaps reluctantly, rejected. In so doing, they turned to

the alternative approaches to culture being suggested by settlement house reformers and emerging professionals.

In probing the question of culture, both Fuller and Herrick may have generated some doubts among Chicago's cultural philanthropists. Their reservations went beyond the issue of support for local work: they challenged the motives and the essential assumptions of their friends. In so doing, they may have helped breach the wall of idealistic faith, making possible the direct support of aesthetic innovation by Chicago's cultural philanthropists in the Progressive period. The time was propitious. Artists and writers, impelled by the enthusiasm of early modernism, were seeking the financial means to produce and communicate their work.

9

The Progressive Period

Progressivism is generally thought of as a political movement—the reform effort that combined the drive for order
and purity in politics with the attempt to arrest or control
bigness in business and to protect the worker and consumer.
But Progressivism clearly was more. It involved a concern
with the quality of social life, particularly in the cities,
that cut across many sectors of American society. We
have seen in Chicago the kinds of issues that engaged
settlement house workers and professionals. The churches,
too, were confronting social questions in the social gospel
movement and in the creation of the institutional church
designed to serve the social and intellectual, as well as the
religious, needs of its members. The Progressive spirit
manifested itself also in cultural endeavors as trustees and
administrators of cultural institutions experimented in
ways to bring them closer to the public and into new
relations with municipal government.

But as others have shown, Progressivism was more
than an institutional movement. Running parallel to
efforts at reform was an attempt to understand the nature
of society and to derive an instrumental approach to

intellectual and social problems. There was, as well, an artistic ferment, an openness to the new, a desire to experiment, and a willingness to be daring that challenged the idealistic aesthetic while it tested the limits of realism.[1]

As we turn to the city-wide cultural institutions of Chicago, we will see that all three elements affecting culture in the Progressive period—a concern with the public nature of the institutions, the new instrumentalism, and aesthetic innovation—came into play. Yet these modern tendencies do not describe cultural promotion in the opening years of the twentieth century. Rather it is the tension between Progressivism and elements of the approach dominant in the 1890s that characterizes the movement of this period, a tension resulting in policies that were diverse and contradictory, yet sometimes innovative.

The institutions responded as they did to the cultural currents of Progressivism because their trustees were seeing their relation to the city in a different way. On the surface this does not seem to have been due to any significant change in composition of the governing boards. To look at a list of backers of the major cultural institutions of Chicago in 1915 gives one a sense of continuity: many of the names were from the 1890s, a testimony to continuous interest and long life. Some of the first names were new, however; it was not unusual for a son or nephew to carry on the commitment of a trustee after his death when his involvement had combined extensive philanthropy with service.[2] Additions to the boards of trustees were, with one significant exception, men from the same economic and social background as the elite of the 1890s.[3]

The new perspective of the cultural philanthropists seems to have come out of their common experience rather than from any new blood. In 1917 as in the 1890s, Charles Hutchinson was a leader in Chicago's cultural movement. While his idealism never wavered, by the twentieth century his sense of the public and of its relation to cultural institutions had altered. As we have seen, at the turn of the century men like Hutchinson had been caught up in the struggle for political reform in the city. While Hutchinson does not seem to have been a member of the Civic Federation, an organization dedicated to good government, morality, and conciliation between classes, some of his culturally inclined friends were. The Municipal Voters League, a Federation offshoot, moved more directly into the political arena, running candidates for public office. As they reached out to recover control of the political world from which they had withdrawn, members of Chicago's business elite began to alter their assumptions about the nature of government, allowing room for a new relation between the city and culture.[4]

Perhaps more important to men whose primary philanthropic interest was culture were the critiques and alternatives offered by other members of the cultural enterprise. Settlement house workers singled out a vast population without access to the center of the city, for whom the scale and magnificence of the city-wide cultural institutions served as a bar to entrance. Professional administrators were developing a spirit that first led them to focus on efficiency and then opened them to reformers' concerns. Certain artists in the city criticized the lack of direct promotion of creativity and the scant support for local work. Others were swept up by the heady excitement of modernism. The most trenchant critics of culture raised questions about art and its relation to society that challenged the basic assumptions behind cultural philanthropy: they sought a fresh examination of the effects of industrialization, the nature of beauty, the social function of art, and the relations between art and morality and between academic standards and creativity. The conclusions that reformers, professionals, writers, and artists reached could not be heeded, for they struck at the heart of cultural idealism. However, their raising may, paradoxically, have served as a stimulant, provoking cultural philanthropists to justify their endeavor by expanding the role of their institutions and making them more open to new artistic currents.

The response of the philanthropists to changes in Chicago's life and to criticism was many-faceted, bringing into play not only the approaches of the past but also the new cultural influences of the Progressive period. Taking the opening years of the twentieth century as a whole, four main themes emerge. Cultural philanthropists began to change their conception of a museum collection or a dramatic repertoire. Whereas in 1890 a collection was a set of great works of the past that embodied the ideal, in 1910 it might include contemporary work, some of it experimental, and serve as a means of supporting living artists. The efforts of city-wide cultural institutions to interest the public now extended beyond the middle class: the goal became to reach all Chicago's citizenry in schools, parks, and clubs. These cultural efforts were bound up in an emerging sense of the city as a corporate enterprise accompanied by a greater awareness of communal responsibility and a willingness to try new approaches. And finally, whereas in the 1890s the business elite looked to art to capture an ideal separate from fragmentary reality which might inspire Chicago's citizenry, in 1910 some of them were willing to take the ideal as a design to be imposed on the physical structure of the city itself.

The nineteenth-century definition of art to which cultural philanthropists subscribed had been self-limiting. Art was that which was not entertainment; hence it could not be popular. In operational terms, art was the great masterpieces, created in the past in Europe, as well as the idealistic works of contemporary times. Moreover, art was limited to certain forms. While no clear separation was made between art and science, the philanthropists did differentiate the higher forms, such as painting, from the lower, such as drama. Moreover, within a given medium there were standards separating true art from the false. This hierarchy channeled endowment and guided selection. But by the first decade of the twentieth century, change was taking place at all levels.

From the beginning the Art Institute had supplemented its permanent collection with temporary exhibitions. Later these exhibitions increased in number and in scale, offering to the Chicago public the works of local and regional artists as well as contemporary European paintings and art objects from the Far East. The openness of the cultural institutions is illustrated by the fact that the Armory Show of 1913 was displayed at the Art Institute, whereas hostility to modernism in New York had forced this exhibit out of the Metropolitan building and into another—the Armory from which it takes its name. A similar receptivity brought Chicago's elite to watch Isadora Duncan dance and allowed her to be accompanied by the Chicago Symphony Orchestra.[5]

Openness to the new should not be confused, however, with endorsement or official sponsorship. Art Institute director W. M. R. French left Chicago during the Post-Impressionist Show, commenting privately that it had in it "a large element of hoax and humbug, and another large element of laziness and incompetence." Charles Hutchinson's public discussion of modernism took his usual restrained, tolerant approach. In the midst of "many ignorant and self-interested men," there were "talented and competent artists who are sincerely experimenting in the craft of their profession." However, these gifted modernists have a responsibility to communicate their visions. They should respect the public whose sense of art is based on the great traditions of the past and who love the beautiful. While every age must find its mode

of expression, "the great artist never ignores the public."
French's and Hutchinson's coolness to modernism was
counterposed by the interest of the Art Institute's future
director N. H. Carpenter and by the enthusiasm of
cultural promoters Arthur Aldis and Jerome Eddy, who
lectured on the International Show to the interested, if
bewildered, public who jammed the Art Institute galleries.[6]

But as important as temporary exhibitions or events
were, they differed from a permanent collection, which far
more definitely established the standards by which the
institution defined a work of art. The curriculum of the
university, the regular repertoire of the symphony orchestra,
the permanent collection of the art museum—these were
the real indices of what was regarded as having value. A
critical turning point in fine arts was the organization in
1910 of the Friends of American Art, an association of
125 Chicagoans, each of whom pledged one thousand
dollars for the purchase of works by living American artists
for the Art Institute's collection. A similar decision was
the establishment of the Ferguson Foundation admin-
istered by the Art Institute. The museum itself had built
its sculpture collection of plaster casts of the great works,
but this new foundation endowed the design and construction of original sculpture. The new works were to be
placed, however, in public parks rather than within the
galleries.[7]

While these efforts began to alter the nature of the
collection, they quite obviously served another function as
well: to offer, as the *Bulletin of the Art Institute of
Chicago* put it, "a patronage very favorable to the artists."
Whereas in the 1890s—much to the dissatisfaction of
Chicago's artists—it was thought that the cultural institution would educate taste so that the public would support
creative art, cultural philanthropists in the twentieth
century set up endowments for commission and patronage.
Furthermore, through individual gifts they established a

structure of awards for works exhibited at Art Institute shows. The effort was not limited to the fine arts, but was extended to drama and to poetry.[8]

It was clearly a significant step for Chicago's cultural life when the business elite extended its cultural philanthropy to the support of the contemporary artist and the purchase of his works. For the artist himself it signaled a change, for it opened the possibility of new sources of patronage and greater recognition of his work. Yet the creation of various kinds of endowment for contemporary art did not necessarily mean either extension of the sense of democracy or support of the creative tendencies of the age. In form this whole effort—the Ferguson Foundation, the Friends of American Art, the Art Institute awards, the support of an art theater and of *Poetry* magazine—can be seen as a further articulation of the elitism of cultural philanthropy to patronage. The various endowments provided a source of support for art separate from the market place, enabling decisions to be made according to standards of aesthetic judgment rather than of public taste.

In 1890 this form of patronage would have largely determined the selection of actual works of art: the choices would have been in keeping with the design of the World's Columbian Exposition of 1893 and the architecture and collection of the Art Institute—that is, in the academic Beaux-Arts tradition. Yet by 1910, the possibilities were more open, largely perhaps because the choice could be in professional rather than in lay trustee hands. The Ferguson Foundation, controlled by the trustees of the Art Institute, continued to select the sculpture of Lorado Taft. However, these same men allowed Harriet Monroe to break both with the academic tradition and with popular judgment in her selection of pieces for *Poetry*. The options and the outcome were not always so free or so clear-cut. The Friends of American Art moved within the range of James McNeill Whistler, George Bellows, Robert

Henri, J. Francis Murphy, and William Kieth: the collection was open to the currents of modernism only to the degree that American painting as a whole in 1910 was open.[9]

Twentieth-century cultural philanthropy not only extended itself to the support of contemporary art; it also broke with the hierarchical conception that limited endowment to certain forms. Drama, which had shared with the newspaper the lowest esteem, came to be seen as an appropriate object of endowment. In 1904 Arthur Aldis and other cultural promoters originated a drive to establish a resident theater in the city, where plays would be chosen because of their dramatic merit rather than because of the requirements of the "star" actor or the desires of an entertainment-seeking public. The trustees intended primarily to support the performance of works from the great dramatic repertoire, but they also sought to encourage contemporary talent by offering to perform, as a kind of award, one work a year chosen from among plays submitted by their authors. Rather than achieving the success of the Chicago Symphony Orchestra, as at least one critic had hoped, the Art Theater failed at the end of its first season. The *Dial* charged that this swift demise was the result of an elitism fostered by its backers: "The idea got abroad that the new playhouse was the resort of a coterie, that it was a 'society' affair, that visitors would feel uncomfortable unless they wore evening clothes and diamonds." Efforts were continually made in the next decade to find a workable structure. Donald Robertson's Players were successively sponsored by a woman's club and the Chicago Theatre Society and were given free use of the Art Institute's Fullerton Hall; but the group was unable to establish a secure footing. In 1911 Maurice Browne, an English newcomer to Chicago, ignored the warnings of failure and established what he called the Little Theater, based on the model of the amateur Hull-House Players.

At the outset he sought from Chicago's cultural philanthropists not endowment, but subscriptions; after his
second season, however, he received an anonymous gift
that allowed him to continue debt-free.[10]

Opera was presented in Chicago only by traveling
companies until conflict between rivals in New York in the
early twentieth century brought a group to the city. In
1910, the Chicago Grand Opera Company was formed,
backed by enthusiasts in Chicago and New York. The
easterners were bought out three years later by Harold
McCormick, leaving only the local supporters, whose names
were familiar from the boards of trustees of other Chicago
cultural institutions. The company's life would remain
financially uncertain in this period. Yet a significant step
had been taken. Like theater, opera had become an art
form worthy of cultural philanthropy.[11]

By far the most significant of these endowments for
the creative arts was the support of *Poetry* magazine.
Harriet Monroe, a native Chicagoan with close ties to
the movement for cultural uplift—her brother-in-law was
the architect John Wellborn Root, one of the initial
designers of the fair, and she had herself composed the
Columbian Ode, performed at the fair's dedicatory exer-
cises—asked herself in 1911 why poetry was in such a low
state when the other arts were flourishing. She found her
answer in the structure of endowment: "Painting, sculpture, music are endowed with museums, exhibitions, opera
houses, orchestras, prizes and scholarships. Poetry alone
receives no assistance." In particular, in Chicago

> the Art Institute, with the arts which it officially represented
> and encouraged, was backed by a group of the most powerful
> and wealthy men and women in the city, and by a devoted
> director and assistants whose salaries depended on successful
> propaganda. The trustees gave large sums for necessary
> increases in gallery space and upkeep, and urged their friends
> to remember the Institute with liberal gifts and legacies.

Their efficient and excellent work was inspired by enthusiasm. . . . But why was poetry left out of it? . . . the chief reason, it seemed to me, was that poetry had no one to speak for it, no group of powerful citizens to take a special interest in it, to plead its cause with a planned and efficient program of propaganda.[12]

Miss Monroe decided to create an institution to support poetry. Taking as her model the Friends of American Art, she began with the list of its donors, asking one hundred men to give fifty dollars a year for five years to support a magazine that would choose from the contemporary offerings the best poetic works, becoming "an exhibition gallery for poets." She found a ready response among Chicago's cultural philanthropists (and others): Charles Hutchinson told her, "You may count on me as long as I live." *Poetry* became an endowed journal, free of the necessity to attract a wide following. It was significant not only because it successfully extended cultural philanthropy to literature but also because it was completely free from the givers' influence. So firm had been the control exercised on the Art Theater that the director, Arthur Mapes, was forced to resign; but *Poetry*'s editor was left alone. For at least one supporter the decision to allow Harriet Monroe a free hand was conscious. As Arthur Aldis noted when he mailed his annual check, "I am also sending my ballot for the administrative committee, in the hope that they are quiet men who will keep their hands off the poetry." When Carl Sandburg's "Hog butcher of the world . . ." struck at the business elite's sense of art and hopes for the city and provoked the *Dial*'s wrath, there was evidently no hint of pressure from the magazine's backers urging more conventional poetry, and no guarantor seems to have withdrawn support.[13]

Both the Little Theater and *Poetry* are significant for yet another reason. Working without restrictions, Maurice Browne and Harriet Monroe opened their institutions to the new cultural forces in Chicago. The Little Theater became a focal point for the Liberation, providing a setting for Rupert Brooke, Rabindranath Tagore, and others to speak to the younger generation of poets and artists gathering in the city. Its repertory combined productions of local playwrights' work with older classics and the new theater of Henrik Ibsen. It experimented with new techniques of scenery, lighting, and costumes that made no attempt at realism, but sought to heighten emotional reaction. *Poetry*'s role in fostering modernism shows the strength of the creative forces surfacing in these years and is a tribute to Harriet Monroe's flexibility. She was a member of Lorado Taft's generation, and her own work in the nineteenth century was thoroughly conventional; yet she opened her office and the pages of her magazine to the voices of modern poetry. She welcomed the work of Vachel Lindsay, Edgar Lee Masters, and Carl Sandburg with their midwestern spirit; and through the agency of its foreign editor, Ezra Pound, *Poetry* published the more conscious formal innovations of the Imagists.[14]

A detailed examination of all the efforts of cultural endowment in Chicago in the Progressive period is beyond the scope of this study. One final example, however, will illustrate the range of these efforts and again underscore the open quality of their possibilities. Francis Fisher Browne, the venerable publisher of the *Dial*, in 1907 found the support of the cultural philanthropists in establishing a bookstore dedicated to the sale of serious literature. While its circular pointed out that it was to operate on "sound commercial principles," its central purpose was clear. At Browne's Bookstore, in the Fine Arts Building, the books were not to be treated only as "merchandise but also as embodiments of 'the best that had been thought and said in the world.'" While the bookstore harked back to the Arnoldian values that had informed the *Dial* and the cultural philanthropists in 1890, visually it looked toward the future: its interior was the design of Frank Lloyd Wright, an architect whose organic approach to form was among the most significant contributions of the Progressive period. Linking old and new, Browne's Bookstore was an appropriate emblem of the early twentieth century.[15] Holding the cultural goals of the 1890s and frequently speaking in the language of that decade, the philanthropists were extending their efforts far beyond the Gallery of Old Masters at the Art Institute. At the museum they had gone beyond temporary exhibitions to bring contemporary American art into the permanent collection. Both within the museum and outside, they were establishing an endowment structure to reward and support working artists. And they were moving out from such traditional areas of endowment as museums and libraries to support a variety of potentially creative endeavors, including an art theater, an opera company, a literary magazine, and even a bookstore.

The cultural enterprise of the 1890s had been two-pronged. It had meant the establishment of collections and programs embodying a set of cultural values; it had involved, as well, efforts to attract a middle-class public in order that exposure to art might lift the city out of materialism and foster creative work. In the twentieth century, as we have seen, the notion of the "collection" was radically revised, particularly in fine arts. Similarly, the whole relation of the institution to the public was redefined, along with the social purposes of art. In 1888 Hutchinson's thinking about materialism and art mainly concerned the businessman who had withdrawn from public life to concentrate on his private affairs while corruption was allowed to go unchallenged in Chicago. But by the twentieth century, Hutchinson's focus had shifted to art's value for the masses. It remained the duty of the philanthropic elite to support aesthetic endeavor: "Art must still be nourished by the few who appreciate its value." But the few acted for the many: "Art is not destined for a small and privileged class. Art is democratic. It is of the people and for the people." "It exists for the common heart and for ordinary culture." Yet, though Hutchinson wrote an essay called "The Democracy of Art," art's basic function had not changed. Art still used "the raw material of leisure, ambition and desire" to create "forces for the refinement of living." It remained the "refining power of the beautiful" that gave a special quality to art's presentation of the Ideal. Now, however, it was the people who would benefit by this process.[16]

Hutchinson remained vague about what refinement could mean. He spoke of the role of the museum in ministering "to the uplifting of the life of the community." The test of the cultural institution is "the service it renders to the community in which it stands." "Art for art's sake is a selfish and erroneous doctrine, unworthy of those who present it. Art for humanity and a service of Art for those who live and work and strive in a humdrum world is the true doctrine and one that every Art Museum should cherish." The Art Institute offered opportunities for the experience of art that strengthened men's souls. Those who appreciated art disciplined their bodies and found their satisfaction in spiritual fruits rather than in material goods. It could be assumed that as their numbers increased, the society would become more ordered and sober. Reaching men one by one and changing them, the city-wide cultural institutions would aid in "the advancement of the civilization of the present age."[17]

Others active in culture were more willing than Hutchinson to draw conclusions in specific terms. Harlow Higinbotham, long-time president of the Field Columbian Museum, wrote of the increasing pressures on both rich and poor. "The tension of life is reaching the limit of human endurance. The rich are overwhelmed with the vast responsibilities of their position; the poor are oppressed with a gloomy apprehension of still worse to come. The laborer is losing individuality; the capitalist is self-centered and absorbed. What is to be done?" The specific solution that Higinbotham found in 1903 was music, which had the power to add to life "the joy of living, the play spirit, the richness of companionship, sympathy, service, and sacrifice." The effects could be far-reaching: "the tension of living will be relieved and the strangling grip of material-ism will be changed to the cordial handclasp of mutual forbearance and fraternity." By focusing on the spirit, businessmen could be broadened and workers could be turned away from preoccupation with their economic condition.[18]

Higinbotham's statement presupposed that there were no irreconcilable divisions within the society. In this his colleagues in cultural institutions would have concurred, as well as in his complementary belief that open opportunity existed in America. Despite their business success, the men involved in culture generally felt themselves to be men in the middle, counseling arbitration between capital and labor, not victory for the former. Their concern was with binding up the divisions of society.

Culture came to promise larger benefits and the Renaissance to have a special appeal. Florence was a model of the "ideal Chicago." As usual Hutchinson gave this idea its fullest expression, dwelling on what he felt were the significant aspects of earlier centuries. "Originally the word Art included almost every form of human endeavor. As late as the Italian Renaissance, no distinction was made between Art and Craft, every craftsman was an artist in his degree, and every artist was a craftsman of a superior sort." Artists gave form to the ideals of the common people. They were the ones "who could best express the life and the hope of the time in painting, sculpture, and architecture, in terms understood by all." The result was harmony and cooperation. Artists were appreciated in their time: "The great masters of the Renaissance from Giotto to Veronese were duly honored in their day and generation." They were responsible workmen and citizens who had a respected place in the community. They tried to communicate with their public. "They did not set their Art upon a pedestal where few could see it. . . . They placed their art upon the ground where children could look and gaze at it, and by it be inspired."[19]

In this look at the past Hutchinson selected those elements of harmony and social integration of which art was the most important expression. Implicitly, the Renaissance provided a model for the Chicago of his hopes. The city in the early twentieth century was the location of heterogeneous communities linked primarily by economic and political ties. It lacked social integration and a shared culture. By the establishment of museums and libraries Hutchinson sought to refine his fellow citizens and in this way render the society ordered and stable. He sought to uplift his city and thus make it cultured and creative. Chicago's citizens would be brought under a new unity. Not only would they be disciplined but, in partaking of art, they would join in a common experience and fill the void caused by the lack of shared values. The city that was searching for its soul would find it and would strive to reach the ideal. As George Adams intoned, "We look through the dust and smoke of Chicago as she is, to see the fair and noble form of our city as she will be, a center of influence, intellectual as well as industrial, a school of the nation, as Pericles declared that Athens was the school of Greece."[20]

With this new sense of the value of culture and with the new commitment to the broader public, the city-wide cultural institutions established new programs and responded to citizens' organizations and to the possibilities of a changing municipal government.

From its beginning the University of Chicago had

injected vitality into the cultural life of the city. One element was of crucial importance for the changes that took place in the twentieth century: this was university extension, promoted by President Harper. The conception of extending the resources of an institution outside its walls had been developed by administrators in the 1890s. Its wide application at the University of Chicago, though initially resisted, captured the imagination of cultural philanthropists. Moreover, extension offered the possibility of moving outside the downtown location to reach people in their neighborhoods, a primary concern of settlement house reformers who strongly influenced a new generation of administrators who were active in the early twentieth century.

The role of the University of Chicago in expanding the technique to museums was direct, for the initiator of museum extension in the city was Wallace W. Atwood, a professor at the University of Chicago. His efforts were undertaken at an institution that until the end of our period seems to have been separate from the other city-wide cultural institutions. The Chicago Academy of Sciences, bypassed when the Field Columbian Museum was established and unable to work out a cooperative arrangement, decided to keep its autonomy, to remain "somewhat independent or aloof from the great endeavors that are taking place within the city." A smaller institution that was seeking a reason for its existence, the academy was perhaps freer and more receptive than the Field to the idea of changing its relation to the public. In 1909, under Atwood's direction, it launched an extraordinary range of activities designed to interest school children in natural history. It established loan collections for the public schools; it sponsored lecture courses for children and supplied literature to supplement them; it opened a children's library and reading room and provided facilities for lectures and laboratory work conducted under the guidance of the classroom teacher. In the process it found that to display academically parts of the collection as if they were textbook illustrations was less interesting to children than the arrangement of animals in their natural settings, and this discovery set a pattern for other museum extension programs.[21]

Through its expansion of activities the Chicago Academy of Sciences not only attracted to itself the support of certain members of the business elite involved in other cultural institutions, it also served as a model for other museums in the city, among them the Field. Norman Wait Harris, a newcomer to the elite, concerned that the Field was not attracting children to its doors "to the extent that the trustees believed was to have been anticipated," gave a quarter of a million dollars to extend the work of the museum to Chicago's public schools. The Field already had its lecture series and welcomed classes to its buildings. With the Harris endowment it followed the lead of the Chicago Academy of Sciences and established loan collections designed to "give light and life to the routine of the schools, instill a love of nature in the scholars, make for good citizenship and constantly increase the friends and frequenters of the Museum." Cabinets and cases of these materials were delivered on a regular short-term basis to the schools.[22]

In Chicago and elsewhere museum extension was deemed a great success, and the Field program became a model of what a museum could do. The Art Institute followed the Field's lead and established loan collections, but its extension effort did not stop with exhibits. It also established a lecture service offered to "Art Clubs, Schools and Colleges, Women's Clubs, Chambers of Commerce, and all who believe in the practical utility of the beautiful and in the development of the art of a community as a means to a richer, finer, and more wholesome community life."[23]

It was service to other organizations rather than extension that was the most distinctive feature of the Art Institute's adjustment to the twentieth century. From the beginning the museum had served as a meeting-ground and exhibition hall for art societies in the city. In the twentieth century the relation of the museum to the societies was extended in range and in depth. By 1914, nearly eighty associations met at the Art Institute each week. A good many of these were federated in the Municipal Art League. Through its Exhibition Committee the league helped manage an annual exhibition at the Art Institute of the work of Chicago artists. At this February exhibition, the individual clubs gave receptions for their members and took them on gallery tours. Many of the clubs made regular purchases at these exhibitions as did the Chicago Municipal Art Gallery. The Exhibition Committee of the league met at the Art Institute; there delegates received news of events at the museum which they reported back to their clubs.[24]

Among these groups were not only those designed to provide fellowship for art lovers and amateur artists but also organizations such as the Public School Art Society founded by Ellen Gates Starr of Hull-House, which purchased paintings to decorate the schools, organized collections, sponsored lectures, and sought to bring the Art Institute into closer relation with the people. The Society led children through the museum on guided tours and organized neighborhood art centers that coordinated activities with the Art Institute.[25]

Other city-wide institutions also benefited from such organizations. While the Chicago Symphony Orchestra maintained a pricing policy that limited attendance at concerts to the middle class throughout this period, associations were set up outside its formal structure to enable a broad spectrum of city residents to hear orchestral music. The Chicago Woman's Club sponsored Sunday afternoon concerts at the Art Institute for several years and spearheaded the formation of the Civic Music Association, which offered free concerts in city parks. Members of the orchestra and its director as well as other local musicians volunteered their talents. The programs of popular concerts were expanded to include community singing and there were hopes that opportunities for performance would encourage Chicago composers.[26] The list of such civic organizations could be expanded. Made up of community-minded citizens, including members of the business elite and their wives, the societies originated outside the city-wide cultural institutions but cooperated with these institutions in combined efforts to bring culture to the community. In so doing they shifted away from the institutions' focus on masterworks to offer to the public, as had the reformers, the music and art that the public wanted. In effect these associations were changing the nature of the collections.

It is no single step taken by any one of the institutions that can adequately convey the newer approaches to the public in the period. Rather it is the very multiplicity itself that is revealing—a kind of explosion of activity on many different levels. Beyond its rigorous schedule of exhibitions the Art Institute in 1916 was offering instruction for adults, with special Sunday evening classes for working people; for children, there were gallery tours, a Children's Hour, and special high school classes; the museum sold reproductions and offered loan collections of paintings, slides, and books for schools and associations; it had extension programs of traveling exhibits with accompanying lectures, classes in a part of the city remote from downtown, noon talks to factory workers, and promotional lecturers. On the night of December 31, 1912, the Art Institute remained open free and provided a lecture on Rembrandt, a musical program, and refreshments as an alternative means of welcoming the New Year. The enthusiasm with which growth in attendance was greeted is indicated by this statement: the Art Institute was seen to be

> constantly growing in its popularity as a center of influence. . . . On November nineteenth, for example the number of visitors reached twelve thousand four hundred. That afternoon William Jennings Bryan made an impromptu address from the steps of the Institute before an assemblage of some twenty thousand people.
>
> It is suggestive of the Art Institute's relation to the city to note that the front steps of its building become the rallying place for spontaneous public gatherings as this.[27]

But it was not just the level of activity that rose between 1890 and 1917; it was the concern behind it. There was a sense of seeking and questioning that itself was new. A weakness once discovered became a problem to be solved. The problem and the solution were seen to involve not merely the institution, but the whole community. Moreover, the issues were those that had been important to reformers and professionals. For example, in 1914 the Art Institute became concerned that as yet "no systematic effort has been made to introduce all Chicago school children to the Art Institute." It met with representatives of the Board of Education, the Municipal Art League, the Public School Art Society, and the General Federation of Women's Clubs, among others, to discuss the question. A committee of representatives from all interested organizations was then constituted to devise a plan to remedy the situation.[28]

Here is a very different sense of the relation of the Art Institute to the community. In 1890 the city-wide cultural institutions were set apart from the city as a sphere in which the philanthropic elite could act to restructure the quality of life in the city. By 1910 they were working with other kinds of citizens' organizations in a cooperative effort to meet the needs of the city as they were then felt. Equally significant, the institutions themselves were joining with agencies of city government to achieve common goals.

Perhaps from the beginning the city-wide cultural institutions had been concerned with their relation to the public schools. Their original charters had established free days and special provisions for school children and teachers. This relationship was enriched by the extension programs at the Field and the Art Institute and through the intermediary role played by such citizens' organizations as the Public School Art Society. The Art Institute received an unexpected strengthening of its bond with the schools when it was inadvertently put on the list of educational institutions where public school teachers could receive credits toward promotion, and more than 1,500 Chicago teachers sought instruction. While such programs clearly deepened the connection of the museum to the city, in themselves they did not signal a new departure.[29]

The really critical moment of change came in 1903. After years of effort the state passed an act that transferred ownership of the Art Institute and the Field Museum, formally in the hands of the city, to the South Park Commission, one of the three autonomous park districts in the city. It authorized the commission to hold a referendum on a tax to contribute to the maintenance of the two museums. The successful outcome of the vote brought $50,000 to each museum annually. The difference was more than merely economic or formal. It meant that the cultural institutions and the city could now expect to work together. Charles Hutchinson became one of the South Park commissioners, his first municipal office. The new city charter of 1905–1906 provided for a board of public libraries, museums, and art galleries. Because of conflicts with the state legislature, the charter was never to go into effect, but this provision expressed the understanding among the city's political leaders of the cooperative relationship between civic and cultural institutions.[30]

At the same time that Chicago's public bodies were beginning to cooperate with cultural institutions in common endeavors, the city was drastically revising its understanding of one of its own institutions, the public library. We have seen how the library, founded with a commitment to serve the public, altered its own priorities. Acquisitions and some neighborhood delivery stations were sacrificed as the available resources went to pay for a handsome building. In the twentieth century, public needs again won out, as the library board and librarians acted on the promptings of reform and professionalism. The board, which included Graham Taylor, the head of the Chicago Commons settlement, was dissatisfied with the response of the library to twentieth-century needs and, declaring the position of librarian to be vacant, called an advisory committee made up largely of professional librarians and academics to restructure the entire system. The plan the committee submitted broke the dominance of the central downtown library building. Taking a hard look at the existing level of library services, the group called for a regional system dividing the city into five library districts, each with a main library servicing neighborhood branches and delivery stations. It also stressed the need for more effective work with children and closer relations with the public schools and for a greater commitment to the immigrant population. It set in motion a civil service examination for the next librarian.[31]

In Henry Legler the board found a man who could carry out their intentions to the full. The plan as he implemented it meant a tremendous change in the extent and quality of library service offered by the public library system. It also signaled a significant shift away from the cultural values of the 1890s to an acceptance of the instrumental approach of the Progressive period, an approach which was the essence of the professional spirit.

The concept of the central downtown building whose location was to symbolize the city's spiritual unity was abandoned in favor of five buildings of equal importance placed throughout the city. The belief in the power of a design to inspire Chicago's citizenry gave way to an emphasis on the building as a service station, which, like a business, should be able to shift its location with population changes. The branches should be placed "on busiest corners of the busiest thoroughfares." Rather than choosing designs from "the classic Greek, or other monumental type of building," the board should look for plans that offered "a business front conforming in character to its neighbors—except as to commonplace ugliness." The collection was important because of its usefulness, not its power to uplift. Emphasis was placed on its ability to convey information helpful for problem solving. The important works were the "fugitive pamphlets, official reports and ephemeral printed matter of all sorts,—all extremely valuable data. . . . The most live and productive printed matter in the library." There was nothing special about the process of library management. It was similar to management of a shop or factory and had a similar goal—efficiency. Reference books should be placed near the reference desk "to bring the working staff nearer the source of supplies."[32]

There were many parallels between the restructuring of the public library and the changes that took place in the park system. In the park system, however, one notion did not supplant the other: the twentieth century concept was merely added to that of the nineteenth. Chicago had long been known for its public parks. In the nineteenth century these were ornamental, designed to embellish the city and to provide islands of beauty. Settlement house reformers had a crucial impact on both libraries and parks. They successfully promoted their understanding of the need for playgrounds for the use of children; moreover, the settlement house itself became a model for an institution originating in Chicago, the field house.[33]

With the establishment of playgrounds, the need was seen to provide recreational facilities for all seasons. As swimming pools and indoor tennis courts were built, the idea took shape that the buildings housing them should not be limited to athletics or activities for children, but should provide meeting rooms and entertainment and educational facilities for all residents of the neighborhood. The result was the field house—the multi-service institution staffed by social workers, seen at the time as a municipally sponsored and supported settlement. In the South Park system, which encompassed the central lake-front area, field houses became a regular feature of the parks.[34]

Emerging out of the same drives that led to the reorganization of the public library system, the field houses were obvious locations for the neighborhood library branches then being promoted. The possibilities seemed endless. The houses set up refectories with inexpensive food and low-priced milk and ran their own ice cream factories. They operated laundries to provide for the needs of bathers. And in 1909 the Art Institute set up loan exhibitions from its permanent collection to rotate among the field houses. Working within the park system, the Art Institute was adopting the reformers' neighborhood approach.[35]

The field house was both an extension of the interest in recreation and play and a return, through its cultural offerings, to the concern for beauty of the older park. Similarly, it was both a neighborhood institution like a settlement house and a kind of distribution center for the culture of the central city, reflecting both the values of reformers and the tenets of the 1890s. Like many efforts at decentralization, the field house was subject to the tension between local involvement and centralized direction, between the development of culture as an outgrowth of neighborhood life and the shaping of taste from collections brought in from the outside. And while the playground was becoming increasingly widespread, the cultural philanthropists continued to work along traditional lines, encouraging the development of the lake front and the erection of public monuments through gifts to the city and through the direction of the Ferguson Foundation.

The inclusion of cultural resources in the field house was seen as neither trivial nor merely ornamental, but as a central element in its definition. As momentum built in the second decade of the twentieth century, an activity was developed that seemed to crystallize the varied hopes of urban reformers, settlement house workers, and cultural enthusiasts: this was the play festival or pageant. Beginning about 1907, massive outdoor gatherings expressed the heterogeneous quality of the city, as ethnic communities in native costume performed their folk songs, dances, and sports. Dramas involving vast numbers of costumed school children commemorated high points of history and culture, as for example in 1912 when 1800 children dressed as Shakespearean characters participated in a tribute to the great English playwright. While settlement house workers may have seen the festival as a way in which the immigrant could locate himself in terms of his past or as a constructive means for the young to express their sexual energies, cultural promoters probably saw the pageant through the lens of idealism. Combining the artistry of costume with music and drama and including vast numbers of participants, the pageant may have seemed an important step away from the materialism that threatened relations between the classes in the city. The excitement and the sense of common participation the pageants generated recalled to one observer the World's Columbian Exposition. With a sense that the millennium was at hand, pageants were held throughout the city, culminating in a week-long festival at Eckhart Park in 1917 in which the Municipal

Art League sponsored an exhibition, the Civic Music Association held concerts, and the local drama leagues sponsored pageants. At the point that the war intervened and this energy became translated into patriotism, hopes were high for a development of the lake front that would include vast parade grounds and a municipal pier with facilities to allow huge audiences for musical and dramatic performances.[36]

Of more lasting influence perhaps than the pageants was a quieter development, also of the Progressive period. For more than a decade the Municipal Art League had been attempting to promote good taste by trying to establish a fund to purchase objects of art for public buildings and by supporting the veto power exercised by the Municipal Art Commission over art in public places. These efforts came to fruition when, in 1914, the city established a $5,000 fund to purchase the works of local painters and sculptors for the decoration of public buildings. The board created to choose the works was made up of official representatives from citizens' organizations such as the Municipal Art League and from the Art Institute. In the development of interest group politics in the Progressive period, the city-wide cultural institutions and citizens' associations were seen as representing the cultural interest and as experts in the field of taste.[37]

It is in the whole area of the relation of the cultural institution to the public, to citizens' groups, and to the municipal government that Chicago seems to have been influential during the Progressive period. In 1909 the American Federation of Arts, designed to link local art societies throughout the country, was organized at a convention in Washington. Chicago's elite constituted a large proportion of its national leadership in its early years: Charles Hutchinson was president; its board of directors included Franklin MacVeagh, Bryan Lathrop, and N. H. Carpenter (the director of the Art Institute after 1914).

Its periodical *Art and Progress*, launched the same year, was a catalogue of the efforts of museums, associations, and city governments to promote culture. The federation's lasting contribution was the organization of art exhibitions to travel throughout the country, supplemented by illustrated lectures. In its early, dynamic years, the American Federation of Arts was, to some degree, a projection of Chicago's approach to culture onto the national scene.[38]

An illuminating contrast is provided by the American Academy of Art. Emerging out of the cooperation of artists during the World's Columbian Exposition, it, too, was a national organization. Its central concern was its professional school in Rome, established to instill the Beaux-Arts tradition into the visual arts. Daniel Burnham, one of its leading promoters, solicited for donations among Chicago's cultural philanthropists, only to find a disappointing response. As he wrote to McKim, "The University, the Art Institute, and the Orchestral Association have, as Dr. Harper told you, each recently gone through the ranks of capable givers, and have gleaned over the field again and again. Ordinary argument will do nothing."[39]

What Burnham hoped would change the situation was a plan to have cultural institutions themselves serve as founders: the Art Institute would, for example, contribute as a body to the school. But Hutchinson, though personally a supporter of the academy, refused to cooperate with Burnham's plan, at least until the museum's own fund-raising drive met success. Later an impassioned appeal at the Commercial Club for contributions to a column in Burnham's memory met with a seemingly chilly response. Despite the identification that the American Academy of Arts offered with great national artistic personages and with the Vanderbilts and the Morgans, it generated relatively little interest in Chicago. Chicago's cultural elite were more likely to focus their interest on their own city or on a national organization devoted to the diffusion of culture to the broad public. Faced with failure in his own city, Burnham consoled himself with the difference between Chicago and New York: "Meanwhile the Rockefeller road to success is an easy one."[40]

Beginning in 1909, the strength of conflicting cultural currents in Chicago—localism and centralization, efficiency and beauty—intensified with the publication of the Chicago Plan. The combined Merchants and Commercial clubs sponsored and, through committees, helped to develop the comprehensive design for the city prepared by Daniel Burnham. After the plan's publication, the Commercial Club promoted it.[41]

The plan reverted to the cultural values of the nineteenth century. It captured the imagination of many of those Chicago businessmen whose interest in culture and the city had been awakened in the 1890s. Their enthusiasm recalled the World's Columbian Exposition. Burnham himself made continual reference to the fair as the forerunner of his city-planning effort, and to some degree it was. The fair had taught the importance of a comprehensive plan permitting a unified arrangement of buildings and also had reinforced an appreciation for traditional architectural approaches. Yet there was an essential difference between 1909 and 1893. The fair was the White City, the dream of a summer, whose essence had been its ideal nature. It was "an epitome of the best we had done and a prophecy of what we could do." The Chicago Plan looked to a City Beautiful, of granite and marble rather than plaster of Paris. It was the scheme of the fair, with its planned groupings, its elegance, its vistas and symmetry, projected onto the city itself as a realizable goal—a master plan that step by step, with the cooperation of the citizenry, could be achieved.[42]

Much of the plan concerned transportation corridors, the routing of the railroad, and commercial development.

It need not concern us, except insofar as it, like the library plan of the advisory committee, showed a new sense of the city as a total entity with various parts functionally interrelated.[43] Yet while the new design of the library system moved toward dividing it into smaller units, the Chicago Plan sought more effective centralization. This was especially true in regard to the city's cultural institutions. Burnham saw the city in terms of concentric circles (or half-circles, because of the lake) with their common center along the lake.

Building on efforts already begun by the South Park Commission, Burnham climaxed his design with a plan for a cultural and civic complex at the center point. Seeing it as re-creating the Sorbonne of Paris, Burnham sought to bring together the city-wide cultural institutions (with the exception of the Newberry and the University of Chicago), in a symmetrical arrangement along the lake. The Field Columbian Museum which gathered "under one roof the records of civilization culled from every portion of the globe," and represented "man's struggle through the ages for advancement," would be set in the middle, flanked by the Crerar Library and the Art Institute. The Chicago Public Library and the Chicago Symphony Orchestra would remain in their existing buildings nearby. The buildings would be connected by porticos and would be surrounded by open park land and wide roads suitable for parades and pageants. Moving radially from the Field Museum would be another wide road, ornamented with a monumental statue, pointing toward the domed civic center, the government buildings several blocks away. Swathed in the trappings of classic and Renaissance magnificence, the institutions of culture and of the city would form an axis at the heart of the city, a symbol of its communal and spiritual life.[44]

One is struck by the contrast between the modern quality of the Burnham Plan's comprehensive design and treatment of technical problems such as transportation on the one hand and the archaic character of its under-standing of culture on the other. The plan restated visually and verbally the conceptions held by cultural philanthropists in 1890, as if the newer currents that had been guiding changes in the institutions in the Progressive period had never been articulated. Such concerns as the placement of the buildings to symbolize the unity of the city and the emphasis on visual impact had been seriously questioned by reformers concerned about reaching the people in their neighborhoods and by professionals inter-ested in efficiency. The decentralized library plan had been devised on the basis of the humanitarian and instru-mental alternatives that reformers and professionals had provided. It seems extraordinary in retrospect that the same men who were most effectively guiding the cultural and civic institutions toward the changes we have under-stood as Progressive accepted the Burnham Plan with no noticeable sense of contradiction. Not only businessmen involved in culture, such as Charles Hutchinson, but also Graham Taylor, the prime exponent of neighborhood institutions, waged an active campaign to convince Chicago's citizenry of the value of the plan.[45]

Yet this was in itself illustrative of the difference between the situations of 1909 and 1890. The Commercial Club was limited in what it could accomplish. It gave early support to the plan and underwrote its publishing costs but found that a base of business leaders was not adequate to win for it the widespread acceptance it needed. To get a larger base, Mayor Fred A. Busse appointed a commission that brought in other interests and engaged a professional staff to explain the plan and advertise its benefits. In the literature that resulted, the comprehensive design for the lake front park was underplayed, in some instances not even mentioned. The elite were no longer working in institutions where they could make all the critical decisions. Beyond their persuasive ability they had only their own votes in the referenda for the separate projects. They had to rely on the masses of voters to choose step by step whether the plan would become a reality. Hence while the lake front plan had its important meanings for them, they and others concentrated on the more immediately practical roads and bridges which the plan suggested.[46]

Yet even without its center of arts and letters, the Chicago Plan emphasized visual beauty and a certain grandeur. Without its Sorbonne, Chicago could still be Paris, the city whose nineteenth-century design by Baron Haussmann had a clear influence on Burnham.[47] As bridges were built, roads widened, and the lake front filled for a park, the mark of the nineteenth century was made indelibly on the twentieth. While the plan would never be carried out fully, enough would be built to provide a visible record of the desire to reshape the city into an ideal form.

The stamp of the past was clear in the plan's concern for the needs of the middle and upper classes. Like cultural institutions of the nineteenth century, the plan was designed for a limited sector of the population. It hoped to create a beautiful city where men of substance would settle, where parks, statues, and culture would exist as the proper background for the leisured life. But the plan showed a fundamental disregard for the essential urban problems of neighborhoods such as that surrounding Hull-House. The University of Chicago settlement located near the stockyards sharply criticized the plan's inattention to the housing of working people, many of whom were forced to live "in dark, unventilated rooms, sometimes in cellars." Burnham thought that the cure for the slums was to cut wide streets through them to expose them to the disinfecting light. Yet, however limited its scope, the plan did raise a central question about the quality of life as it was led in the city. The time had passed when the city should be concerned about growth. In the twentieth century Chicago should take as its "dominant idea . . . conservation. The people of Chicago have ceased to be impressed by rapid growth or the great size of the city. What they insist asking now is, How are we living?"[48]

The Burnham Plan was an effort to remake Chicago physically as the cultural philanthropists of the 1890s had hoped to do spiritually through art. It was true that these businessmen had moved in the Progressive period from the purchase of the art of the past to a concern for the living artist, an acceptance of certain elements of modernism, and a broader definition of those efforts worthy of endowment. From a concentration on a centrally located building, they had reshaped their institutions to extend outward and to enter into the life of the neighborhoods. And perhaps most significant, they had entered into a new working arrangement with the city, cooperating with its instrumental approach to achieve common goals. Yet despite these changes, a common core of assumptions still bound the cultural philanthropists of the Progressive period with the 1890s. While settlement house workers, professionals, and artists questioned the value of art, these businessmen retained their belief in its power to ennoble the beholder. And while reformers moved to a concern with the social and economic problems of the city, these members of the city's elite kept their belief in the primacy of cultural reform. They would go far in the Progressive period to broaden their understanding and to make their efforts more effective, but as their support of the Chicago Plan showed, they could still respond to Daniel Burnham and his conception of the city.

Thus at the point in which the Great War intervened, Chicago's cultural philanthropists stood caught between the old and the new. Progressivism had lent to the cultural movement its esprit. In the early years of the twentieth century, members of the business elite had reaffirmed their commitment to the public and had become aware of new aesthetic and social possibilities. Yet the air of enthusiasm and the sheer level of activity obscured the fundamental contradictions between Progressive tendencies and the older tradition.

Cultural philanthropy in Chicago did not end in 1917. In the decades to follow, the city would gain the John G. Shedd Aquarium, the Museum of Science and Industry, the Max Adler Planetarium, and the Chicago Zoological Park. The Field Museum would move into its permanent building. The Art Institute would be significantly expanded. And the Civic Opera Building would be planned and built. Step by step, major elements of the Burnham Plan would be realized: Michigan Avenue, Walker Drive, Grant Park, and the extension of the shoreline of Lake Michigan. Forty years after 1893, Chicago again hosted a World's Fair. Charles L. Hutchinson would live until 1924; Martin A. Ryerson, until 1936.[49]

But World War I marked a significant turning point. The war itself drained the energies of the cultural philanthropists and shifted their commitments. After the Armistice the names of the cultural elite were still invoked, but except for their important bequests, their roles seem largely symbolic. As their hold on cultural affairs slackened, their sons and nephews were joined by others. The names of women and members of formerly excluded ethnic groups appeared on some lists of trustees, perhaps because new sources of financial support were now sorely needed. Most dramatically with the industrial exhibits of the Museum of Science and Industry, the concept of the collection, which had expanded in the Progressive period, now became so inclusive as to lose any distinctive meaning. Any distinction between the commercial spirit and cultural enterprise evaporated as Samuel Insull speculated to finance the

Civic Opera Building, combining the opera house with a potentially profitable office building as its source of support.

History began to catch up with the city. Demography and economic reality fixed New York's primacy, making the boasts of Chicago's loyal seem empty. To this was added the humiliation of organized crime in the Prohibition years.[50] Chicago was a different city after World War I, and its cultural philanthropy a different phenomenon. While some elements remained, recalling the past, they became more and more intertwined with new impulses. Increasingly, the distinctive configurations of Chicago's cultural philanthropy, as developed between the 1880s and 1917, would recede, making way for different conceptions of culture and the city.

Appendix A
Participation of the Cultural Philanthropists

I have examined the backgrounds of thirty-four of the business and professional men who were active in cultural promotion in Chicago. My concern has been with those men who felt a generalized responsibility for culture rather than a specific interest in one of the arts or sciences. Hence the basis of selection was service as a trustee in two or more of the city-wide cultural institutions: the Art Institute, the Field Columbian Museum, the University of Chicago, the Chicago Symphony Orchestra (here members of the Orchestral Association were included as well as trustees), and the Newberry and Crerar libraries. Ten men who sat on three or more boards I have regarded as leaders within the larger group.

Many of these men were also members of the Auditorium Association and guarantors of the World's Columbian Exposition. Two decades later, a significant proportion of the cultural philanthropists backed *Poetry* magazine and were on the Chicago Plan Commission. I have noted these extensions of involvement for the thirty-four men most active in cultural concerns in the city. However, because of the different kind of involvement that these four associations entailed, except in one case, I have not regarded participation as equivalent to trusteeship.

Biographical data on the cultural philanthropists come from several different kinds of sources. Of primary importance are local biographical dictionaries, such as *The Book of Chicagoans: A Biographical Directory of Leading Living Men of the City of Chicago*, ed. John W. Leonard (Chicago: A. N. Marquis & Co., 1905). The fair occasioned an important source of this kind: *The Biographical Dictionary and Portrait Gallery of Representative Men of Chicago, Minnesota Cities and the World's*

Columbian Exposition, 3 vols. (Chicago and New York: American Biographical Publishing Co., 1892). The *Social Register* contains useful information as does the general list *The Elite Directory and Club List of Chicago, 1889–90* (Chicago: The Elite Directory Co., 1889), also published in other years. The manuals of particular organizations, such as the Citizens Association, prove helpful as do collections of college alumni biographies. Newspaper obituaries, especially in the *Chicago Tribune*, are of value, though information is not fully reliable. Biographies are sparse but helpful, especially Charles Blatchford, Jr., *The Story of Two Chicagoans, Eliphalet W. Blatchford and Mary E. W. Blatchford* (privately printed, 1962). Where printed material is lacking, manuscript records are particularly important, such as the Municipal Voters League Papers at the Chicago Historical Society.

George E. Adams
    Art Institute: trustee, 1882/83–1888/89; vice-president, 1882/83
    Field Columbian Museum: trustee, 1894–1917
    Chicago Symphony Orchestra: trustee, 1894–1917; president, 1894–98; member Orchestral Association
    Newberry Library: trustee, 1892–1917; second vice-president, 1904–10; first vice-president, 1911–17
    Auditorium Association stockholder

Allison Armour
    Art Institute: trustee, 1892/93–1898/99
    Chicago Symphony Orchestra: trustee, 1894–97

Edward E. Ayer
    Art Institute: trustee, 1891/92–1927
    Field Columbian Museum: trustee, 1894–1927; president, 1894–97
    Chicago Symphony Orchestra: member Orchestral Association
    Newberry Library: trustee, 1892–1911
    Auditorium Association stockholder

Adolphus C. Bartlett
    Art Institute: trustee, 1888/89–1922
    University of Chicago: trustee, 1900–1922
    Chicago Symphony Orchestra: trustee, 1891–93; member Orchestral Association
    Chicago Plan Commission

Watson F. Blair
    Art Institute: trustee, 1882–88
    Field Columbian Museum: trustee, 1894–1928; second vice-president, 1909–28
    Chicago Symphony Orchestra: member Orchestral Association

Eliphalet W. Blatchford
 Art Institute: trustee, 1882/83–1892/93
 Newberry Library: trustee, 1892–1914; president, 1892–1914
 Crerar Library: trustee, 1894–1914

Daniel H. Burnham
 Art Institute: trustee, 1906–12
 Chicago Symphony Orchestra: trustee, 1894–1912; member Orchestral
  Association
 Poetry magazine guarantor

Edward B. Butler
 Art Institute: trustee, 1907/8–1924
 Chicago Symphony Orchestra: member Orchestral Association
 World's Columbian Exposition guarantor
 Poetry magazine guarantor
 Chicago Plan Commission

Clyde M. Carr
 Art Institute: trustee, 1908/9–1923
 Chicago Symphony Orchestra: trustee, 1912–1922/23; member Orches-
  tral Association
 Chicago Plan Commission

Frederic A. Delano
 University of Chicago: trustee, 1913–14
 Chicago Symphony Orchestra: trustee, 1905–1917/18; member Orches-
  tral Association
 Poetry magazine guarantor
 Chicago Plan Commission

Nathaniel K. Fairbank
 Art Institute: trustee, 1882/83–1899/1900
 Chicago Symphony Orchestra: trustee, 1891–93; president, 1891–93
 Auditorium Association director and first vice-president

Marshall Field
 Art Institute: trustee, 1883/84–1905
 Crerar Library: trustee, 1894–1906; second vice-president, 1895–99
 Auditorium Association stockholder

John J. Glessner
 Art Institute: trustee, 1891/92–1935
 Chicago Symphony Orchestra: trustee, 1898–1935/36; member Orches-
  tral Association
 Auditorium Association stockholder
 Poetry magazine guarantor

Charles D. Hamill
  Art Institute: trustee, 1883/84–1905
  Chicago Symphony Orchestra: trustee, 1891–1905

William Rainey Harper
  University of Chicago: trustee, 1890–1906
  Chicago Symphony Orchestra: trustee, 1903–6; member Orchestral Association

Harlow N. Higinbotham
  Field Columbian Museum: trustee, 1894–1918; president, 1898–1908
  World Columbian Exposition guarantor and president of the Directory
    (An exception to the rule of two trusteeships is made here, because of
    Higinbotham's role as leader.)

Charles L. Hutchinson
  Art Institute: trustee, 1882/83–1924; president, 1882/83–1924
  University of Chicago: trustee, 1890–1924; treasurer, 1890–1924
  Chicago Symphony Orchestra: trustee, 1914–1923/24; member Orchestral Association
  World's Columbian Exposition guarantor
  Poetry magazine guarantor

Huntington W. Jackson
  Field Columbian Museum: trustee, 1894–99
  Crerar Library: trustee, 1894–1901; first vice-president, 1896–1900;
    president, 1900–1901

David B. Jones
  Chicago Symphony Orchestra: member Orchestral Association
  Newberry Library: trustee, 1902–23

Chauncey Keep
  Field Columbian Museum: trustee, 1915–28
  Chicago Symphony Orchestra: trustee, 1906–1928/29; member Orchestral Association
  Crerar Library: trustee, 1906–29

Edson Keith
  Art Institute: trustee, 1882/83–1896/97; vice-president, 1882/83–1889/90
  Crerar Library: trustee, 1895–96
  Auditorium Association stockholder

Bryan Lathrop
  Art Institute: trustee, 1893/94–1916

Chicago Symphony Orchestra: trustee, 1894–1916; vice-president, 1894–98; president, 1899–1916; member Orchestral Association
Newberry Library: trustee, 1896–1916
Poetry magazine guarantor

Frank O. Lowden
University of Chicago: trustee, 1905–12
Chicago Symphony Orchestra: trustee, 1898–1912; member Orchestral Association
Poetry magazine guarantor

Cyrus H. McCormick
Field Columbian Museum: trustee, 1894–1936
Chicago Symphony Orchestra: member Orchestral Association
Auditorium Association stockholder
World's Columbian Exposition guarantor

Harold F. McCormick
University of Chicago: trustee, 1899–1928
Chicago Symphony Orchestra: trustee, 1901–41; member Orchestral Association

Franklin MacVeagh
University of Chicago: trustee, 1901–13
Newberry Library: trustee, 1892–96
Auditorium Association stockholder

George Manierre
Field Columbian Museum: trustee, 1894–1923
Newberry Library: trustee, 1898–1919

John J. Mitchell
Art Institute: trustee, 1900/1901–1918
Crerar Library: 1900–27
World's Columbian Exposition guarantor
Poetry magazine guarantor

Arthur Orr
Art Institute: trustee, 1902/3–1905
Chicago Symphony Orchestra: trustee, 1898–1905; member Orchestral Association

Julius Rosenwald
University of Chicago: trustee, 1912–32
Chicago Symphony Orchestra: member Orchestral Association
Chicago Plan Commission

Martin A. Ryerson

    Art Institute: trustee, 1890/91–1924; vice-president, 1902–24; honorary trustee and honorary president, 1925–32

    Field Columbian Museum: trustee, 1894–1932; vice-president, 1894–1932

    University of Chicago: trustee, 1890–1932; vice-president of board, 1890–92; president of board, 1893–1922

    Chicago Symphony Orchestra: member Orchestral Association

    Auditorium Association stockholder and director

    World's Columbian Exposition guarantor

    Poetry magazine guarantor

Albert A. Sprague

    Art Institute: trustee, 1889/90–1914

    Chicago Symphony Orchestra: member Orchestral Association

    Auditorium Association director

    World's Columbian Exposition guarantor

Albert A. Sprague II

    Field Columbian Museum: trustee, 1910–46

    Chicago Symphony Orchestra: trustee, 1916–1945/46; member Orchestral Association

    Crerar Library: trustee, 1914–46

Lambert Tree

    Art Institute: trustee, 1883/84–1884/85

    Newberry Library: trustee, 1892–1910; second vice-president, 1902–3; first vice-president, 1904–10

Appendix B
The Chicago Institutions

Art Institute of Chicago
  1869   Chicago Academy of Design founded
  1879   Chicago Academy of Design reorganized; name changed to Chicago Academy of Fine Arts
  1882   Presidency of Charles L. Hutchinson began; name changed to Art Institute
  1883   Building opened, a Romanesque design by Burnham and Root
  1893   New building opened, a Renaissance design by Shepley, Rutan, and Coolidge
  1894   Acquisition of Dermidoff Collection
  1898/99   Award system for contemporary artists begun
  1903   Act concerning Museums in Public Parks
  1906   Ferguson Foundation organized
  1910   Friends of American Art organized
  1913   Post-Impressionist show
  1914   Death of William M. R. French, director; Newton H. Carpenter named director pro-tem

Field Columbian Museum
  1893   Incorporated; Frederick J. V. Skiff appointed director; Marshall Field gift of $1 million
  1894   Name changed from Columbian Museum of Chicago to Field Columbian Museum
  1905   Name changed to Field Museum of Natural History
  1906   Death of Marshall Field; bequest of $8 million from his estate

1911   Loan collection endowed by Norman Wait Harris
1915   Construction begun for new building in Grant Park to be completed in 1920

Chicago Symphony Orchestra
1877   Theodore Thomas Orchestra's annual summer concerts inaugurated
1881   Chicago Biennial Musical Festival organized; first festival in 1882
1889   Opening of Auditorium
1890   The Chicago Orchestra organized; Thomas, director
1904   Orchestra Hall dedicated
1905   Death of Theodore Thomas; Frederick Stock named conductor; name changed to Theodore Thomas Orchestra
1913   Name changed to Chicago Symphony Orchestra, Founded by Theodore Thomas
1913/14   Civic Music Association founded

Newberry Library
1868   Death of Walter L. Newberry
1885   Death of Mrs. Newberry, releasing endowment
1887   Newberry Library founded; William Frederick Poole chosen librarian
1893   Building opened, designed by Cobb; Poole demoted to consulting librarian
1894   John Vance Cheney chosen librarian
1909   Resignation of Cheney; W. N. C. Carlton named librarian

John Crerar Library
1889   Death of John Crerar
1893   Crerar's will upheld in courts, releasing endowment
1894   John Crerar Library incorporated
1895   Clement W. Andrews selected as librarian; decision that Crerar emphasize science (leaving the humanities to the Newberry, popular books to Chicago Public)
1897   Library opened to public
1910   Hope ended for Grant Park site
1912   Purchase of property, Michigan Avenue and Randolph Street; building by Holabird and Roche completed in 1921

University of Chicago
1889   Rockefeller pledged initial gift of $600,000 if $400,000 raised from other sources
1890   University of Chicago incorporated; structure outlined in *Bulletin* #1
1891   Presidency accepted by William Rainey Harper, to whom it had been offered in 1890

1892 Buildings occupied, designed by Cobb in late Gothic style; formal opening
1906 Death of Harper; Harry Pratt Judson named successor

Chicago Public Library
1841 Young Men's Association formed
1871 Chicago Fire; English gift; William Frederick Poole brought to Chicago to become librarian
1872 Illinois Free Public Library Act; first board appointed
1873 Formal opening
1884 Delivery station initiated
1887 Frederick H. Hild chosen librarian
1890 Branch reading room established
1897 Building dedicated, designed by Shepley, Rutan, and Coolidge
1904 Blackstone branch built
1906 Branches established in field houses
1909 Hild's resignation forced; advisory commission established; Henry E. Legler chosen librarian
1915 Branches total thirty-two
1916 A *Library Plan for the Whole City* published

Notes

Preface

1. [Price Collier], *America and the Americans from a French Point of View* (New York: G. Scribner's Sons, 1897), p. 254.

2. The Field Columbian Museum and the Chicago Symphony Orchestra have had various name changes. I have chosen to retain their original designations throughout to avoid confusion. I have generally shortened the John Crerar Library to Crerar Library.

Chapter 1

1. Charles Eliot Norton to Henry Blake Fuller, 30 October 1893, quoted in Kermit Vanderbilt, *Charles Eliot Norton: Apostle of Culture in a Democratic Age* (Cambridge, Mass.: Harvard University Press, Belknap Press, 1959), p. 203.

2. This process has been a continuing one in American history. Jane Maloney Johnson, " 'Through Change and Through Storm': A Study of Federalist-Unitarian Thought, 1800–1860," (Ph.D. diss., Radcliffe College, 1958), traces the Boston development to the Jeffersonian period, while Frederic Cople Jaher, "The Boston Brahmins in the Age of Industrial Capitalism," in Jaher, ed., *The Age of Industrialism in America: Essays in Social Structure and Cultural Values* (New York: Free Press, 1968), pp. 188–262, follows the process in the post–Civil War years. Probably the Jacksonian period is the decisive one because of its scale, as suggested by Neil Harris, *The Artist in American Society: The Formative Years, 1790–1860* (New York: George Braziller, 1966).

3. Johnson, " 'Through Change and Through Storm,' " pp. 23–52; George M. Fredrickson, *The Inner Civil War: Northern Intellectuals and*

the Crisis of the Union (New York: Harper & Row, 1965), pp. 29–35, discusses this phenomenon in somewhat different terms.

4. Harris, *Artist in American Society*, pp. 13, 127–32, 146–68, 182–86. Harris does not make it clear that the elite did not hold political power.

5. Meyer Howard Abrams, *The Mirror and the Lamp: Romantic Theory and the Critical Tradition* (New York: Oxford University Press, 1953), p. 56, clarifies the meaning of idealism in considering English writers and critics. My thinking on idealism has been greatly influenced by Roger B. Stein's penetrating and subtle study, *John Ruskin and Aesthetic Thought in America, 1840–1900* (Cambridge, Mass.: Harvard University Press, 1967). See especially comments on Horatio Greenough's functionalism, pp. 12–13.

6. My understanding of the meaning of art to Americans and of art's relation to the society in the early and middle years of the nineteenth century has been shaped by the provocative work of Harris, *Artist in American Society*. For specific reference, see pp. 28–38.

7. Lillian B. Miller, *Patrons and Patriotism: The Encouragement of the Fine Arts in the United States, 1790–1860* (Chicago: University of Chicago Press, 1966), pp. 8–23.

8. Katherine Everett Gilbert, *A History of Esthetics*, rev. ed. (Bloomington: Indiana University Press, 1953), pp. 218–23, 263–65; Miller, *Patrons and Patriotism*, pp. 14–18; Stein, *John Ruskin*, pp. 20–21; Harris, *Artist in American Society*, pp. 41–48.

9. Stein, *John Ruskin*, pp. 11, 15–16.

10. Stein, *John Ruskin*, pp. 18–19; Monroe C. Beardsley, *Aesthetics from Classical Greece to the Present: A Short History* (New York: Macmillan Co., 1966), pp. 245–62; Harris, *Artist in American Society*, pp. 178–79.

11. Both Harris, *Artist in American Society*, pp. 172–81, and Stein, *John Ruskin*, pp. 26–30, discuss transcendentalism, but they see the problem in somewhat different terms. Also useful is Vivian C. Hopkins, *Spires of Form: A Study of Emerson's Aesthetic Theory* (Cambridge, Mass.: Harvard University Press, 1951). See especially pp. 17–19, 35–37, 198–208.

12. Hopkins, *Spires of Form*, p. 15.

13. Stein, *John Ruskin*, especially pp. 39–41.

14. Allen F. Davis, *Spearheads for Reform: The Social Settlements and the Progressive Movement* (New York: Oxford University Press, 1965), pp. 3–8; see also chapter 6 below.

15. John D. Rosenberg, *The Darkening Glass: A Portrait of Ruskin's Genius* (New York: Columbia University Press, 1961), pp. 92–105; George P. Landow, *The Aesthetic and Critical Theories of John Ruskin* (Princeton, N.J.: Princeton University Press, 1971), pp. 90–91, 315–16.

16. Rosenberg, *Darkening Glass*, pp. 154–60; Stein, *John Ruskin*, deals largely with Ruskin's influence on the pacification of art in America. The influence of Ruskin's understanding of the social uses of art is clear from the writing of Norton and Jarves. Unlike English writers, Americans were

less concerned with industrialization and urbanization than with democracy. Ruskin himself was full of contradictions, countering the major thrust of his later argument with statements suggesting that art had moral force (John Ruskin, "A Museum or Picture Gallery: Its Functions and Its Formation," in *The Works of John Ruskin*, ed. E. T. Cook and Alexander Wedderburn [London: George Allen, 1880], 34:247–62).

17. Harris, *Artist in American Society*, pp. 156–62. While there had been a suggestion of spiritual development in neoclassicism, it remained quite subordinate to the dominant use of art to provide models and to shape gracious behavior.

18. Miller, *Patrons and Patriotism*, pp. 90–120; Theodore Sizer, "The American Academy of the Fine Arts," and Charles E. Baker, "The American Art-Union," in Mary Bartlett Cowdrey, ed., *American Academy of Fine Arts and American Art-Union: Introduction, 1816–1852* (New York: New-York Historical Society, 1953), pp. 3–240; Harris, *Artist in American Society*, pp. 92–97.

19. The Central Park Association, *The Central Park* (New York: T. Seltzer, 1926), pp. 19–26 (quotation from p. 25); Andrew Jackson Downing, *A Treatise on the Theory and Practice of Landscape Gardening*, 6th ed. (1859; facsimile ed., New York: Funk & Wagnalls, 1967), p. 51.

20. Albert Fein, ed., *Landscape into Cityscape: Frederick Law Olmsted's Plan for a Greater New York City* (Ithaca, N.Y.: Cornell University Press, 1967), pp. 1–44. Olmsted's design for the park is best understood through the plan itself: Frederick Law Olmsted and Calvert Vaux, "Description of a Plan for the Improvement of the Central Park: Greensward," ibid., pp. 63–88. H. W. Bellows, "Cities and Parks: With Special Reference to the New York Central Park," *Atlantic Monthly* 7 (1861): 416–22 (quotation from p. 422).

21. For Jarves's life and thought see *Dictionary of American Biography*, s.v. Jarves, James Jackson; and Francis Steegmuller, *The Two Lives of James Jackson Jarves* (New Haven, Conn.: Yale University Press, 1951), especially pp. 125–27, 135–225. Jarves's most complete statement is *The Art-Idea* (New York: Hurd and Houghton, 1864), pp. 337–53.

22. [James Jackson Jarves], "Can We Have an Art-Gallery?" *Christian Examiner* 72 (1862): 204–5; Jarves, *The Art-Idea*, pp. 314–53; Steegmuller, *Two Lives*, p. 205.

23. My thinking about the meaning of the Civil War and its aftermath has been shaped by Fredrickson, *Inner Civil War*, especially his brilliant discussion of the Sanitary Commission, pp. 98–112. *The Diary of George Templeton Strong*, ed. Allan Nevins and Milton Halsey Thomas, 4 vols. (New York: Macmillan Co., 1952), vol. 3, gives a good sense of what the Civil War meant. See, for example, Strong's pleasure at Stillé's being considered for an important post (16 January 1863, 3:288).

24. Henry W. Bellows, *Historical Sketch of the Union League Club of New York: Its Origin, Organization, and Work, 1863–1879* (New York: press of G. P. Putnam's Sons for private distribution, 1879), quotation from

confidential circular sent to organizers of the Union League Club in New York, p. 21 (Olmsted quotation from p. 13). Will Irwin, Earl Chapin May, and Joseph Hotchkiss, *A History of the Union League Club of New York City* (New York: Dodd, Mead, & Co., 1952), pp. 7–47. See also for the sense of crisis, *Diary of George Templeton Strong*, vol. 3, entry for 5 November 1862, pp. 271–72, for example; and for how the Union League Club functioned during the war, entries for 25 June–6 July 1863, pp. 324–31.

25. Fredrickson, *Inner Civil War*, pp. 23–165; Henry W. Bellows, *The New Man for the New Times: A Sermon Preached in all Souls' Church on New Year's Day, 1865* (New York: J. Miller, 1865); *Letters of Charles Eliot Norton*, ed. Sara Norton and M. A. DeWolfe Howe, 2 vols. (Boston: Houghton Mifflin Co., 1913), 1:221–82.

26. Broadus Mitchell, *Frederick Law Olmsted: A Critic of the Old South*, Johns Hopkins University Studies in Historical and Political Science, ser. 42, no. 2 (Baltimore, Md.: Johns Hopkins Press, 1924), pp. 62–66; Rollo Ogden, ed., *Life and Letters of Edwin Lawrence Godkin*, 2 vols. (New York: Macmillan Co., 1907), 1:225–39 (see especially the copy of the prospectus for the *Nation*, 1:237–39); Edwin Lawrence Godkin, *Problems of Modern Democracy: Political and Economic Essays*, ed. Morton Keller (Cambridge, Mass.: Harvard University Press, 1966), pp. xiv–xix. The most comprehensive source for this and the following discussion of Mugwumpery is John G. Sproat, *The Best Men: Liberal Reformers in the Gilded Age* (New York: Oxford University Press, 1968).

27. Willie Lee Rose, *Rehearsal for Reconstruction: The Port Royal Experiment* (Indianapolis, Ind.: Bobbs-Merrill Co., 1964), pp. 217–41; Sproat, *Best Men*, pp. 12–50, 143–68; Edward C. Kirkland, *Industry Comes of Age: Business, Labor and Public Policy, 1860–1897*, Economic History of the United States, vol. 6 (New York: Holt, Rinehart, and Winston, 1961), pp. 163–94; Geoffrey Blodgett, "Reform Thought and the Genteel Tradition," in H. Wayne Morgan, ed., *The Gilded Age*, rev. ed. (Syracuse, N.Y.: Syracuse University Press, 1970), pp. 57, 62–68.

28. Bellows, *Historical Sketch*: for confidential prospectus, p. 22; for Bellows's sense of change, p. 123; cf. p. 93 for the reality of politics. The experience of the Union League of Philadelphia was similar. See George Parson Lathrop, *History of the Union League of Philadelphia* (Philadelphia: J. B. Lippincott & Co., 1884).

29. *Dictionary of American Biography*, s.v. Bellows, Henry Whitney; Charles Capen McLaughlin, "Selected Letters of Frederick Law Olmsted" (Ph.D. diss., Harvard University, 1960), pp. 52–53; Vanderbilt, *Charles Eliot Norton*, pp. 100–102.

30. Harris, *Artist in American Society*, p. 278; Fredrickson, *Inner Civil War*, p. 112.

31. Fredrickson, *Inner Civil War*, pp. 211–15; Sproat, *Best Men*, pp. 143–68, 244–71; *Dictionary*, s.v. Bellows, p. 169; McLaughlin, "Selected Letters of Frederick Law Olmsted," pp. 66ff.

32. [Charles Eliot Norton], *Considerations on Some Recent Social Theories* (Boston: Little, Brown & Co., 1853), pp. 19–20; Vanderbilt, *Charles Eliot Norton*, pp. 21–66 (quotation from p. 53).

33. [Charles Eliot Norton], "Goldwin Smith," *North American Review* 99 (1964):526; Norton quoted in Vanderbilt, *Charles Eliot Norton*, p. 95, see pp. 67–102, for this phase of Norton's life; [Charles Eliot Norton], "American Political Ideas," *North American Review* 101 (1865):551.

34. Letter to Miss Gaskell, 2 October 1865, in *Letters of Charles Eliot Norton*, 1:285–86; quotation from Norton to George W. Curtis on Lincoln, 10 December 1863, ibid., p. 266.

35. Vanderbilt, *Charles Eliot Norton*, pp. 103ff.

36. Ibid., pp. 120ff. Henry F. May, *The End of American Innocence: A Study of the First Years of Our Own Time, 1912–1917* (New York: Alfred A. Knopf, 1959), calls Norton "perhaps the most important late-nineteenth-century arbiter of elegant American taste (p. 35). Quotation from Charles Eliot Norton, "A Definition of the Fine Arts," *Forum* 7 (1889):34.

37. Vanderbilt, *Charles Eliot Norton*, pp. 130–32; Charles Eliot Norton, *Historical Studies of Church-Building in the Middle Ages: Venice, Siena, Florence* (New York: Harper Brothers, 1880), p. 29.

38. Norton, "Definition," p. 36.

39. John Tomsich, *A Genteel Endeavor: American Culture and Politics in the Gilded Age* (Stanford, Calif.: Stanford University Press, 1971).

40. The best source for understanding realism in the period is William Dean Howells, "Editor's Study," a monthly column in *Harper's*, January 1886–March 1892.

41. W. S. Lilly, "The Ethics of Art," *Forum* 7 (1889):138. Walter Edwards Houghton, *The Victorian Frame of Mind, 1830–1870* (New Haven, Conn.: Yale University Press, 1957), pp. 154–60, has suggested that doubt and anxiety underlay English dogmatism in the Victorian period, a hypothesis that has shaped my own thinking about American parallels.

42. John Bascom, *Aesthetics; or, The Science of Beauty* (Boston: Crosby and Nichols, 1862), p. 33; William Torrey Harris, "Editor's Preface," *Journal of Speculative Philosophy* 2 (1868):v–vi, quoted in Stein, *John Ruskin*, p. 192; Lilly, "Ethics of Art," p. 140; Matthew Arnold, *Culture and Anarchy: An Essay in Political and Social Criticism* (London: Smith, Elder and Co., 1869), p. viii. On Arnold see Lionel Trilling, *Matthew Arnold* (New York: W. W. Norton & Co., 1939) and Raymond Williams, *Culture and Society, 1780–1950* (New York: Columbia University Press, 1958), pp. 120–36. Williams's study of British thought is an important introduction to the question of idealism and the meaning of culture.

43. Rosenberg, *Darkening Glass*, pp. 94–100; Howard Mumford Jones, "The Renaissance and American Origins," *Ideas in America* (Cambridge, Mass.: Harvard University Press, 1944), pp. 140–51, relates this discovery to "the special quality of the relation between wealth and culture" in the period (quotation from p. 146); Stein, *John Ruskin*, pp. 187, 236–37,

256–57; James Jackson Jarves, *Italian Rambles: Studies of Life and Manners in New and Old Italy* (New York: G. P. Putnam's Sons, 1883), p. 379. This analytic model makes distinctions more clear-cut than the somewhat ambiguous reality. For example, James M. Hoppin mediated between Ruskinian understandings and love of the Renaissance by putting, with some reservations, the Ruskinian sense of medieval life into the Renaissance *(The Early Renaissance and Other Essays on Art Subjects* [Boston: Houghton Mifflin Co., 1892], pp. 1–55).

44. Jarves, *Art-Idea*, p. 166.

45. Charles Moore, *The Life and Times of Charles Follen McKim* (Boston: Houghton Mifflin Co., 1929), pp. 308–9.

46. Irving Kolodin, *The Metropolitan Opera, 1883–1966: A Candid History* (New York: Alfred A. Knopf, 1966), pp. 3–6, 49–64; Laurence Vail Coleman, *The Museum in America: A Critical Study*, 2 vols. (Washington, D.C.: American Association of Museums, 1939), 1:17; René Brimo, *L'Évolution du Goût aux États-Unis d'après l'histoire des collections* (Paris: James Fortune, 1938), p. 173.

47. Henry Ward Beecher, "Be Generous of Beauty," in his *Eyes and Ears* (Boston: Tichnor and Fields, 1862), p. 282. On Beecher, see William G. McLoughlin, *The Meaning of Henry Ward Beecher: An Essay on the Shifting Values of Mid-Victorian America, 1840–1870* (New York: Alfred A. Knopf, 1970). Beecher played an important role in the development of public concepts of the nature and meaning of art. See Harris, *Artist in American Society*, pp. 134–35, 307–12.

48. Henry Ward Beecher, "Christian Liberty in the Use of the Beautiful," in his *Star Papers* (New York: J. C. Derby, 1855), p. 296.

49. Winifred E. Howe, *A History of the Metropolitan Museum of Art*, 2 vols. (New York: Gillis Press, 1913), 1:99–104. While Boston's Museum of Fine Arts developed out of the Atheneum, similar pressures contributed to its foundation. C. C. Perkins promoted the museum through the Social Science Association whose membership reads like a Mugwump roster. See Charles Callahan Perkins, "Art Education in America," *Journal of Social Sciences*, no. 3 (1871): 37–57.

50. [George Fiske Comfort], "Art Museums in America," *Old and New* 1 (1870):505; Neil Harris, "The Gilded Age Revisited: Boston and the Museum Movement," *American Quarterly* 14 (1962):551–55; Howe, *Metropolitan Museum*, 1:131; Daniel M. Fox, *Engines of Culture: Philanthropy and Art Museums* (Madison: State Historical Society of Wisconsin, 1963) is a valuable introduction to museum development and its ideological roots.

51. Frederick Law Olmsted, "Public Parks and the Enlargement of Towns" (paper read before the American Social Science Association, 1880), in his *Public Parks* (Brookline, Mass., 1902), pp. 54, 63; Brimo, *L'Évolution du Goût*, p. 173.

52. [Comfort], "Art Museums in America," p. 511; James Jackson Jarves, "Museums of Art, Artists, and Amateurs in America," *Galaxy* 10

(1870):50–59; see, for example, *Nation* 18 (5 March 1874):156–58.

53. [Comfort], "Art Museums in America," p. 510; Perkins, "Art Education in America," pp. 46–49.

54. Walter Muir Whitehill, *Museum of Fine Arts, Boston: A Centennial History*, 2 vols. (Cambridge, Mass.: Harvard University Press, 1970) 1:10–39, 62–63, 147–48, 172–217; Harris, "Gilded Age Revisited"; Howe, *Metropolitan Museum of Art*, 1:202; Metropolitan Museum of Art, *Annual Report of the Trustees of the Association*, during the period, especially the speeches of Joseph H. Choate, 30 March 1880, 10:172–78, and Henry E. Howland, 5 November 1894, 25:614–18; Brimo, *L'Évolution du Goût*, p. 101.

55. Daniel J. Kevles, unpublished manuscript (a social interpretation of physics in American society to be published by Knopf), pp. 19–38, 42–44, quotation from Charles William Eliot, p. 38; Henry Fairfield Osborn, *The American Museum of Natural History: Its Origin, Its History, the Growth of Its Departments to December 31, 1909* (New York: Irving Press, 1911), pp. 9–21.

56. Moore, *Charles Follen McKim*, pp. 62–94 (quotation from pp. 62–63). John C. Cawelti, "America on Display: The World's Fairs of 1876, 1893, 1933," in Jaher, ed., *Age of Industrialism in America*, pp. 317–63, supports these distinctions between generations as reflected in world's fairs. See pp. 334–46 for consideration of the World's Columbian Exposition.

Chapter 2

1. Robert Knutson, "The White City: The World's Columbian Exposition of 1893" (Ph.D. diss., Columbia University, 1956), pp. 9–15.

2. John J. Ingalls, "Lessons of the Fair," *Cosmopolitan* 16 (1893–94): 142.

3. See Bessie Louise Pierce, *A History of Chicago*, 3 vols. (New York: Alfred A. Knopf, 1937–57), 3:64–233, for details of economic development.

4. Constance McLaughlin Green, *American Cities in the Growth of the Nation* (London: Athlone Press, University of London, 1957), pp. 100–128; Wyatt Winton Belcher, *The Economic Rivalry between St. Louis and Chicago, 1850–1880* (New York: Columbia University Press, 1947); Pierce, *History of Chicago*, 2:113, 109.

5. Pierce, *History of Chicago*, 2:93–94; Green, *American Cities*, pp. 108–9; Pierce, *History of Chicago*, 3:9–19.

6. Ray Ginger, *Altgeld's America: The Lincoln Ideal versus Changing Realities* (New York: Funk & Wagnalls Co., 1958), p. 5.

7. Pierce, *History of Chicago*, 3:22, 516, 20–63, passim.

8. Ibid., 1:44–49, 317; 3:333; Donald S. Bradley and Mayer N. Zald, "From Commercial Elite to Political Administrator: The Recruitment of the Mayors of Chicago," *American Journal of Sociology* 71 (1965–66): 160–64; Humbert S. Nelli, *Italians in Chicago, 1880–1930: A Study in*

Ethnic Mobility (New York: Oxford University Press, 1970), pp. 88–124.

9. Two Chicago novels that capture this sense are Robert Herrick, *The Web of Life* (New York: Macmillan Co., 1900); and Henry Blake Fuller, *The Cliff-Dwellers* (New York: Harper & Brothers, 1893).

10. Blake Nevius, *Robert Herrick: The Development of a Novelist* (Berkeley and Los Angeles: University of California Press, 1962), pp. 88–97, discusses this in reference to the novel.

11. Gwladys Spencer, *The Chicago Public Library: Origins and Backgrounds* (Chicago: University of Chicago Press, 1943), pp. 328–31, 346; quotation from p. 351.

12. Pierce, *History of Chicago*, 3:470–92, discusses these commercial ventures and other forms of entertainment, as does Alfred Theodore Andreas, *History of Chicago: From the Earliest Period to the Present Time*, 3 vols. (Chicago: A. T. Andreas Co., 1884–86), 3:628–73; Ellis A. Johnson, "The Chicago Symphony Orchestra, 1891–1942: A Study in American Cultural History" (Ph.D. diss., University of Chicago, 1955), p. 25; Theodore Thomas, *Theodore Thomas: A Musical Autobiography*, ed. George P. Upton, 2 vols. (Chicago: A. C. McClurg & Co., 1905), 1:317–18.

13. Andreas, *History of Chicago*, 3:419–20; one short-lived example was the Chicago Art League (founded 1880) which lasted from two to three years (ibid., p. 419).

14. Pierce, *History of Chicago*, 3:489; Philo Adams Otis, *The Chicago Symphony Orchestra: Its Organization, Growth and Development, 1891–1924* (Chicago: Clayton F. Summy Co., 1924), p. 14; Andreas, *History of Chicago*, 3:629–33; Lawrence L. Edlund, *The Apollo Musical Club of Chicago: A Historical Sketch* (Chicago: Apollo Musical Club, 1946).

15. Pierce, *History of Chicago*, 3:23–24, considers the German organizations; Archibald Byrne, "Walter L. Newberry's Chicago," *Newberry Library Bulletin*, 2d ser. 3(1955):261–73, discusses the native-born group in the years before the Fire, detailing the organizational affiliations of one of its members; Paul M. Angle, *The Chicago Historical Society, 1856–1956: An Unconventional Chronicle* (New York: Rand McNally & Co., 1956), pp. 15–60; William Kerr Higley, *Historical Sketch of the Academy*, Chicago Academy of Science, Special Publication no. 1 (Chicago: Stromberg, Allen & Co., 1902), p. 5.

16. This inward orientation also characterized those eager associations devoted to culture, the women's clubs (such as the Fortnightly).

17. Higley, *Historical Sketch of the Academy*, p. 5; this is a national rather than a local phenomenon, as demonstrated by Frances W. Gregory and Irene D. Neu, "The American Industrial Elite in the 1870's: Their Social Origins," in *Men in Business*, ed. William Miller (Cambridge, Mass.: Harvard University Press, 1952), pp. 198–99.

18. "The Second Father of the Newberry," *Newberry Library Bulletin* 1, no. 7 (June 1947):3–18, is a perceptive discussion of Blatchford. Social recognition is clearly reflected in the newspaper articles written about the

Twentieth Century Club. Membership in the club was by invitation and seems to have been limited to the wealthy members of the native-born elite. A gathering of members is referred to as "A Brilliant Assemblage," for example, and the words *society* and *fashion* are prominent in the "Scrapbook of Clippings Concerning the Activities of the Club, 1889–19-?," p. 1, Payne Papers, Newberry Library.

19. Andreas, *History of Chicago*, 1:670–71; Otto M. Nelson, "The Chicago Relief and Aid Society, 1850–1874," *Journal of the Illinois State Historical Society* 59 (1966):48–66; Pierce, *History of Chicago*, 2:446; Sarah Edwards Henshaw, *Our Branch and Its Tributaries: Being a History of the Work of the Northwestern Sanitary Commission* (Chicago: Alfred L. Sewell, 1868), pp. 25, 226–27, 29; Andreas, *History of Chicago*, 2:315–23.

20. William Quentin Maxwell, *Lincoln's Fifth Wheel: The Political History of the United States Sanitary Commission* (New York: Longmans, Green & Co., 1956), pp. 216–19.

21. Byrne, "Walter L. Newberry's Chicago," p. 266; Newberry's will was far more complicated than this suggests ("Second Father of the Newberry," pp. 13–17).

22. Pierce, *History of Chicago*, 3:419. The legend of the Fire is best conveyed through the literature of the grandchildren, Janet Ayer Fairbanks, *The Smiths* (Indianapolis, Ind.: Bobbs-Merrill Co., 1925), pp. 160–63 and Margaret Ayer Barnes, *Within this Present* (Boston: Houghton Mifflin Co., 1933), pp. 14–18.

23. Pierce, *History of Chicago*, 3:475; the *Chicago Tribune*, 25 September 1873, has a historical account of the exposition's beginnings, while the issue for 14 September 1879 describes some of the industrial exhibits.

24. *Chicago Tribune*, 25 September 1873; four years later concern was expressed over the narrowness of support (ibid., 18 November 1877).

25. *Chicago Tribune*, 18 November 1877; John D. Kysela, S.J., "Sara Hallowell Brings 'Modern Art' to the Midwest," *Art Quarterly* 27 (1964): 150–55.

26. *1883 Catalogue of the Art Hall of the Inter-State Industrial Exposition*, copy in Chicago Historical Society, Chicago, Ill.; *Charter, Constitution and By-Laws of the Chicago Academy of Design* (Chicago, 1874), pp. 4–5, 13–14, copy in Chicago Historical Society; Charles N. Baker, *Life and Character of William Taylor Baker* (New York: Premier Press, 1908), pp. 268–69; call for meeting to organize the "Institution for the Encouragement of the Fine Arts," 13 May 1879, Art Institute of Chicago Scrapbook, no. 3, n.p., Ryerson Library, Art Institute of Chicago; quotation from Chicago Academy of Fine Arts Records, p. 5, Art Institute of Chicago.

27. "Art Matters: Establishment of the Art Institute of Chicago under Most Favorable Auspices," *Chicago Tribune*, 24 December 1882, in Art Institute of Chicago Scrapbook, no. 2, n.p., Ryerson Library, Art Institute of Chicago.

28. *Chicago Tribune*, 25 September 1873; ibid., 17 November 1877; Otis, *Chicago Symphony Orchestra*, pp. 15, 17–20; Johnson, "Chicago

Symphony Orchestra," pp. 21–22; "Program: First Musical Festival, Chicago," copy in Chicago Historical Society.

29. Otis, *Chicago Symphony Orchestra*, pp. 19–20; Johnson, "Chicago Symphony Orchestra," p. 24; Bruce Grant, *Fight for a City: The Story of the Union League Club of Chicago and Its Times, 1880–1955* (Chicago: Rand McNally & Co., 1955), pp. 120–23; W[illiam] S[mythe] B[abcock] Mathews, ed., *A Hundred Years of Music in America* (Chicago: G. L. Howe, 1889), pp. 322–24 (Mathews states the cost as $70,000, p. 322; as $60,000, p. 324).

30. Grant, *Fight for a City*, pp. 124–28; "Auditorium Supplement," *Chicago Daily Inter Ocean*, 11 December 1889, p. 1.

31. "Auditorium Supplement," p. 1.

32. Rose Fay Thomas, *Memoirs of Theodore Thomas* (New York: Moffat, Yard and Co., 1911), pp. 352–54; Otis, *Chicago Symphony Orchestra*, pp. 28–29.

33. Richard J. Storr, *Harper's University: The Beginnings: A History of the University of Chicago* (Chicago: University of Chicago Press, 1966), pp. 18–40.

34. Goodspeed to sons, 27 October 1889, copy, Rockefeller Papers, University of Chicago Library; Storr, *Harper's University*, pp. 35–40; Goodspeed to Harper, 1 June 1890, Harper Papers, University of Chicago Library, outlines categories of membership on the board of trustees: "Baptists from abroad. . . . city Baptists. . . . citizens, not Baptist. . . . the Jewish representative"; quotation from Goodspeed to Harper, 1 October 1890, Harper Papers.

35. Goodspeed to Harper, 5 October 1890, Harper Papers.

36. Knutson, "The White City," pp. 14–17; while there were more than 29,000 individual stockholders, 90 of them held 40 percent of the stock. For the selection of the Directory each share was worth one vote. The national Commission which competed with the Directory for authority was given responsibility for setting general guidelines and for approving the plans of the Directory (ibid., pp. 16–17); *A History of the World's Columbian Exposition, Held in Chicago in 1893*, ed. Rossiter Johnson, 4 vols. (New York: D. Appleton and Co., 1897–98), 1:22.

37. Diary of Charles L. Hutchinson, 27 March 1890, p. 4, typescript copy, Hutchinson Papers, Newberry Library.

38. *History of the World's Columbian Exposition*, ed. Johnson, 1:102–5; Knutson, "The White City," p. 18. This sense of identification was expressed by Harlow N. Higinbotham in his *Report of the President to the Board of Directors of the World's Columbian Exposition* (Chicago: Rand McNally & Co., 1898), p. 78: "One who had not shared in some way in that task can not appreciate its gravity and the deep, heartfelt thankfulness of those who had borne it when they saw the end of their labors, and the great Exposition practically complete, unfolding its noble and beautiful proportions to the eyes of the world."

39. *An Historical and Descriptive Account of the Field Columbian*

Museum, publication 1, vol. 1, no. 1 (Chicago: Field Columbian Museum, 1894), p. 11; McCagg to Hutchinson, 17 March 1885, Hutchinson Papers, Newberry Library.

40. For John Crerar's bequest, see Thomas Wakefield Goodspeed, "The Founder: John Crerar," in J. Christian Bay, *The John Crerar Library, 1895–1944* (Chicago: Directors of the John Crerar Library, 1945), pp. 23–24.

41. The University of Chicago reserved a seat for a representative of the German Jewish Standard Club (Storr, *Harper's University,* pp. 40, 42); perhaps because of Theodore Thomas, the Chicago Symphony Orchestra's board of trustees was open to a few persons of German descent; Rabbi Emil Hirsch was an original trustee of the Field Columbian Museum.

42. See correspondence between Edward E. Ayer and Sidney C. Eastman, 30 August–1 September 1893, letterbook no. 1, files, Field Museum of Natural History. Quotation from Ayer to Eastman, 31 August 1893. Despite his origins as the son of immigrant parents, Kohlsaat did not belong to the German community of Chicago. As the son-in-law of the prominent Nelson Blake and a leading newspaper editor and powerful Republican, Kohlsaat moved in elite circles. Eastman did include some men with German surnames in his final backup list, although these men did not serve on the board of trustees.

43. Ayer to Eastman, 31 August 1893, McCagg to Blatchford, 19 February 1892, and McCormick to Blatchford, 9 February 1892, Poole Papers, Newberry Library.

44. Eastman to Ayer, 1 September 1893. The question is complex, involving both individual motivation and social recognition. Swift's total dedication to the intricate processes of his packing business was obviously important; but the cultural philanthropists in the nineteenth century were also linked by friendship and private social life, which did not include this packer (it was not involvement in the packing business per se, for P. D. Armour was sought as a potential trustee of the Field [Eastman to Ayer, 30 August 1893]).

45. Carnegie to Hutchinson, 30 April 1901, Hutchinson Papers, Chicago Historical Society.

Chapter 3

1. Hutchinson was asked to speak at such organizations as the Commercial Club when matters of cultural interest were discussed, as, for example, during the club year 1911–1912 when he made an address entitled "The Welfare of Chicago." He was introduced by the club president as "one of those members who perhaps more than anyone else does things in Chicago and never says anything about it. I do not know of anyone who has done more than he" *(Commercial Club of Chicago Yearbook, 1911–12* [Chicago: Executive Committee, 1912], p. 182).

2. This account of Hutchinson's career draws heavily on the biographical

sketch by Thomas Wakefield Goodspeed, "Charles Lawrence Hutchinson," *University Record* 11 (1925):50–76, which is the best review of Hutchinson's life. Specific page references to biographical details have been omitted; further references are given only for those aspects of Hutchinson's career not treated by Goodspeed.

3. Bessie Louise Pierce, *A History of Chicago*, 3 vols. (New York: Alfred A. Knopf, 1937–57), 3:86–87; Ernest Poole, *Giants Gone: Men Who Made Chicago* (New York: McGraw-Hill Book Co., 1943), p. 268.

4. Goodspeed, "Charles Lawrence Hutchinson," p. 61 for quotation.

5. Alfred Theodore Andreas, *History of Chicago: From the Earliest Period to the Present Time*, 3 vols. (Chicago: A. T. Andreas Co., 1884–86), 3:422.

6. Poole, *Giants Gone*, pp. 271–72.

7. Acquisitions are recorded in the annual reports of the Art Institute and the Field Columbian Museum—for example, *Publications of the Field Museum of Natural History*, Report Series 1 (1895/96):103; Ryerson sat with Hutchinson on almost all the boards of the city-wide cultural institutions: he was president of the board of trustees of the University of Chicago while Hutchinson was treasurer, and he was vice-president of the board of the Art Institute while Hutchinson was president; a sense of Hutchinson's social life and his most important personal ties is conveyed by his diary, 1881–1911, typescript copy, Hutchinson Papers, Newberry Library.

8. See chapter 8 for a discussion of the Cliff Dwellers; Robert Morss Lovett, *All Our Years: The Autobiography of Robert Morss Lovett* (New York: Viking Press, 1948), p. 62; for relationship with Fuller and Herrick see diary, 6 September 1900, p. 37, and 11–12 August 1900, p. 36, typescript copy, Hutchinson Papers, Newberry Library.

9. Charles Fabens Kelly, "Chicago: Record Years," *Art News* 51, no. 4 (June–August 1952):62, 107; Benjamin Hutchinson quoted in "Some Anecdotes of 'Old Hutch,'" clipping, scrapbook of Charles Hutchinson, Hutchinson Papers, Newberry Library. A note from Benjamin Hutchinson to Charles Foote (later Charles Hutchinson's secretary) March 1891, conveys a vivid sense of how father and son differed: "How long have you been drawing $125 a month? did I ever agree to give you over $100 was you not man enough when you drew your pay and quit to notify me of the same" (Hutchinson Papers, Chicago Historical Society).

10. For Hutchinson's mother's influence, see Goodspeed, "Charles Lawrence Hutchinson," pp. 51, 55–56; diary of Hutchinson, honeymoon trip May–June 1881, p. 1 and a European trip April 1890, pp. 11–12, typescript copy, Hutchinson Papers, Newberry Library; Daniel M. Fox considered the personal element in the foundation of art museums in his provocative study, *Engines of Culture: Philanthropy and Art Museums* (Madison: State Historical Society of Wisconsin, 1963), pp. 9–10.

11. The model comes through in the obituaries of the members of the Commercial Club, as for example, that of A. A. Sprague, *Commercial Club of Chicago Yearbook, 1914–15* (1915), pp. 294–95; P. D. Armour quoted

in Wayne Andrews, *Battle for Chicago* (New York: Harcourt, Brace & Co., 1946), p. 88. The one exception is Berthe Honoré Palmer. Potter Palmer took what may have been his wife's place on the board of the Art Institute (fully accepting this, Mrs. Palmer would later fight to so establish her son Honoré). But Mrs. Palmer was cut from a different cloth, taking her cues from eastern models as she attempted to project her career on a national scale (Ishbel Ross, *Silhouette in Diamonds: The Life of Mrs. Potter Palmer* [New York: Harper & Brothers, 1960], especially pp. 158–59).

12. Each of these men was on the boards of three or more of the city-wide cultural institutions: George E. Adams, Edward E. Ayer, Adolphus C. Bartlett, Watson F. Blair, E. W. Blatchford, Charles L. Hutchinson, Chauncey Keep, Byron Lathrop, Martin A. Ryerson, and Albert A. Sprague II. See Appendix for a more complete listing and a discussion of kinds of sources used to assemble biographical data.

13. Such a member of the new generation was Eliphalet Wickes Blatchford, president of the board of trustees of the Newberry Library ("The Second Father of the Newberry," *Newberry Library Bulletin* 1, no. 7 [June 1947]: 3–18).

14. Such were the observations of Edward Hungerford in *The Personality of American Cities*, quoted in Bessie Louise Pierce, *As Others See Chicago: Impressions of Visitors, 1673–1933* (Chicago: University of Chicago Press, 1933), p. 437.

15. David Heathcote Crook, "Louis Sullivan, the World's Columbian Exposition and American Life" (Ph.D. diss., Harvard University, 1964), p. 206.

16. "Those most involved in Chicago's cultural institutions" includes along with the ten men who were on the boards of three or more city-wide cultural institutions, the twenty-four who were trustees of two before 1917: Allison Armour, Daniel Burnham, Edward B. Butler, Clyde M. Carr, Frederic A. Delano, Nathaniel K. Fairbank, Marshall Field, John J. Glessner, Charles D. Hamill, William R. Harper, Harlow N. Higinbotham, Huntington W. Jackson, David B. Jones, Edson Keith, Frank O. Lowden, Cyrus H. McCormick, Harold F. McCormick, Franklin MacVeagh, George Manierre, John J. Mitchell, Arthur Orr, Julius Rosenwald, Albert A. Sprague, and Lambert Tree.

17. Chicago Manual Training School, *Tenth Annual Catalogue, 1892–93*, p. 2, Blatchford Papers, Newberry Library; Emmett Dedmon, "A Short History of the Commercial Club," (1968), p. 11, Chicago Historical Society; John J[acob] Glessner, *The Commercial Club of Chicago: Its Beginning and Something of Its Work* (Chicago: privately printed, 1910), p. 133; for meeting to discuss permanent art building, see *Annual Report of the Chicago Art Institute* 13 (1891/92):15.

18. Homer Hoyt, *One Hundred Years of Land Values in Chicago* (Chicago: University of Chicago Press, 1933), pp. 196–97; Crook pointed out the special relation to Chicago of the members of the Directory of the World's Columbian Exposition in "Louis Sullivan," p. 296.

19. Hoyt, *Land Values*, pp. 197–98.

20. For consideration of these developments, see Alfred D. Chandler, "The Beginnings of 'Big Business' in American Industry," *Business History Review* 33 (1959):1–31; see also Edward C. Kirkland, *Industry Comes of Age: Business, Labor, and Public Policy, 1860–1897*, The Economic History of the United States, vol. 6 (New York: Holt, Rinehart and Winston, 1961), pp. 199–215; list of nonresident members, Glessner, *The Commercial Club*, pp. 194–95.

21. Hoyt, *Land Values*, pp. 189–90, 201–2, 214–15; Hoyt gives examples of the precipitous decline in values: the property at 1922 Calumet which had cost $100,000 to build in the nineteenth century, sold in 1908 for $33,500 (ibid., p. 214); Ray Ginger argues that after 1890 Chicago had reached economic maturity, and capital was beginning to flow outward (*Altgeld's America: The Lincoln Ideal versus Changing Realities* [New York: Funk & Wagnalls Co., 1958], pp. 110–11).

22. Pierce, *History of Chicago*, 3:112, fn. 9. The exceptions to this were the occupant of a position on the University of Chicago's board of trustees reserved for a member of the Standard Club and several trustees of the Chicago Symphony Orchestra. Until the day of Julius Rosenwald in the twentieth century, no Jew or person of German descent was active in more than one city-wide cultural institution.

23. Pierce, *History of Chicago*, 3:340–80, passim; Nick Alexander Komons, "Chicago, 1893–1907: The Politics of Reform" (Ph.D. diss., George Washington University, 1961), pp. 35, 42–45. On the surface it would seem that the inability to win local office may have been related to party loyalties: of those most active in culture before 1900 whose political affiliations are known, all but two were Republicans. Unlike many cities, however, Chicago had two active political parties. Democrats predominated as mayors during the period, but Republicans largely controlled the city council. The relation of cultural involvement and the Republican party seems to have been that both commanded the support of those with ties to New England. Lambert Tree and Franklin MacVeagh, the two Democrats were from Washington, D.C., and Pennsylvania, respectively.

24. Komons, "Chicago, 1893–1907," pp. 435–36; Sidney I. Roberts, "The Municipal Voters' League and Chicago's Boodlers," *Journal of the Illinois State Historical Society* 53 (1960):117–25; for municipal reform in general see Samuel P. Hays, "The Politics of Reform in Municipal Government in the Progressive Era," *Pacific Northwest Quarterly* 55 (1964):166–67.

25. Pierce, *History of Chicago*, 3:244–56, 281, fn. 28.

26. Claudius O. Johnson, *Carter Henry Harrison I: Political Leader*, University of Chicago, Local Community Research Committee, Social Science Studies, no. 11 (Chicago: University of Chicago Press, 1928), pp. 188–97.

27. Franklin MacVeagh, "Municipal Government of Chicago," in *Proceedings of the National Conference for Good City Government*, 1894, pp. 85–86; Hays, "Politics of Reform," pp. 177–78.

28. Address by President Franklin MacVeagh, 11 September 1874, in

Addresses and Reports of the Citizens' Association of Chicago, 1874 to 1876 (Chicago: Hazlitt & Reed, 1876), pp. 3–12 (quotation from p. 11); Franklin MacVeagh, "A Programme of Municipal Reform," *American Journal of Sociology* 1 (1895–96):551–63 (quotation from pp. 556–57); Frederic A. Delano, "Authority and Responsibility" (Paper given before the Chicago Literary Club, 31 January 1910), pp. 7–8, Chicago Literary Club Papers, Newberry Library.

29. Charles Norman Fay, "Is Democracy a Failure? Another Plain Tale from Chicago," *Outlook* 97 (1911):777 (original in italics). Because his cultural involvement was limited to the orchestra, Fay is not included in the tabulation of members of the cultural elite.

30. George E. Adams, *Lincoln* (Petersboro, N.H.: Transcript Printing Co., 1908), p. 11, copy in Newberry Library; Harlow N. Higinbotham, "Patriotism," *America* 5 (1891):384.

31. Franklin H. Head, "The President and the Facts," *America* 1 (1888):2 (Head was trustee of only one city-wide cultural institution, the Newberry Library, but as an active member of the Commercial Club and of the Little Room, and as a future guarantor of *Poetry* magazine he can be regarded as a Chicago businessman interested in culture); "Cheers on Young Men," report of a speech by Charles Hutchinson to the Polytechnic Society, 2 December 1905, clipping in scrapbook, 1899–1920, n.p., Hutchinson Papers, Newberry Library; Mary McDowell, "Beginnings" (Address given at the University of Chicago, 10 February 1914, revised 15 December 1927), p. 37, McDowell Papers, Chicago Historical Society; Louise C. Wade, "The Heritage from Chicago's Early Settlement Houses," *Journal of the Illinois State Historical Society* 60 (1967):430; Adolphus C. Bartlett, "A Letter to His Fellow Citizens from an Employer of Labor," (Chicago, 25 September 1903), copy in Presidential Papers, University of Chicago Library.

32. Franklin H. Head, "What Shall We Do with Our Indians," *America* 5 (1891):523, 525; Edward E. Ayer, "The North American Indians and Their Treatment" [1892] (Paper never delivered), Ayer Papers, Newberry Library; George E. Adams, "Color in Certain Poets" (Paper delivered to Chicago Literary Club, 16 January 1905), p. 1, Chicago Literary Club Papers.

33. Emma Burbank Ayer, *A Motor Flight through Algeria and Tunisia* (Chicago: A. C. McClurg & Co., 1911), pp. 104, 107, for example; Francis Cummins Lockwood, *The Life of Edward E. Ayer* (Chicago: A. C. McClurg & Co., 1929); "Hutchinson Is Back to Boom City's Art," clipping (probably from *Chicago* [?] *Post*, 18 April 1898), Scrapbook B, p. 2, Hutchinson Papers, Newberry Library.

Chapter 4

1. Quotation from minutes of meeting, [no date], pp. 18–19, Blatchford Papers, Newberry Library.

2. Quotations from McCagg, ibid., pp. 7, 15, 16.

3. Quotation from Lincoln, ibid., pp. 20–21.

4. *Proceedings of the Trustees of the Newberry Library, July 1, 1887–Jan. 5, 1888*, p. 9.

5. Diary of Hutchinson, 29 March 1890, p. 6, Hutchinson Papers, Newberry Library; Joseph F. Newton, *David Swing: Poet-Preacher* (Chicago: Unity Publishing Co., 1909), pp. 147–51, 219–23; see discussion, chapter 3, on eastern influences.

6. The following discussion is based on the reprint of a lengthy lecture before the Art Institute by Charles L. Hutchinson, "Art: Its Influence and Excellence in Modern Times," *Saturday Evening Herald*, 31 March 1888.

7. Charles L. Hutchinson, report as Sunday school superintendent, 1882, in notebook, p. 34, Hutchinson Papers, Newberry Library.

8. Charles L. Hutchinson, report as Sunday school superintendent, [no date], in notebook, pp. 2, 3–4, Hutchinson Papers, Newberry Library.

9. This quotation and the following discussion return to Hutchinson, "Art."

10. Hutchinson was hardly a consistent psychologist. At one point in the lecture he also asks, "In such a state as this can art be made to play an important part in the cultivation of the affection, the intellect and the will?"

11. Theodore Thomas, "Music in Chicago," *Chicago Tribune*, 23 January 1894, quoted in Theodore Thomas, *Theodore Thomas: A Musical Autobiography*, ed. George P. Upton, 2 vols. (Chicago: A. C. McClurg & Co., 1905), 1:276–77; quotation opposite copyright page, ibid. (original in italics); Thomas, "Music in Chicago," quoted ibid., pp. 278–79.

12. "The Chicago Orchestra," *Dial* 22 (1897):270.

13. Quoted in Rose Fay Thomas, *Memoirs of Theodore Thomas* (New York: Moffat, Yard and Co., 1911), p. 516; Williams to Edward G. Mason, 8 December 1894, quoted in J. Christian Bay, *The John Crerar Library, 1895–1944* (Chicago: Directors of the John Crerar Library, 1945), p. 52.

14. The name was an evocation of the transcendentalist journal of the 1840s by a transplanted New Englander (Lloyd Lewis, "Francis Fisher Browne," *Newberry Library Bulletin* 1, no. 2 [September 1945]:29). The *Dial* published articles by Horatio N. Powers, Arnold's most enthusiastic supporter in the United States (John Henry Raleigh, *Matthew Arnold and American Culture* [Berkeley and Los Angeles: University of California Press, 1957], pp. 67–68); quotations from Ruskin also sprinkle its pages. See also Fredric John Mosher, "Chicago's 'Saving Remnant': Francis Fisher Browne, William Morton Payne, and the *Dial* (1880–1892)" (Ph.D. diss., University of Illinois, 1950); "The Chicago Orchestra," p. 270.

15. "Chicago's Higher Evolution," *Dial* 13 (1892):205–6.

16. William Morton Payne, "Literary Chicago," *New England Magazine* 7 (1893):685; "Chicago's Higher Evolution," p. 206. The *Dial* was critical, however, of the university's organization, believing that its best governors were faculty members, not trustees.

17. Thomas, "Music in Chicago," quoted in Theodore Thomas, *Theodore Thomas*, 1:277; *Annual Report of the Chicago Art Institute* 17 (1895/96):14.

18. *Proceedings of the Trustees of the Newberry Library*, 1914, p. 19; Higinbotham quoted in *A History of the World's Columbian Exposition, Held in Chicago in 1893*, ed. Rossiter Johnson, 4 vols. (New York: D. Appleton and Company, 1897–98), 1:276.

19. Charles L. Hutchinson, "Chicago as an Art Center," *World To-day* 13 (1907):913.

20. Hutchinson, "Art."

21. Charles Moore, *Daniel H. Burnham: Architect, Planner of Cities*, 2 vols. (Boston: Houghton Mifflin Co., 1921), 1:53–68; Charles Moore, *The Life and Times of Charles Follen McKim* (Boston: Houghton Mifflin Co., 1929), pp. 308–9; St. Gaudens quotation from "Design," report of the department of construction, World's Columbian Exposition, [p. 36], typescript copy, James W. Ellsworth Papers, Chicago Public Library.

22. "Organization," report of the department of construction, World's Columbian Exposition, typescript copy, James W. Ellsworth Papers; Burnham quoted in Moore, *Daniel H. Burnham*, 1:72.

23. Charles L. Hutchinson, "The Democracy of Art," *American Magazine of Art* 7 (1916):398, 399, 400, 399; "Energy and Art," *Dial* 24 (1898):37.

24. Hutchinson, "Democracy of Art," pp. 400, 399.

25. Burnham to Thomas, [1893] and 26 October 1901, Thomas Papers, Newberry Library.

26. Martin A. Ryerson, speech delivered 2 July 1894, quoted in Thomas Wakefield Goodspeed, *A History of the University of Chicago: The First Quarter-Century* (Chicago: University of Chicago Press, 1916), p. 238; Oliver C. Farrington, "Frederick J. V. Skiff," *Museum Work* 3 (1920–21):197–98.

27. Howard Mumford Jones, "The Renaissance and American Origins," *Ideas in America* (Cambridge, Mass.: Harvard University Press, 1944), pp. 143–51, deals with this question, making specific reference to Chicago's cultural philanthropists.

28. George E. Adams, address at dedication of Orchestra Hall, 14 December 1904, quoted in Theodore Thomas, *Theodore Thomas*, 1:289. Perhaps with hope of broadening support, Adams saw the association as one "in which rich and poor, learned and unlearned men and women, merchants and bankers, professional men and workingmen, join hands to serve the higher life of the community in which they live" (ibid.).

29. This is explicitly stated by Alfred Theodore Andreas in his discussion of the Art Institute, *History of Chicago: From the Earliest Period to the Present Time*, 3 vols. (Chicago: A. T. Andreas Co., 1884–86), 3:419.

30. Hutchinson, "Art"; *Annual Report of the Chicago Art Institute* 20 (1898/99):38.

Chapter 5

1. Minutes of the Art Committee, 17 June 1902–22 January 1912; French to Hutchinson, 27 February 1909, copy in letterpress book, 14 December 1908–24 April 1909; French to Hutchinson, 3 October 1900, copy in letterpress book, 27 December 1899–26 October 1900; French to Carpenter, 8 September 1909, copy in letterpress book, May–September 1909; Hutchinson to Charles B. Foote, 28 April 1914, letter scrapbook; C. H. Burkholder to French, 9 May 1912, copy in letterpress book, 19 April–26 September 1912, Art Institute of Chicago.

2. An expense as small as $3.25 had to be approved by the trustees of the Field (Minutes, 11 May 1908, p. 246); see also correspondence in Higinbotham file, letterbook, Field Museum of Natural History, regarding an expedition to the Saint Francis River in Arkansas: Higinbotham questioned, 14 October 1897, "What fishes can be obtained in that river that are different from those in the other tributaries of the Mississippi"; the 1895–96 annual report of the Field Columbian Museum summarized: "President Ayer passed the winter in Egypt adding much valuable material to the archeologic collections from that country. . . . Vice-President Ryerson and Mr. C. L. Hutchinson, on their trip around the world, procured and presented to the Museum a large and unique amount of material. . . . Mr. Owen F. Aldis invited O. P. Hay, Assistant Curator of Ichthyology to accompany him on an excursion to the waters of Southern Florida" *(Publications of the Field Museum of Natural History,* Report Series 1 [1895/96]:103); for efforts to limit Ayer, see, for example, Minutes, 26 February 1908, p. 235, Field Museum of Natural History.

3. Ayer to trustees, 20 December 1910, Trustees' Letters and Papers, Newberry Library; see chapter 7.

4. Rose Fay Thomas, *Memoirs of Theodore Thomas* (New York: Moffat, Yard and Co., 1911), p. 356; the nature of the Orchestral Association's authority is inferred from Philo Adams Otis, *The Chicago Symphony Orchestra: Its Organization, Growth, and Development, 1891–1924* (Chicago: Clayton F. Summy Co., 1924), pp. 69, 319, and also from a letter by the president of the Orchestral Association, Bryan Lathrop, regarding the need for "a man of energy and of business experience" on the executive committee. It would also seem that the committee made the routine ongoing decisions at their weekly meetings (Lathrop to Frank O. Lowden, 29 November 1911, Lowden Papers, University of Chicago Library).

5. Thomas issued an ultimatum to the Orchestral Association: either the orchestra would be provided with a permanent home and an endowment to meet deficits or he would resign (Charles Edward Russell, *The American Orchestra and Theodore Thomas* [Garden City, N.Y.: Doubleday, Page & Co., 1927], p. 293); a sense of the personal relationships between administrators and trustees can be gleaned from institutional correspondence, as, for example, French's newsy letters to Hutchinson

(20 March 1909, copy in letterpress book, 14 December 1908–24 April 1909, Art Institute of Chicago) and from comments by trustees to administrators, as, for example, Higinbotham to Skiff, 31 July 1905, Higinbotham file, letterbook, Field Museum of Natural History. Thomas was in a special position, having married Charles Norman Fay's sister.

6. Goodspeed to Harper, 14 April 1891, 1 November 1890, copy in Rockefeller Papers, University of Chicago Library; H. E. Hinckley to Ryerson, 15 September 1893, Secretary of the Board of Trustees Papers, University of Chicago Library; Harry Pratt Judson to Hutchinson, 10 October 1892, Hutchinson Papers, Newberry Library.

7. *The President's Report* [1892–1902], University of Chicago, Decennial Publications, 1st ser. (Chicago: University of Chicago Press, 1903), 1:xiv–xv; Hutchinson negotiated successfully with J. Laurence Laughlin and George E. Hale (Hutchinson to Harper, 3 January 1892, Presidential Papers, University of Chicago Library).

8. Diary of Hutchinson, 9 April 1890, typescript copy, p. 11, Hutchinson Papers, Newberry Library; see, for example, French to Hutchinson, 26 April 1902, copy in letterpress book, 3 January–25 October 1902, p. 407, Art Institute of Chicago.

9. See chapter 1; also René Brimo, *L'Évolution du Goût aux États-Unis d'après l'histoire des collections* (Paris: James Fortune, 1938); Daniel M. Fox, *Engines of Culture: Philanthropy and Art Museums* (Madison: State Historical Society of Wisconsin, 1963); James Steel Smith, "The Beauty of Collected Things," *Antioch Review* 26 (1966–67):528–51; Robert G. Smith, "The Museum of Art in the United States," *Art Quarterly* 21 (1958):297–316.

10. "The Endowments of Culture in Chicago," *Dial* 15 (1893):286.

11. Will of John Crerar, quoted in the biographical sketch by Thomas Wakefield Goodspeed, "The Founder: John Crerar," in J. Christian Bay, *The John Crerar Library, 1895–1944* (Chicago: Directors of the John Crerar Library, 1945), p. 24.

12. Ibid., pp. 18–20.

13. Ibid., pp. 26–34; William Landram Williamson, *William Frederick Poole and the Modern Library Movement* (New York: Columbia University Press, 1963), pp. 138–50.

14. [Harlow N. Higinbotham], *Report of the President to the Board of Directors of the World's Columbian Exposition* (Chicago: Rand McNally & Co., 1898), pp. 85–86.

15. Robert Knutson, "The White City: The World's Columbian Exposition of 1893" (Ph.D. diss., Columbia University, 1956), pp. 151–76, 197–202.

16. *Publications of the Field Museum of Natural History*, Report Series 1 (1899/1900):433.

17. While certain aspects of the University of Chicago can be considered as a part of cultural uplift, one counterpart to the collection of the museum—its curriculum—does not reflect this attempt to represent the

ideal. Only when one looks at the debate over the requirements for the A.B. degree does one find, among advocates of the classical course, a comparable concern with structuring the students' experience (Richard J. Storr, *Harper's University: The Beginnings: A History of the University of Chicago* [Chicago: University of Chicago Press, 1966], pp. 311–20); the clearer substitute for the "collection" is scientific research: among the University of Chicago's trustees, the commitment to scientific research was understood in idealistic terms.

18. See, for example, the list of acquisitions, *Annual Report of the Chicago Art Institute* 21 (1899/1900):47–48, and the discussion of the purchase of sculptural casts, ibid., p. 53. It is interesting in this regard that though Hutchinson personally preferred the works of those such as the Pre-Raphaelites, his own collection, frequently on loan to the Art Institute, included a wide range of examples from the history of art.

19. *An Historical and Descriptive Account of the Field Columbian Museum*, publication 1, vol. 1, no. 1 (Chicago: Field Columbian Museum, 1894):14; George A. Dorsey, "The Department of Anthropology, of the Field Museum—A Review of Six Years," *American Anthropologist*, n.s. 2 (1900):265; Rose Fay Thomas, *Theodore Thomas*, p. 390.

20. *Annual Report of the Chicago Art Institute* 9 (1887/88):12; Chicago, Art Institute, *Catalogue of Objects in the Museum, Sculpture and Painting*, 3d ed. (Chicago: printed for the Art Institute, 1898). I have profited from the suggestive discussion of Brimo, *L'Évolution du Goût aux États-Unis*, pp. 171–75.

21. "The Field Columbian Museum," *Scientific American*, Supplement 51 (1901):21,168; *Historical and Descriptive Account of the Field Columbian Museum*, p. 14.

22. W[illiam] S[mythe] B[abcock] Mathews, "Music in the Columbian Fair," *Music* 1 (1891):42–43; Rose Fay Thomas, *Theodore Thomas*, p. 375; Russell, *American Orchestra and Theodore Thomas*, p. 286.

23. American museums are characterized as "encyclopedic" in Smith, "The Museum of Art," p. 313.

24. Bay, *John Crerar Library*, pp. 29–34; *The John Crerar Library* (Chicago: n.p., 1897), n.p.; "Chicago, Ill.: John Crerar L.," *Library Journal* 21 (1896):334–35.

25. For example, in 1900 the Art Institute transferred its metal collection to the Field, while the Field sent its Egyptian and Assyrian casts to the Art Institute (*Annual Report of the Chicago Art Institute* 21 [1899/1900]:26–27). Given that the two institutions shared many members of their boards of trustees, it is noteworthy that the arrangements made by the two were formal: the collections were exchanged on a purchase basis (Higinbotham to Skiff, 4 January 1900, historical file, Field Museum of Natural History).

26. W. M. R. French to Harper, 30 April 1895, and H. N. Higinbotham to Harper, 20 May 1902, Harper Papers, University of Chicago Library; Theodore Thomas to Harper, 26 February 1901, Presidential Papers, University of Chicago Library.

27. For Hutchinson, see Ernest Poole, *Giants Gone: Men Who Made Chicago* (New York: McGraw-Hill Book Co., 1943), p. 272.

28. *Annual Report of the Chicago Art Institute* 15 (1893/94):35; *Publications of the Field Museum of Natural History*, Report Series 1 (1897/98):263; ibid., 2 (1901/2):91–92.

29. [Higinbotham], *Report of the President*, pp. 158–59; *A History of the World's Columbian Exposition, Held in Chicago in 1893*, ed. Rossiter Johnson, 4 vols. (New York: D. Appleton and Co., 1897–98), 1:477–79, quoted from p. 477; "A Midway Review," *Dial* 15 (1893):106.

30. The Art Institute lectures were generally held on weekday afternoons, the most important of which was the Tuesday afternoon Lecture Course. These educational opportunities would not, of course, have been available to those required to work during the week *(Annual Report of the Chicago Art Institute* 21 [1899/1900]:32–35; 27 [1907/8]:43–47; 37 [1915]:62–65; *Publications of the Field Museum* 2 [1903/4]:253).

31. Thomas Wakefield Goodspeed, *A History of the University of Chicago: The First Quarter-Century* (Chicago: University of Chicago Press, 1916), p. 319; *Programs of the Chicago Symphony Orchestra* 1–26 (1891/92–1916/17).

32. Charles Fabens Kelly, "Chicago: Record Years," *Art News* 51, no. 4 (1952):106; *Annual Report of the Chicago Art Institute* 21 (1899/1900): 36; *Publications of the Field Museum* 1 (1897/98):293.

33. *The Newberry Library: Trustees, Officers, and Committees; By-Laws* (n.p., 1894), p. 18.

34. W[illiam] S[mythe] B[abcock] Mathews, "The Chicago Orchestra Commercially Considered," *Music* 1 (1892):576, 579.

35. John H. Mueller, *The American Symphony Orchestra: A Social History of Musical Taste* (Bloomington: Indiana University Press, 1951), pp. 104–5; Theodore Thomas, *Theodore Thomas: A Musical Autobiography*, ed. George P. Upton, 2 vols. (Chicago: A. C. McClurg & Co., 1905), 1:107.

36. Box office statements, beginning 14 December 1904, Orchestra Hall, Chicago, Ill.; many members of the Orchestral Association favored Sunday performances. As Fay wrote to Hutchinson, "A large majority favored them, as you did. . . . A Sunday performance means to us an opportunity to reach, with a programme of a popular and attractive, but not trivial or worthless character, at low prices, a large class of people for whom our educational programmes are perhaps too advanced" (Fay to Hutchinson, 1 February 1894, Hutchinson Papers, Newberry Library). Sunday performances were successfully opposed by several of the original guarantors, perhaps on religious grounds.

37. Fay to W. R. Michaelis, 11 January 1905, copy sent to trustees of the Orchestral Association, Harper Papers; Ellis A. Johnson, "The Chicago Symphony Orchestra, 1891–1942: A Study in American Cultural History" (Ph.D. diss., University of Chicago, 1955), p. 259.

38. [Higinbotham], *Report of the President*, pp. 242–43. His action was short-lived: the fair was reopened on Sunday by the courts (ibid.).

39. David Heathcote Crook, "Louis Sullivan, the World's Columbian Exposition, and American Life" (Ph.D. diss., Harvard University, 1964), pp. 180–97.

40. *Annual Report of the Chicago Art Institute* 25 (1903/4):61; Crook, "Louis Sullivan," p. 421; W. A. Otis, "Library Buildings from the Viewpoint of the Architect," *Public Libraries* 8 (1903):202.

41. Goodspeed, *History of the University of Chicago*, p. 233.

42. Mary Catherine Laux, diary entry, 29 January 1883, quoted in Allan McNab, "The School of the Art Institute—A Brief History," *Art Institute of Chicago Quarterly* 55 (1961):26; Lee de Forest, *Father of Radio: The Autobiography of Lee de Forest* (Chicago: Wilcox & Follett, 1950), p. 105.

43. *Annual Report of the Chicago Public Library* 10 (1882):24.

44. *Annual Report of the Chicago Art Institute* 32 (1910/11):14.

45. [Higinbotham], *Report of the President*, p. 294.

46. "Literary Tributes to the World's Fair," *Dial* 15 (1893):177–78.

47. *History of the World's Columbian Exposition*, 1:33–34; Crook, "Louis Sullivan," p. 239.

48. *Annual Report of the Chicago Art Institute* 9 (1887/88):8. Perhaps the clearest example is the Crerar. Though intended by its donor to serve the South Side, the Crerar was, in fact, located downtown. Its trustees regarded a central location as crucial to its usefulness (Bay, *John Crerar Library*, p. 191).

49. Goodspeed to Harper, 14 April 1891, quoted in Goodspeed, *History of the University of Chicago*, p. 219; Orchestral Association circular, 1904, quoted in Rose Fay Thomas, *Theodore Thomas*, p. 517.

50. *Annual Report of the Chicago Art Institute* 14 (1892/93):30–35; ibid., 22 (1900/1901):16–17.

51. Ibid., 23 (1901/2): 19; *Publications of the Field Museum* 3 (1907): 129.

52. Goodspeed, *History of the University of Chicago*, pp. 233–34 (the building in this instance was Kent Chemical Hall); Storr, *Harper's University*, pp. 71, 66–67; when traveling, Hutchinson and Ryerson constantly sent back reminders to Harper of the necessity to hold down expenses. As Hutchinson jokingly wrote to Harper in 1896, "Go slow. . . . Is it not a relief to have the two bugbears of the Board of Trustees away? No one at home to oppose you" (26 January 1896, Presidential Papers, University of Chicago Library).

53. Knutson, "The White City," pp. 14–15, 35–41; *Annual Report of the Chicago Art Institute* 21 (1899/1900):21. This speculative drive was not true of the Crerar which lived on its income (Bay, *John Crerar Library*, p. 51).

54. *Annual Report of the Chicago Art Institute* 21 (1899/1900):56.

55. *Annual Report of the Chicago Public Library* 1 (1873):5; ibid., 5 (1878): 7–9; ibid., 3 (1875):23.

56. Ibid., 18 (1890):8.

57. Charles S. Thornton, dedicatory address, quoted ibid., 26 (1898): 31; ibid., 3 (1875):26.

58. Ibid., 2 (1874):16; "Library Economy and History: Chicago (Ill.) P.L.," *Library Journal* 22 (1897):361.

59. *Annual Report of the Chicago Public Library* 26 (1898):75; Chicago Library Club, *Libraries of the City of Chicago* (Chicago: Library Club, 1905), pp. 69–70, 77–78.

60. Ibid., p. 67; Forrest Crissey, "Chicago's New Public Library Building," *Outlook* 57 (1897):278–87.

61. *Annual Report of the Chicago Public Library* 31 (1903):9; Chicago Library Club, *Libraries of the City*, p. 77.

Chapter 6

1. Diary of Hutchinson, 10 April 1901, typescript copy, p. 52, Hutchinson Papers, Newberry Library; Thomas Wakefield Goodspeed, "Charles Lawrence Hutchinson," *University Record* 11 (1925):61; *Hull House Bulletin* 3, no. 6 (October 1898) copy in Chicago Historical Society; Robert McCaul, "Dewey's Chicago," *The School Review* 67 (1959): 276–77; Bernard R. Bowron, "Henry Blake Fuller: A Critical Study," (Ph.D. diss., Harvard University, 1948), pp. 413–14, 422–23; Allen F. Davis and Mary Lynn McCree, eds., *Eighty Years at Hull-House* (Chicago: Quadrangle Books, 1969), p. 109. Hutchinson was also an important contributor and active member of the board of directors of the University of Chicago Settlement (material re: settlement, McDowell Papers, Chicago Historical Society).

2. Christopher Lasch's discussions of Jane Addams have shaped my thinking about her, especially his introduction to her life and thought and his selection of her writings in *The Social Thought of Jane Addams* (Indianapolis, Ind.: Bobbs-Merrill Co., 1965). See also his *The New Radicalism in America, 1889–1963: The Intellectual as a Social Type* (New York: Alfred A. Knopf, 1965), pp. 3–37. There is now a fine intellectual biography of Jane Addams: John C. Farrell, *Beloved Lady: A History of Jane Addams' Ideas on Reform and Peace* (Baltimore, Md.: Johns Hopkins Press, 1967). Material on Miss Addams's life is based on these sources, unless otherwise noted. The recent study by Daniel Levine, *Jane Addams and the Liberal Tradition* (Madison: State Historical Society of Wisconsin, 1971), focuses on Miss Addams's political and social thought. It does include a discussion of her views on children and education, pp. 89–110. Unfortunately Allen F. Davis, *American Heroine: The Life and Legend of Jane Addams* (New York: Oxford University Press, 1973) was received too late to shape my thinking.

3. Addams to Ellen Gates Starr, 7 February 1886, in Lasch, ed., *Social Thought of Jane Addams*, p. 5; Farrell, *Beloved Lady*, pp. 44–52; Jane Addams, *Twenty Years at Hull-House* (New York: Macmillan Co., 1911), pp. 81–88.

4. Addams, *Twenty Years*, p. 101; Davis and McCree, *Eighty Years*, a splendid collection of documents relating to Hull-House, with useful notes, has an informative discussion "Beginnings," pp. 15–23, on the early years;

Jane Addams, "The Art-Work Done by Hull-House, Chicago," *Forum* 19 (1895):614–15; Jane Addams, "The Subjective Necessity for Social Settlements," in *Philanthropy and Social Progress* (New York: T. Y. Crowell & Co., 1893), p. 7.

5. Addams, "Subjective Necessity for Social Settlements," p. 4.

6. See photographs in *Hull House Maps and Papers* (New York: T. Y. Crowell & Co., 1895).

7. Jane Addams, "The Objective Value of a Social Settlement," in *Philanthropy and Social Progress*, pp. 45–46.

8. *Hull-House Yearbook*, 1 May 1910, copy in Chicago Historical Society; Allen F. Davis, *Spearheads for Reform: The Social Settlements and the Progressive Movement, 1890–1914* (New York: Oxford University Press, 1967) is a valuable discussion of the settlement house movement (specific reference is on p. 76); Graham Taylor, "Survival and Revival of Neighborship," *Survey* 28 (1912):226–31. The Chicago Commons was an important Chicago settlement house.

9. "Hull House: A Social Settlement," in *Hull House Maps and Papers*, pp. 207–30 (quotation, p. 225); Davis, *Spearheads for Reform*, pp. 40–59; Addams, "Art-Work Done by Hull-House," pp. 614–17; Davis and McCree, *Eighty Years*, p. 22.

10. Addams, "Objective Value of a Social Settlement," p. 33.

11. Addams, "Subjective Necessity for Social Settlements," p. 21. Farrell in *Beloved Lady* (pp. 80–108) considers Jane Addams's changing conceptions of culture in the light of the intellectual influences impinging upon her, as well as of her experiences at Hull-House.

12. Addams, "Objective Value of a Social Settlement," p. 35; Addams, *Twenty Years*, pp. 234–46; Addams, "Art-Work Done by Hull-House," p. 615.

13. Jane Addams, "A Function of the Social Settlement," *Annals of the American Academy of Political and Social Science* 13 (1899):326–27.

14. Ibid., 335–37; W[illiam] S[mythe] B[abcock] Mathews, "Editorial Bric-a-Brac," *Music* 17 (1899):179–82.

15. Addams, "Function of the Social Settlement," p. 332; Ellen Gates Starr, "Art and Labor," in *Hull House Maps and Papers*, pp. 165–78 (quotation from p. 178).

16. Starr, "Art and Labor," pp. 178–79.

17. Davis and McCree, *Eighty Years*, p. 83.

18. "First Report of a Labor Museum at Hull House," pamphlet, Chicago Historical Society; Addams, *Twenty Years*, pp. 235–46 (quotation from p. 242); Jane Addams, *Democracy and Social Ethics* (New York: Macmillan Co., 1902), pp. 209–14 (quotation from p. 190); *Hull House Yearbook*, 1 May 1910, pp. 50–51, copy in Chicago Historical Society.

19. For one exposition of his views, see John Dewey, *Democracy and Education* (New York: Macmillan Co., 1916); Davis, *Spearheads for Reform*, p. 58.

20. John Dewey, *Lectures in the Philosophy of Education, 1899*, ed. Reginald D. Archambault (New York: Random House, 1966), pp. 299–

300; Dewey, *Democracy and Education*, p. 88; John Dewey, "Culture and Industry in Education," 1906, reprinted in *Teachers College Bulletin*, ser. 10, no. 10 (1 March 1919), p. 18; Dewey, *Democracy and Education*, p. 279.

21. John Dewey, *The School and Society* (Chicago: University of Chicago Press, 1899), p. 102.

22. Addams, "Objective Value of a Social Settlement," p. 35; Jane Addams, *The Spirit of Youth and the City Streets* (New York: Macmillan Co., 1909) (quotation from p. 20).

23. Jane Addams, *Spirit of Youth*, pp. 20, 90, 96–101, 103. Farrell, in *Beloved Lady* (pp. 104–19), first led me to Jane Addams's reappreciation of culture.

24. Elizabeth Halsey, *The Development of Public Recreation in Metropolitan Chicago* ([Chicago]: Chicago Recreation Commission, 1940), p. 17; Davis, *Spearheads for Reform*, pp. 61–65.

25. John Dewey, "An Undemocratic Proposal," *Vocational Education* 2 (May 1913):374–77 (quotations from pp. 376, 375).

26. Davis and McCree, *Eighty Years*, pp. 107–8.

27. Allen Davis emphasizes this shift, although he attributes it to a realization on the reformers' part that their educational program was impractical (*Spearheads for Reform*, pp. 49–58); Addams, *Democracy and Social Ethics*, pp. 153, 154, 163–64.

28. Jane Addams, "Opening of the Exhibit," in her *The Child in the City* (Chicago: Blakely Printing Co., 1911), pp. 4–5.

29. Addams, *Democracy and Social Ethics*, pp. 165, 222–23.

30. Louise C. Wade, "The Heritage from Chicago's Early Settlement Houses," *Journal of the Illinois State Historical Society* 60 (1967):430; Hutchinson to Addams, 5 August 1912, and Frances Hutchinson to Addams, 2 December 1910, Addams Papers, Swarthmore Peace Collection, Swarthmore, Pa.

Chapter 7

1. See, for example, the letters of Norman Williams and Edward G. Mason to Huntington W. Jackson, March 1895, about a prospective candidate, printed in "Appointment of the First Librarian," *Crerar Current* 2, nos. 1–9 (1955):11–12.

2. William Landram Williamson, *William Frederick Poole and the Modern Library Movement* (New York: Columbia University Press, 1963), pp. 39–40, 61–62, 84–86, 113.

3. Robert H. Wiebe, *The Search for Order, 1877–1920* (New York: Hill and Wang, 1967), considers professionalization at the turn of the century. He links the drive toward professionalization to the movements of reform in the Progressive period in a way that has influenced my own thinking.

4. William Warner Bishop, "Some Chicago Librarians of the Nineties: Fragments of Autobiography," *Library Quarterly* 14 (1944):343–44;

Winsor to Poole, 8 April 1892, and Dewey to Poole, 5 May 1892, Poole Papers, Newberry Library; Mrs. H. L. Elmendorf, "The Public Library, 'A Leaven'd and Prepared Choice,'" *Library Journal* 37 (1912):419–22.

5. For a trustee's definition, see, for example, the address by Frank S. Johnson, trustee of the Crerar Library, reported in "Library Meetings: Chicago," *Public Libraries* 10 (1905):88; G. E. Wire, "Chicago Library Club," *Library Journal* 17 (1892):28–29. The speaker was evidently referring to the statement, infamous among librarians, by William W. Greenough, once president of the trustees of the Boston Public Library, about planning the new library building: "We have consulted no librarians, not even our own. Librarians are not practical men and have bees in their bonnets" (quoted in Houghton Wetherold, "The Architectural History of the Newberry Library," *Newberry Library Bulletin* 6 [1962]:17).

6. Minutes of meeting, 11 December 1891, Chicago Library Club, Minutes December 1891 to March 1905, p. 10, Chicago Historical Society.

7. For example, the president of the board of trustees wrote to Skiff before the director went abroad, "I cannot say that I enjoy the thout [*sic*] as it means another pretty long straight line for me." Higinbotham was reminded of his child who once said about his mother's being away, "It was so hard to be good all the time" (Higinbotham to Skiff, 31 July 1905, Higinbotham file, Field Museum of Natural History). In contrast, Charles F. Millspaugh, curator of botany, wrote formally, as on 29 July 1907, when he requested a vacation extension and signed the letter "Respectfully yours" (Millspaugh Correspondence, Field Museum of Natural History). For letter informing Skiff, see D. C. Davies to Skiff, 29 August 1906, copy in Skiff General Correspondence, 1893–1907, Field Museum of Natural History.

8. A. R. Crook, "The Training of Museum Curators," *Proceedings of the American Association of Museums* 4 (1910):59–63; "Democracy and Education," *Dial* 14 (1893):352; "The Crerar Library," *Dial* 17 (1894): 324–25.

9. *Annual Reports of the John Crerar Library* 4 (1898):12; Charles F. Millspaugh, "Botanical Installation," *Proceedings of the American Association of Museums* 4 (1910):52–56.

10. William Frederick Poole, *The Construction of Library Buildings*, U.S. Bureau of Education, Circulars of Information, no. 1 (Washington, D.C.: Government Printing Office, 1881), pp. 8–15 (quotations from pp. 8, 14, 15).

11. Lloyd to Poole, 21 September 1890, Poole Papers; Wetherold, "Architectural History of the Newberry Library," pp. 3–23 (quotation from p. 17). In fact, the design of the exterior of the library was a modified Romanesque of great simplicity.

12. *Publications of the Field Museum of Natural History*, Report Series 2 (1901/2), p. 85.

13. Clement Walker Andrews, "The Economics of Library Architecture," *Public Libraries* 21 (1916):112.

14. *Proceedings of the Trustees of the Newberry Library*, 1911, p. 16; Clement Walker Andrews, "The Use of Books," *Library Journal* 32 (1907):249–52 (quotation from p. 251); Clement Walker Andrews, "The Field of Co-Operation between Libraries of Learning," *Library Journal* 41 (1916):319.

15. *Annual Report of the Chicago Art Institute* 32 (1910/11):31; Thomas to Fay, copy of portion of letter, 14 . . . [illegible word] 1900, Thomas Papers, Newberry Library.

16. Williamson, *William Frederick Poole*, p. 144; Rose Fay Thomas, *Memoirs of Theodore Thomas* (New York: Moffat, Yard and Co., 1911), p. 392.

17. Burnham quoted in Charles Moore, *Daniel H. Burnham: Architect, Planner of Cities*, 2 vols. (Boston: Houghton Mifflin Co., 1921), 1:43; Higinbotham quoted in [Harlow N. Higinbotham], *Report of the President to the Board of Directors of the World's Columbian Exposition* (Chicago: Rand McNally & Co., 1898), p. 33. Harper and Burnham played many roles in Chicago's cultural life; thus they were professionals in one capacity and members of the cultural elite in another. In addition, Burnham, as an architect, may be considered a member of Chicago's artist community.

18. George A. Dorsey, "The Aim of a Public Museum," *Proceedings of the American Association of Museums* 1 (1907):98–100 (quotation from p. 100).

19. See, for example, N. H. Carpenter's comments, *Chicago Daily Tribune*, 4 June 1914, in scrapbook, Newspaper Tributes to the Memory of William M. R. French, Ryerson Library, Art Institute of Chicago; French to Hutchinson, 5 March 1904, copy in letterpress book, 6 July 1903–7 March 1904, and 6 January 1905, copy in letterpress book, 5 November 1904–22 March 1905, Art Institute of Chicago.

20. Flyers, beginning 1892, Newberry Library Centre for University Extension, Blatchford Papers, Newberry Library.

21. William Rainey Harper, *The Trend in Higher Education* (Chicago: University of Chicago Press, 1905); Richard J. Storr, *Harper's University: The Beginnings: A History of the University of Chicago* (Chicago: University of Chicago Press, 1966), pp. 61, 196–206. The following discussion is based on the material Storr selected, pp. 196–97.

22. *Annual Register of the University of Chicago* 1, no. 1 (Chicago, 1897):80; "The President's Statement on the Condition of the University," *University Record* 1 (1886–97):6; "University Extension: Class-study Day," *University Record* 1 (1896–97):395.

23. Chapter 5; Harper to Gates, 21 December 1891, Gates Papers, University of Chicago Library. Harper was a trustee of the Orchestral Association from 1903 until his death in 1906.

24. Hutchinson to Harper, 26 January 1896, Presidential Papers; Ryerson to Harper, 13 February 1896, Presidential Papers; Hutchinson to Goodspeed, 20 April 1898, Goodspeed Papers; Jenkin Lloyd Jones to Hutchinson, 25 June 1902, Secretary of the Board of Trustees Papers; Harper to Hutchinson, 19 February 1894, Presidential Papers, University of Chicago Library.

25. Wiebe, *Search for Order*, pp. 111–32.

26. [Editorial], *Public Libraries* 1 (1896):16.

27. Chicago Library Club, *Libraries of the City of Chicago* (Chicago: Library Club, 1905), p. 84; "Library Meetings: Chicago," *Public Libraries*, a regular monthly feature, conveys the broad concerns of the Chicago Library Club; see 7 (1902):205 and 8 (1903):29 for specific reference.

28. "Library Meetings: Chicago," *Public Libraries* 11 (1906):214.

29. Kenneth S. Lynn, *The Dream of Success: A Study of the Modern American Imagination* (Boston: Little, Brown and Co., 1955), pp. 220–23, relates Veblen's glorification of the engineer as professional to Robert Herrick.

30. Thorstein Veblen, *The Theory of the Leisure Class: An Economic Study in the Evolution of Institutions* (New York: Macmillan Co., 1899), pp. 44–45, 15.

31. Ibid., pp. 49, 48, 340–41.

32. Ibid., pp. 150–52, 159–62, 128–30, 133–39.

33. Ibid., pp. 391–94.

34. See Morton White, *Social Thought in America: The Revolt against Formalism* (New York: Viking Press, 1949).

35. Henry Eduard Legler, "The World of Print, and the World's Work," *Library Journal* 38 (1913): 442, 439. On Legler, see Pearl I. Field and Althea Warren, "Henry Eduard Legler, 1861–1917," in *Pioneering Leaders in Librarianship*, ed. Emily Miller Danton (Chicago: American Library Association, 1953), pp. 120–29.

Chapter 8

1. Walter Dwight Moody, *What of the City?* (Chicago: A. C. McClurg & Co., 1919), p. 184.

2. Diary of Hutchinson, 20 January–8 April 1906, typescript copy, pp. 89–92, Hutchinson Papers, Newberry Library; Charles Moore, *Daniel H. Burnham: Architect, Planner of Cities*, 2 vols. (Boston: Houghton Mifflin Co., 1921), 1:236–37.

3. Kenyon Cox, "Art: An Example from Chicago," *Nation* 92 (1911): 455.

4. Ada Bartlett Taft, *Lorado Taft: Sculptor and Citizen* (Greensboro, N.C.: [Mary T. Smith], 1946), pp. 28–33, 42–52.

5. Herbert S. Stone to Harriet Monroe, 2 January 1895, Monroe Papers (personal), University of Chicago Library; Hamlin Garland to Robert Herrick, [1897?], Herrick Papers, University of Chicago Library; Little Room membership list, 1903, Little Room Papers, Newberry Library; Bernard Duffey, *The Chicago Renaissance in American Letters: A Critical History* ([East Lansing]: Michigan State College Press, 1954), pp. 51–57. Duffey provides a good introduction to the artistic milieu of this group.

6. Harriet Monroe to sister [Lucy], 15 January 1899, Monroe Papers (personal).

7. Copy of letter, unsigned, from executive committee, Hamlin Garland chairman, n.d., Little Room Papers; Frances Hooper, "Giving the O.O. to Our Very Esteemed Highbrows, the Cliff Dwellers; They Starve Not, Neither Do They Sin," *Chicago Sunday Herald*, 10 September 1916.

8. Charles Francis Browne, "Lorado Taft: Sculptor," *The World To-Day* 14 (1908):191, 192.

9. Taft, *Lorado Taft*, p. 20; Bernard R. Bowron, "Henry Blake Fuller: A Critical Study" (Ph.D. diss., Harvard University, 1948), p. 361; Henry Blake Fuller, *With the Procession* (New York: Harper & Brothers Publishers, 1895), pp. 86–87; Hamlin Garland, *Roadside Meetings* (New York: Macmillan Co., 1930), p. 262.

10. Taft, *Lorado Taft*, pp. 27, 79–80.

11. Hamlin Garland, "Work of an Art-Association in Western Towns," *Forum* 19 (1895):606–9; see cover for motto, *The Arts* (initial name of *Arts for America*) 4, no. 3 (September 1895), counselors and patrons are found on the inside of the front cover.

12. [Finley Peter Dunne], "The Carnegie Libraries," in his *Dissertations by Mr. Dooley* (New York: Harper & Brothers Publishers, 1906), p. 181; "How to Make Chicago an Art Center," *Arts for America* 7 (1897): 107.

13. Ralph Clarkson, "The Art Situation in Chicago," *Arts for America* 7 (1898): 272, 270, 271; see also article by C. F. B. (probably Charles Francis Browne), "Chicago, 1897," *Arts for America* 7 (1898):300–302.

14. This consideration of Fuller's life draws heavily on Bowron, "Henry Blake Fuller."

15. Henry Blake Fuller, "The Upward Movement in Chicago," *Atlantic Monthly* 80 (1897):534–47; see, for example, Fuller to I. K. Pond, 15 April 1897, Fuller Papers, Newberry Library; diary of Hutchinson, 6 September 1900, p. 37; 10 April 1901, p. 52, typescript copy, Hutchinson Papers, Newberry Library.

16. Henry Blake Fuller, "Howells or James," 1885, Fuller Papers.

17. Duffey, *Chicago Renaissance*, pp. 37–38; [Henry Blake Fuller], *The Chevalier of Pensieri-Vani* (Boston: J. G. Cupples Co., 1890), p. 1. Fuller used the pseudonym Stanton Page.

18. [Fuller], *Chevalier of Pensieri-Vani*, pp. 160, 161.

19. Henry Blake Fuller, *The Cliff-Dwellers* (New York: Harper & Brothers, 1893), pp. 134, 238, 240, 241, 243.

20. Fuller, *With the Procession*, p. 25.

21. Hamlin Garland catches both sides of Fuller in his *Companions on the Trail: A Literary Chronicle* (New York: Macmillan Co., 1931), pp. 368–69; Fuller, *With the Procession*, p. 87; Fuller to A. B. Pond, 24 August 1908, Fuller Papers.

22. Henry Blake Fuller, "The Downfall of Abner Joyce," in his *Under the Skylights* (New York: D. Appleton and Co., 1901), pp. 5, 36, 41.

23. Program for "The First Twelfth Night Frolic of the Little Room in the Twentieth Century," Little Room Papers; for Herrick's life and

his relations with the wealthy I rely on Blake Nevius, *Robert Herrick: The Development of a Novelist* (Berkeley and Los Angeles: University of California Press, 1962), pp. 67, 109–11, 155; diary of Hutchinson, 28 January 1900, p. 30; 11–12 August 1900, p. 36; 7 October 1901, p. 57, typescript copy, Hutchinson Papers, Newberry Library.

24. Robert Herrick, literary notebook, 1895 (but including other years), Herrick Papers. Frances Hutchinson was to provide an annual income of $3,000 a year to Herrick after her death (will of Frances K. Hutchinson, vault files, Art Institute of Chicago).

25. Robert Herrick, "The University of Chicago," *Scribner's Magazine* 18 (1895):401.

26. Nevius, *Robert Herrick*, pp. 288–89, 158–59; see Herrick's self-characterization as Clavercin in *Chimes* (New York: Macmillan Co., 1926).

27. Herrick, literary notebook, 1895, Herrick Papers.

28. Robert Herrick, *The Gospel of Freedom* (New York: Macmillan Co., 1898).

29. Robert Herrick, *The Common Lot* (New York: Macmillan Co., 1904) (quotation from p. 55).

30. Robert Herrick, *One Woman's Life* (New York: Macmillan Co., 1913) (quotation from p. 178).

31. Floyd Dell's memorandum "First Impressions of Chicago" includes the entries "Thomas Concert," and "Grand Opera," as well as "Arrival in Chi; dark, crowds, big buildings," "Anarchist meeting," "Meeting when I saw Jane Addams, her voice & eyes," and "Vegetarian restaurant," Floyd Dell Papers, Newberry Library; Floyd Dell, *Moon-Calf* (New York: Alfred A. Knopf, 1920), p. 394.

32. G. Thomas Tansell, "The 'Friday Literary Review' and the Chicago Renaissance," *Journalism Quarterly* 38 (1961):332–36.

33. *Sherwood Anderson's Memoirs: A Critical Edition*, ed. Ray Lewis White (Chapel Hill: University of North Carolina Press, 1969), pp. 335–36, 334; Eunice Tietjens, *The World at My Shoulder* (New York: Macmillan Co., 1938), pp. 17–19; Margaret Anderson, *My Thirty Years' War* (New York: Covici Friede Publishers, 1930), p. 39.

34. *Sherwood Anderson's Memoirs*, p. 337; Donald F. Tingley, "The 'Robin's Egg Renaissance,' " *Journal of the Illinois State Historical Society* 63 (1970):35–54; Anderson, *Thirty Years' War*, pp. 66–67, 85–92; Floyd Dell conveys these connections dramatically in a letter to Arthur Ficke: "We were all down at Elaine's the other night, E wearing a flame colored gown with one seam. Maurice Browne read some of your poems, so that they sounded grand and conveyed nothing at all. . . . I undertook to prove to somebody you are a great poet. . . . The girl next door has just about finished a second bust of me, being a jim dandy, the bust I mean, though the girl is too—quoting me Nietzsche in the original, and expressing the most amusing views on the subject of love & marriage. . . . I have been reading Gertrude Stein's stuff. . . ." n.d., Floyd Dell Papers.

35. Duffey has dealt with this well in his *Chicago Renaissance*. My own understanding differs from Duffey's, however, regarding the meaning of culture of Herrick's generation and for Dell's and regarding the powerful impulse for cultural uplift of Chicago businessmen in the twentieth century.

36. Cook quoted in Susan Glaspell, *The Road to the Temple* (New York: Frederick A. Stokes Co., 1927), p. 224.

37. Irving Howe, *Sherwood Anderson*, The American Men of Letters Series ([New York]: Sloane, [1951]), p. 61; Floyd Dell expressed this sense of Chicago in his fictionalized memoir, *The Briary-Bush* (New York: Alfred A. Knopf, 1921).

38. Duffey, *Chicago Renaissance*, pp. 242–44; Anderson, *Thirty Years' War*, pp. 35–43.

39. In considering this issue I profited from a conversation with Kenneth S. Lynn, April 1972. Obviously since rewards and communication involve selection, the real issue here is not standards per se, but whether the standards are traditional or modernist.

Chapter 9

1. Morton White, *Social Thought in America: The Revolt against Formalism* (New York: Viking Press, 1949); Henry Farnham May, *The End of American Innocence: A Study of the First Years of Our Own Time, 1912–1917* (New York: Alfred A. Knopf, 1959).

2. Marshall Field's nephew Stanley Field, for example, began service as president of the board of trustees of the Field Museum in 1906; Charles D. Hamill's son Charles H. Hamill was elected to fill the position on the Chicago Symphony Orchestra's board vacated by the father's death.

3. One change should be noted, however. It was during this period that the first truly significant inclusion of Jews came, with the choice of Julius Rosenwald for the board of trustees of the University of Chicago. The extent of his philanthropy and his personal prestige put him on a par with members of Chicago's cultural elite. While membership on the official boards of the city-wide cultural institutions was still confined to men, women were coming to play increasingly active roles on many different levels. Mrs. Arthur Aldis, whose husband was a prominent cultural promoter, was seriously involved in drama both as a playwright and as a benefactor. Harriet Monroe was a poet and the founder and editor of *Poetry* magazine. The Chicago Women's Club creatively promoted the program of the settlement house workers within existing cultural and municipal organizations.

4. For example, A. C. Bartlett and Franklin MacVeagh were members of the Civic Federation; A. A. Sprague and his nephew A. A. Sprague II were both active in the Municipal Voters League; three works deal with politics and reform in Chicago in the period: Nick Alexander Komons, "Chicago, 1893–1907: The Politics of Reform" (Ph.D. diss., George

Washington University, 1961); Sidney I. Roberts, "Businessmen in Revolt: Chicago, 1874–1900" (Ph.D. diss., Northwestern University, 1960); Douglas Sutherland, *Fifty Years on the Civic Front* (Chicago: Civic Federation, 1943). Samuel P. Hays, "The Politics of Reform in Municipal Government in the Progressive Era," *Pacific Northwest Quarterly* 55 (1964):157–69, puts civic reform into perspective.

5. *Chicago Tribune*, 1 December 1908.

6. French to Hutchinson, 20 March 1913, copy in letterpress book 6 February–9 August 1913, p. 271, Art Institute of Chicago; Charles L. Hutchinson, "The Democracy of Art," *American Magazine of Art* 7 (1916):400; Burkholder to French, 27 March 1913, copy in letterpress book 6 February–9 August 1913, p. 289, Art Institute of Chicago.

7. *Annual Report of the Chicago Art Institute* 31 (1909/10):28; the museum explained the relative lack of American paintings purchased in the past as an accident, rather than as policy—an accident that the new fund was designed to remedy ("A New Movement—The Friends of American Art," *Bulletin of the Art Institute of Chicago* 3 [1910]:53); *Annual Report of the Chicago Art Institute* 27 (1905/6):14–15. The Chicago Symphony Orchestra under Theodore Thomas was always open to contemporary compositions.

8. "A New Movement," p. 54; *Annual Report of the Chicago Art Institute*, beginning 20 (1898/99): see, for example, the list of prizes, ibid. 38 (1916):69–71.

9. *Annual Report of the Chicago Art Institute* 32 (1910/11):62–65.

10. Wallace Rice, "'The New Theater' of Chicago," *The World To-Day* 11 (1906):844–48; James L. Highlander, "America's First Art Theatre: The New Theatre of Chicago," *Educational Theatre Journal* 11 (1959):285–90; "A Theatrical Autopsy," *Dial* 42 (1907):129–31 (quotation from p. 130); "The Drama," *The World To-Day* 13 (1907):770–72; "The Drama," *The World To-Day* 15 (1908):899; "The Chicago Theatre Society," *Dial* 51 (1911):63–65; Bernard Frank Dukore, "Maurice Browne and the Chicago Little Theatre" (Ph.D. diss., University of Illinois, 1957), pp. 11–37; Maurice Browne, *Too Late to Lament: An Autobiography* (London: Victor Gollancz, 1955), pp. 118–52. Subscriptions, paralleling membership in the Art Institute, were a departure for theater groups. Browne was later seen as an originator of the Little Theater movement.

11. Edward C. Moore, *Forty Years of Opera in Chicago* (New York: Horace Liveright, 1930).

12. Harriet Monroe, *A Poet's Life: Seventy Years in a Changing World* (New York: Macmillan Co., 1938), pp. 247, 241–42 (p. 247 quotes a *Chicago Tribune* article of 19 November 1912).

13. Harriet Monroe, "Poetry and the Other Fine Arts," *Dial* 54 (1913):497; Monroe, *A Poet's Life*, pp. 244–48 (quotation from p. 244); Aldis to Monroe, 18 July 1912, *Poetry* Collection (business), University of Chicago Library.

14. Bernard J. Duffey, *The Chicago Renaissance in American Letters:*

A *Critical History* ([East Lansing]: Michigan State College Press, 1954), pp. 239–46; Dukore, "Maurice Browne," pp. 63–121.

15. Fredric John Mosher, "Chicago's 'Saving Remnant': Francis Fisher Browne, William Morton Payne, and the *Dial* (1880–1892)" (Ph.D. diss., University of Illinois, 1950), pp. 138–42; "Circular sent to Stockholders of the Dial Co.," quoted, p. 142. The bookstore was short-lived, closing in 1912, for in the long run its successful operation was dependent on sales, not on philanthropic backing.

16. Hutchinson, "Democracy of Art," pp. 397–400.

17. Ibid., p. 398.

18. Harlow N. Higinbotham, "Music as an Ethical and Spiritual Force in Education," *The World To-Day* 5 (1903):1,177.

19. Hutchinson, "Democracy of Art," pp. 397, 399.

20. George E. Adams, address at dedication of Orchestra Hall, 14 December 1904, quoted in Theodore Thomas, *Theodore Thomas: A Musical Autobiography*, ed. George P. Upton, 2 vols. (Chicago: A. C. McClurg & Co., 1905), 1:290.

21. "Wallace Walter Atwood," *University of Chicago Magazine* 5 (1912–13):142–43; Thomas C. Chamberlain, "Address," *Proceedings of the American Association of Museums* 2 (1908):110; Wallace Walter Atwood, "Proposed Educational Work of the Chicago Academy of Sciences," *Bulletin of the Chicago Academy of Sciences* 3 (1909):35–37; Wallace Walter Atwood, "A Natural History Museum and Workshop for Children," *The Child in the City* (Chicago: Blakely Printing Co., 1911), pp. 405–6.

22. S. C. Simms, "The Development of the N. W. Harris Public School Extension of the Field Museum of Natural History," *Proceedings of the American Association of Museums* 10 (1916):56; *Publications of the Field Museum of Natural History*, Report Series 4 (1911):241.

23. *Bulletin of the Art Institute of Chicago* 10 (1916):241.

24. Lena M. McCauley, "Promoting an Interest in Art," *Art and Progress* 5 (1914):204–6; "Notes," *Art and Progress* 3 (1912):754–55; "Notes," *Art and Progress* 5 (1914):224.

25. "Notes," *Art and Progress* 5 (1914):305.

26. Dora Allen, "Bringing Music to the People of Chicago," *Survey* 31 (1913–14):803–4; Civic Music Association, *First Annual Report, 1913–14* (May 5, 1914), copy in Newberry Library; Clippings re: Civic Music Association, Chicago Historical Society.

27. *Annual Report of the Chicago Art Institute* 38 (1916):27–39; clipping from *Chicago Examiner*, 27 December 1912, Art Institute of Chicago Scrapbook, Ryerson Library, Art Institute of Chicago; *Bulletin of the Art Institute of Chicago* 11 (1917):252.

28. "Notes: Instruction for Children," *Bulletin of the Art Institute of Chicago* 13 (1914):21.

29. *Annual Report of the Chicago Art Institute* 29 (1907/8):54–55.

30. *Annual Report of the Chicago Art Institute* 24 (1902/3): 11–13;

Report of the South Park Commission to the Board of County Commissioners of Cook County, 1906–8, [p. 3]; reported in *Public Libraries* 10 (1905):89; Charles Edward Merriam, *Chicago: A More Intimate View of Urban Politics* (New York: Macmillan Co., 1929), p. 14.

31. *A Report Presented to the Board of Directors of the Chicago Public Library by the Advisory Commission* (n.p., 1909), p. 7; Carleton Bruns Joeckel and Leon Carnovsky, *A Metropolitan Library in Action: A Survey of the Chicago Public Library* (Chicago: University of Chicago Press, 1940), p. 47; *A Library Plan for the Whole City: Proposed System of Regional and Auxiliary Branches* ([Chicago]: Chicago Public Library, 1916).

32. *Annual Report of the Chicago Public Library* 43 (1914/15):32–33 (quotation from p. 32); *Annual Report of the Chicago Public Library* 40 (1911/12):24, 22.

33. Allen F. Davis, *Spearheads for Reform: The Social Settlements and the Progressive Movement, 1890–1914* (New York: Oxford University Press, 1967), pp. 62–65, 81.

34. Elizabeth Halsey, *The Development of Public Recreation in Metropolitan Chicago* ([Chicago]: Chicago Recreation Commission, 1940), pp. 30–31; Davis, *Spearheads for Reform*, p. 81.

35. *Report of the South Park Commission,* 1903/4, pp. 7–8; 1905/6, pp. 31–33; *Bulletin of the Art Institute of Chicago* 2 (1909):63.

36. "Park Pageant Honors Poet," *Chicago Daily Tribune,* 24 April 1912, clipping in Art Institute of Chicago Scrapbook vol. 29, p. 36, Ryerson Library, Art Institute of Chicago; in 1909 the students of the Art Institute, with members of art societies, gave a pageant, taking as their theme a favorite period, the Italian Renaissance *(Bulletin of the Art Institute of Chicago* 2 [1909]:33, 49–51); Lena M. McCauley, "The Spirit of Art in Chicago," *Art and Progress* 8 (1917):288. Charles Merriam cast a different light on the pageants: he portrayed them as a "pyrotechnic display" designed to cover up the corruption of city politics after 1915 *(Chicago,* p. 22).

37. "Notes," *Art and Progress* 6 (1914):67; Robert H. Wiebe considered this general development in *The Search for Order, 1877–1920* (New York: Hill and Wang, 1967), pp. 174–75.

38. "The American Federation of Arts," *Outlook* 110 (1915):294; "The American Federation of Arts," *Outlook* 113 (1916):549–50; "The Convention," *Art and Progress* 2 (1910/11):272–73.

39. Charles Moore, *Daniel H. Burnham: Architect, Planner of Cities,* 2 vols. (Boston: Houghton Mifflin Company, 1921), 2:75–80; Daniel H. Burnham to Charles Follen McKim, 20 May 1905, quoted ibid., 2:85.

40. Jesse Benedict Carter, "The American Academy in Rome," *Commercial Club of Chicago Yearbook, 1913–14* (Chicago: Executive Committee, 1914), pp. 144–46; Christopher Grant LaFarge, *History of the American Academy in Rome* ([New York?], 1915), p. 16; Moore, *Daniel H. Burnham,* 2:85.

41. Daniel Hudson Burnham and Edward H. Bennett, *Plan of Chicago*, ed. Charles Moore (Chicago: Commercial Club, 1909). The impetus of the plan caused the two clubs to merge, taking the name of the Commercial Club.

42. For example, see Moore, *Daniel H. Burnham*, 2:169; Charles Moore, "Lessons of the Chicago World's Fair: An Interview with the Late Daniel H. Burnham," *Architectural Record* 33 (1913):33–44; Thomas S. Hines, *Burnham of Chicago: Architect and Planner* (New York: Oxford University Press, 1974), pp. 312–45; Jon Alvah Peterson, "The Origins of the Comprehensive City Planning Ideal in the United States, 1840–1911" (Ph.D. diss., Harvard University, 1967), p. 139; Charles Zueblin, A *Decade of Civic Development* (Chicago: University of Chicago Press, 1905), p. 62.

43. Burnham and Bennett, *Plan of Chicago*, illustration XLIV, between pp. 44 and 45.

44. *Report of the South Park Commission*, 1906–8, pp. 8–14, 90, photographs between pp. 88 and 89, photograph opposite p. 90; Burnham and Bennett, *Plan of Chicago*, pp. 110–18. It is interesting that in the Burnham Plan the University of Chicago does not figure at all. This is one indication that, while important as a cultural force in Chicago, the university was not seen as a civic institution in the years after Harper's death. A more direct indication is an article by William Gardner Hale arguing that the university had been given a bad press, unlike the Art Institute. As a result Chicagoans did not feel that the University of Chicago belonged to the city in the same way that the museum did ("The Continuing City," *University of Chicago Record* 11 [1906–7]:1–8).

45. Peterson, "Origins of Comprehensive City Planning Ideal," and Wiebe, *Search for Order*, both equate the understanding of functional interrelationships and the sense of the city as a total entity with modern (though not necessarily better) American thought; Louise C. Wade, *Graham Taylor: Pioneer for Social Justice, 1851–1938* (Chicago: University of Chicago Press, 1964), pp. 196–97.

46. Robert Averill Walker, *The Planning Function in Urban Government* (Chicago: University of Chicago Press, 1941), pp. 235–41, describes how the Chicago Plan was sold to the city; see, for example, Chicago Plan Commission, *Chicago's Greatest Issue: An Official Plan* ([Chicago]: Chicago Plan Commission, 1911).

47. "The task which Haussmann accomplished for Paris corresponds to the work which must be done for Chicago" (Burnham and Bennett, *Plan of Chicago*, p. 18).

48. Draft of a letter by the board of the University of Chicago Settlement to the City Plan Commission, 5 October 1910, University of Chicago Settlement, Board Meeting minutes, February 1896–October 1910, McDowell Papers, Chicago Historical Society; Burnham and Bennett, *Plan of Chicago*, p. 108; Daniel H. Burnham, address to Merchants Club, 1897, quoted in Moore, *Daniel H. Burnham*, 2:107; Burnham and Bennett, *Plan of Chicago*, p. 32.

49. Carl W. Condit, *Chicago, 1910–29: Building, Planning, and Urban Technology* (Chicago: University of Chicago Press, 1973), pp. 178–216; Hines, *Burnham of Chicago*, p. 340.

50. Moore, *Forty Years of Opera*, pp. 378–92; Condit, *Chicago, 1910–29*, p. 125; Herman Kogan, *A Continuing Marvel: The Story of the Museum of Science and Industry* (Garden City, N.Y.: Doubleday & Co., 1973), pp. 83ff.

Index

Academy of Design, 38, 146

Adams, George E., 39, 55, 62, 66, 67, 230; on art patronage, 90–91; on Chicago as cultural center, 208

Addams, Jane, 126–27, 170; and Hull-House, 127–31, 133–34; and neighborhood, 130; early cultural elitism of, 131; view of art and culture of, 131–32, 134, 136–37, 139; and John Dewey, 132–33, 137; and Ruskinian vision of industrial society, 134–37, 141–42; and immigrants, 136, 138; and youth, 138–39; and cultural philanthropists, 140, 141–42; and political reform, 142, 143, 144; and philanthropy, 142–43; on branch libraries, 161. See also Hull-House; Ethnic groups; Neighborhood; Settlement houses

Administrators: relationships of, with trustees, 145–46; qualifications and social background of, 146; professional community among, 147; power of, 148; values of, 149; and authority of the expert, 149;

and sense of utility, 150–54; and economy, 155; and discipline, 155; as scholars, 156; and public, 156–57; as source of innovation, 160; and reformers' concerns, 161, 196; concern of, for immigrants and children, 161; instrumental approaches of, 215–16; and Chicago Plan, 223. See also Trustees

Aldis, Arthur, 199, 201, 203

Aldis, Mary, 53

American Academy of Art, 220–21

American Academy of Fine Arts, 7–8

American Art-Union, 7

American cities, harshness of, 2–3, 75

American Federation of Arts, 219–20

American Library Association, 147

American Museum of Natural History (New York), 25

Anderson, Margaret, 189, 191

Anderson, Sherwood, 188, 189, 190

Andrews, Clement W., 153, 154

Annual reports, 118, 150

Apollo Club, 34, 47, 57

Armory Show, 198

Armour, Allison, 230

Armour, P. D., 55

Art: nature of, 3, 8; idealism in, 3,
16, 18–19, 77, 86; nationalism
and, 3; neoclassic, 3–4; Ruskin
on, 5–7; for the elite, 7–8;
Norton on, 14–17; genteelists'
understanding of, 17; German
idealism and, 18; realistic approaches to, 18, 86; Hegelianism
and, 18–19; as counterworld,
18–19, 87–88; Matthew Arnold
on, 18; medieval architecture
and, 19, 20, 24, 87, 113; and
unity of the arts, 23–26, 89;
eastern influences on, 73–74;
Hutchinson's view of, 74–79,
88–89, 91, 205–6, 207–8; and
religion, 75; and process of
refinement, 78, 80, 81, 83, 87;
and social change, 79; economics
of, and public taste, 82; pre-
Raphaelite, 86; Impressionist, 86;
Romanesque, 87, 112; Addams's
views of, 128, 132, 134–37,
138–39; Dewey's views of,
137–38, 141; Starr's views of,
134–36; administrators' views of,
150–56; Veblen's views of,
163–64; Fuller's views of,
171–81; Herrick's views of,
184–88; and modernism, 188–93,
195, 197–205. See also Idealism;
Renaissance art and architecture

Art and Progress, 220

Art Institute of Chicago, 235;
founded, 38; Hutchinson's role
in, 51–52; trustees' role in,
51–52, 93–94, 101, 105, 120;
designed for public, 57–58;
concern of, for excellence, 85;
architecture of, 87, 112, 114,
115, 124; and use of reproductions, 101; acquisition of
Dermidoff Collection and El

Greco paintings, 101, 118;
collection, 101–3, 106; and Field
Columbian Museum, 104; and
resistance to University of
Chicago, 104; attendance at,
105, 108; lecture series of, 107;
and temporary exhibitions, 108;
downtown location of, 116–17;
speculative drive of, 118–20;
membership categories of, 120;
role of administrator in, 146;
opened to public, 156–57;
extension program of, 157, 159,
210; International Show at,
198–99; Monroe's observation of,
202–3; loan collections of, 210;
service to organizations by, 211;
concerts at, 211–12; varied
activities of, during Progressive
period, 212; and new sense of
relation to city, 213; and schools,
214; and Act Concerning
Museums and Public Parks, 214;
and field houses, 217; representative of cultural interest, 219; in
Burnham Plan, 222; expansion
of, after World War I, 226

Artist, role of, 5, 77, 91–92

Artistic establishment, 169–74;
"missionary" efforts of, 172;
decrying failure to support local
artists, 173–74, 196. See also
Endowment; Patronage; Support
of contemporary artists

Art museums. See Cultural
institutions

Arts and crafts movement, 135–36

Arts for America, 173

Art Theater, 201, 203

Atlantic Monthly, 14, 73

Atwood, Charles, 153

Atwood, Wallace W., 209

Auditorium, 40, 47, 57, 110, 112,
116

Ayer, Edward E., 45, 46, 52, 58,
230; as collector, 67–68; and
American Indians, 67; link

between collecting and imperialism, 67–68; as trustee, 94

Baker, William T., 39
Balatka, Hans, 33
Barbizon School, 37
Bartlett, Adolphus C., 67, 168
Bartlett, Frederick Clay, 53, 168
Bartlett family, 53
Bascom, John, 19
Beecher, Henry Ward, 21–22, 74
Bellows, George, 200
Bellows, Henry, 9, 10–11, 12, 13, 14, 15, 77–78
Berenson, Bernard, 184–85
Black, John, 45
Blair, Watson F., 58, 230
Blatchford, Eliphalet Wickes, 34–36, 71, 73, 148, 231
Boston, Mass., 9–10, 11
Boston Atheneum, 8, 10
Boston Public Library, 25–26, 86
Bowen, George S., 37
Bradley, William H., 148
Brooke, Rupert, 204
Browne, Charles Francis, 170–73
Browne, Francis Fisher, 83, 204
Browne, Maurice, 191, 201–4
Browne's Bookstore, 204–5
Buckingham, Clarence, 67
Buildings of cultural institutions, 111–20; architectural styles of, 86–88, 112, 113, 123–24; and relation to public, 111–12, 114; architects of, 112; and functional efficiency, 112–13; symbolic function of, 113; World's Columbian Exposition and, 115; downtown location of, 116–17; as spiritual forces, 117; as expressions of philanthropists' business sense, 117–18; and use of master plan, 118; as understood by administrators, 151–53, 165; and decentralization, 215–16, 217; in Chicago Plan, 222–23; after World War I, 226.

See also Renaissance art and architecture
Burnham, Daniel H., 79, 224, 231; as administrator of World's Columbian Exposition, 44, 86–87, 89, 155–56; on unity of arts, 89; and Root, architects of Art Institute, 112; and cultural elite, 168–69; as promoter of Chicago Plan, 220–21. See also Chicago Plan
Burnham Plan. See Chicago Plan
Busse, Fred A., 223
Butler, Edward B., 131, 168, 231

Calumet Club, 56
Carnegie, Andrew, 46
Carpenter, N. H., 199, 219
Carr, Clyde M., 231
Cassatt, Mary, 54
Central Art Association, 172–73
Central Park (New York), 8–9, 23, 54
Century, 17
Chatfield-Taylor, Hobart C., 170–71
Cheney, John Vance, 170
Chevalier of Pensieri-Vani, The (Fuller), 176–77
Chicago, 1, 2; as site of World's Columbian Exposition, 27–28; economic and social development of, 28–30; political life of, 31; epitomizing America, 31; cultural life of, 31–35, 81–86, 208; emergence of philanthropic elite in, 34–48; economic position of, 58–60; loyalty to, 60–61, 84–85; economic and political changes in, 61–63; analogy of, with Florence, 90, 207–8; in Fuller's The Cliff-Dwellers, 177–78; in Fuller's With the Procession, 180; in Herrick's The Common Lot, 186–87; as seen by younger artists, 188, 190–91; and changing relation to cultural

Chicago (*continued*):
institutions, 214–15; park system of, 216; field houses of, 217–18; pageants in, 218–19; Municipal Art League of, 219. *See also* Cultural institutions (Chicago); Cultural philanthropists; Cultural philanthropy; Ethnic groups

Chicago Academy of Design, 38, 44, 47. *See also* Art Institute of Chicago

Chicago Academy of Fine Arts, 51

Chicago Academy of Sciences, 34–37, 44, 47, 57; extension program of, 209–10; habitat exhibits at, 210

Chicago art associations, 33, 108, 211

Chicago Biennial Music Festival Association, 39–41, 47

Chicago businessmen: in economic growth, 28–29; and Inter-State Industrial Exposition, 37; outside circle of cultural philanthropists, 45–46; and business combination, 59–60; and local and national ties, 60–61; and politics, 61–65; criticized by Hutchinson, 75–77; in Fuller's *The Cliff-Dwellers*, 177–78; in Herrick's *The Common Lot*, 186–87. *See also* Chicago; Cultural philanthropists; Trustees

Chicago Club, 56, 112

Chicago Commons, 130

Chicago Grand Opera Company, 202

Chicago Grand Opera Festival, 40

Chicago Historical Society, 34, 36, 57, 73

Chicago Library Club, 147–48, 160–61

Chicago Municipal Art Gallery, 211

Chicago Musical Directory, The, 33

Chicago Plan, 57, 87, 169, 197, 221–26; sponsored by Merchants and Commercial clubs, 221; and spirit of World's Columbian Exposition, 221; described, 222; and Progressive tendencies, 223; campaign for, 223–24; middle- and upper-class bias of, 224

Chicago Public Library, 34, 237; founded, 32; and commitment to broad public, 47, 121, 122; distinguished from Newberry and Crerar, 98, 103; and "unwashed," 114; in nineteenth century, 120–25; board of, 121; as repository of culture, 122; popular use of, 123; new building of, 123–24; task of, redefined by Legler, 165; and changes in twentieth century, 215–16; advisory committee of, 215; and regional system, 215; and instrumental approach, 215–16; and utilitarianism and efficiency, 216; in Chicago Plan, 222

Chicago Relief and Aid Society, 35

Chicago school of architecture, 112

Chicago Society for University Extension, 157

Chicago Symphony Orchestra, 47, 52, 57, 236; founded, 41; Thomas's philosophy of, 80; role of trustees and director of, 95; programming of, 102–3, 109–10; and resistance to University of Chicago, 104; program notes of, 108; and the public, 109–10; and immigrants, 110–11; and use of membership categories, 120; and role of Thomas, 146; pricing policy of, 211; popular concerts of, 211–12; in Chicago Plan, 222. *See also* Endowment; Orchestral Association; Standards and popular taste; Thomas, Theodore

Chicago University, 41, 44

Chicago Women's Club, 211

Chicago Zoological Park, 226

Choirs, 33–34

Cincinnati, Ohio, 28
Citizens Association, 63
City Beautiful movement, 221
City charter of 1905–1906, 214–15
Civic Federation, 63, 196
Civic Music Association, 212, 219
Civic Opera Building, 226, 227
Civic organizations, 212
Civil War, 10–13, 14–15
Clark, John M., 61
Clarkson, Ralph, 170, 173–74
Classical Greek architecture, 113
Cliff Dwellers, 53, 169, 171,
    181–82
Cliff-Dwellers, The (Fuller), 177–
78
Clubs, 56–57
Cobb, Henry Ives, 112, 152
Collections and musical programs:
    nature of, 98–101, 103, 124–25;
    comprehensiveness of, 101–3;
    organization of, 102–3; and
    needs of the public, 104; display
    of, 106; additions to Art
    Institute's, 118; definition of
    success of, 120; and Chicago
    Public Library, 121–23; rethink-
    ing of, by settlement house
    reformers, 134, 136–37, 139, 161;
    rethinking of, by administrators,
    153–54, 156–57; changed con-
    ception of, for philanthropists,
    197–99; nature of, altered by
    civic organizations, 211–12; all-
    inclusive concept of, after World
    War I, 226. *See also* Buildings of
    cultural institutions; Cultural
    institutions (Chicago); Public
Combination, 59–60
Comfort, George Fiske, 22–24
Commercial Club (Chicago), 40,
    41, 56–57, 60, 63, 141, 220, 221,
    223
Commercial ventures into culture,
    32–33, 47
Common Lot, The (Herrick),
    186–87

Concerts, popular, 39, 211–12. *See
    also* Chicago Symphony Orchestra
Cook, George Cram, 189, 190
Cox, Kenyon, 169
Crerar, John, 45
Crerar Library, 41, 45, 65, 82–83,
    236; and Newberry Library,
    98–99, 103; and relation to
    public, 109; atmosphere of, 113;
    downtown location of, 116–17;
    librarian's annual report, 150;
    and utilitarian standard, 154; in
    Chicago Plan, 222
Cultivated gentlemen, image of,
    54–55, 68–69, 75
Cultural evolution of society, 79,
    83–84
Cultural idealism. *See* Idealism
Cultural institutions: development
    of, before Civil War, 7–8, 9–10;
    development of, after Civil War,
    20–22, 24; governance models of,
    23; changing purposes of, 24–26;
    as Hutchinson's teachers, 54, 96;
    traditions governing, 96–97
Cultural institutions (Chicago):
    development of, before 1880,
    32–39; development of, after
    1880, 39–48; and cultural
    philanthropists, 51–53; city-wide,
    57–58; purposes of, 65, 68–69,
    78, 81–83; and city's evolution,
    83–85; as informal "Academy,"
    84; and excellence, 85–86; as
    indirect patronage, 91–92; role
    of, summarized, 91–92; and
    traditions, 96–97; kinds of,
    chosen, 97–100, 103–4;
    cooperation among, 103–4, 107;
    attendance at, 103, 108–9, 123,
    129; and commitment to growth,
    118–19; speculation of, 118–20;
    and membership categories, 120;
    as viewed by Addams, 128–29;
    as viewed by younger artists and
    writers, 190–91; and Progressive
    period, 195, 197, 225; after

Cultural institutions, Chicago (*cont.*):
World War I, 226–27. *See also* Buildings of cultural institutions; Collections and musical programs; Public; *names of individual institutions*

Cultural nationalism, 3, 4

Cultural philanthropists, 52–53; drawn from Protestants of British descent, 34, 35–36, 38, 39–47; emergence of, as group, 36–47; younger generation of, 44–45; friendships among, 52–53; image of the good life held by, 53–54; association of, with artists, 53, 168–70, 171, 174–75, 181, 182, 184; eastern ties of, 55, 73; club life of, 56; wealth of, 58–59; threatened loss of prestige of, 60; loyalty to Chicago of, 60–61, 84–85; lacking in local political power, 61–62, 63; political ideas of, 64–68, 206–7; role of, in cultural institutions, 93–96; and settlement house reformers, 126–27, 143–44; and administrators, 145–49, 155, 158–59; in Progressive period, 195–97; openness of, to new forms, 198; and support of contemporary artists, 199–205; and broadened sense of public, 206; hold of Renaissance on, 207–8; and extension, 209–22; and American Federation of Arts, 219–20; and American Academy of Art, 220–21; and Chicago Plan, 223–24; as straddling 1890s and Progressivism, 225; after World War I, 226–27. *See also* Cultural philanthropy; Elites and elitism; *names of individual institutions* and *individual philanthropists*

Cultural philanthropy: and national developments, 21, 24, 25–26; Henry Ward Beecher on, 21–22; and establishment of Chicago institutions, 36, 38, 40–43, 44; and younger generation, 44–45; as prerogative of elite, 45–46, 47–48, 61; desired role in Chicago of, 65; elitism underlying, 67–69, 200; and idealism, 73–81, 88–89; and standards, 82–83, 100; and Chicago's spiritual development, 83–84; and artistic creation, 84, 91–92; and unity of arts and sciences, 90; and Renaissance model, 90–91; influence of eastern models on, 96–97; and institutions chosen, 97–98; speculative quality of, 119–20; Addams's view of, 128–29, 134, 136–37, 142–43; settlement alternative to, 140–41; Veblen's view of, 162–64; artists' and writers' view of, 173–74, 178–80, 183–84, 190–93; changing nature of, in twentieth century, 197, 225; and contemporary artists, 199–201; and drama, opera, and poetry, 201–5; and extension, 210; after World War I, 226–27. *See also* Cultural institutions; Cultural philanthropists; Elites and elitism; *names of individual institutions*; *names of individual philanthropists*

Culture. *See* Art

Currey, Margery, 189

Curtis, George William, 17

Dearborn Park, 123

Decentralization. *See* Neighborhood

Delano, Frederic A., 64, 65, 231

Dell, Floyd, 168, 188–89, 191

Dewey, John, 126–27, 132, 133, 137–38, 141

Dewey, Melvil, 147

Dial, 74, 79, 81, 88, 204; and understanding of culture, 83; on

Chicago as a cultural center, 83–84; sense of social evolution of, 83–88; and endowment, 97; and criticism of World's Columbian Exposition, 107; and support of administrators, 149–50; and elitism of Art Theater, 201
Discipline, 155–56
Donald Robertson's Players, 201
Dooley, Mr., 173
Dorsey, George A., 156
Downing, Andrew Jackson, 8
Drake, John B., 37
Drama, 201, 218–19. *See also* Art Theater; Little Theater
Dreiser, Theodore, 169
Duncan, Isadora, 198
Dutch Masters, 86, 101, 118

Eastman, Sidney C., 45
Eddy, Jerome, 199
El Greco, 86, 101
Elites and elitism: in early nineteenth century, 2–3; and understanding of Ruskin, 6; and cultural institutions, 7–8, 9; role in Civil War of, 10–13, 14–15; in post–Civil War period, 13–14, 20–22, 23; exemplified by Charles Eliot Norton, 14–17; in Chicago, 34–47; and responsibility for culture, 36, 38, 43, 47, 48, 83; as expressed by Chicago's cultural philanthropists, 67–68, 110–11, 159; and Newberry Library, 72–73; culture of, 75; Hutchinson's belief in, 77; in policies of cultural institutions, 109–11, 114, 128–29; in Addams's early thought, 131; and patronage, 200; in Chicago Plan, 224–25. *See also* Cultural institutions; Cultural philanthropists; Cultural philanthropy
Emerson, Ralph Waldo, 15, 77
Endowment, 82–83, 199. *See also*

Artist, role of; Artistic establishment; Patronage; Support for contemporary artists
Entertainment, 107, 109
Ethnic groups, 30–31; and Chicago Public Library, 32, 47, 121–23; as centers for cultural expression, 33–34; political power of, 61–63; and interest in music, 110–11; and Sunday closing of World's Columbian Exposition, 111; and Addams's view of culture, 129, 132–33, 138, 139, 140; and Hull-House Labor Museum, 136; and administrators, 161; and pageants, 218
European city, 2–3; as setting for art, 78–79
Extension, 133, 157–59, 160–61. *See also* Museum extension; Public; University of Chicago; *names of individual institutions*

Fair. *See* World's Columbian Exposition
Fairbank, Nathaniel K., 39, 41, 58, 74, 231
Fay, Charles Norman, 41, 64, 65, 111, 155
Ferguson Foundation, 199, 200
Ficke, Arthur Gordon, 189
Field, Marshall, 29, 39, 45, 46, 59, 64, 231
Field and Leiter, 39
Field Columbian Museum, 41, 52, 65, 66, 67, 235–36; founded, 44; trustees of, 45–46, 94; building of, 87, 153, 226; collection of, 100–103, 106; and Art Institute, 104; and University of Chicago, 104; and lecture series, 107; publications of, 107–8; attendance at, 108–9; downtown location of, 116–17; and growth, 119; and use of membership categories, 120; and Hull-House Labor Museum, 136; and administra-

Field Columbian Museum (*cont.*): tors, 149–50; extension program of, 159, 210; ownership of, transferred to city, 214
Field houses, 217–19
Field Museum of Natural History. *See* Field Columbian Museum
Florence, Italy, 16, 90, 207
Forest Hills Cemetery (Brookline), 54
Fort Sheridan, 63
Freie Presse, 111
French, Daniel Chester, 115
French, William M. R., 96, 146, 156–57, 159–60, 198
Friday afternoon concert series, 110
Friday Literary Review, 188
Friends of American Art, 199, 200, 203
Fuller, Henry Blake, 1, 53, 126–27, 167, 170, 171, 172; as friend of cultural philanthropists, 174, 175; life and pertinent works of, 174–81; as cultural observer and reporter, 175; "The Upward Movement in Chicago," 175; on meaning of art, 175, 176–77; and realism, 175–76, 180, 181; and *The Chevalier of Pensieri-Vani*, 176–77; on cultural philanthropy, 177–80; on feelings about Chicago, 177–78, 180; and *The Cliff-Dwellers*, 177–78; and *With the Procession*, 178–80; and *Under the Skylights*, 180; cosmopolitan tastes of, 180
Fullerton Hall, 107

Gage, Lyman J., 39
Garland, Hamlin, 170, 171, 172; portrayed by Fuller, 180–81
Gaskell, Miss, 15
Genteelists, 17, 70, 74
German community, 33–34, 110–11. *See also* Ethnic groups
German idealism, 18

Gibbs, Woolcott, 11
Gilder, Richard Watson, 17, 116
Glaspell, Susan, 189, 190
Glessner, John J., 53, 231
Godkin, E. L., 11
Good government movement. *See* Political reform
Goodspeed, Thomas W., 42, 51, 117
Gospel of Freedom, The (Herrick), 184–85
Gothic architecture, 20, 87, 112, 113
Great Fire of 1871, 29, 36; recovery from, 36–37
Great Northern Trust, 59
Greenough, Horatio, 4–5
Gunsaulus, Frank W., 74

Hackett, Francis, 188
Hall, Elbridge G., collection, 102
Hallowell, Sara, 37–38
Hamill, Charles D., 39, 232
Harper, William Rainey, 41, 55, 168, 232; relationship of, with trustees, 95, 146, 159; and effort to subsume cultural institutions, 104; and university publications, 108; speculation of, 119; praised by *Dial*, 150; ideas of, 157–58; and extension, 158–60. *See also* University of Chicago
Harper's, 17
Harris, Norman Wait, 210
Harrison, Carter, 63
Harvard University, 55
Haussmann, Baron, 224
Haymarket Riot, 57, 63
Head, Franklin H., 66, 67
Hegelianism, 18–19, 88
Henri, Robert, 200–201
Herrick, Harriet, 187
Herrick, Robert, 53, 167, 181–88; relationship of, with cultural philanthropists, 181–82; and University of Chicago, 183–84;

support of endowed art theater, 184; and *The Gospel of Freedom* and culture as self-indulgence, 184–85; and importance of service, 185; and *The Common Lot*, 186; and *One Woman's Life* and the relation between sexual and artistic energies, 187–88

Higinbotham, Harlow N., 44, 58, 66, 85, 100, 111, 206–7, 232

Howells, William Dean, 18

Hull-House, 66, 175; founded, 127–29; early years of, 129–30; and art, 130–31; evolving experience of, 133; and university extension, 133; concerts at, 134; arts and crafts society of, 136; Labor Museum of, 136–37; and labor movement, 137; playground of, 140–41; and reform, 142; Players, 201. *See also* Addams, Jane; Starr, Ellen Gates

Hunt, Richard Morris, 115

Hutchinson, Benjamin, 49–50, 53

Hutchinson, Charles L., 232; role in Art Institute of, 38, 94, 101; subscribed to Biennial Music Festival, 39; as president of Commercial Club, 42; and University of Chicago, 42–43; and thoughts on New York, 43; McCagg letter, 44; Carnegie letter, 46; life and cultural involvement of, 49–55; as opposing labor unions, 66–67; on Egypt and imperialism, 68; on art, 74–79, 81, 88–89, 91–92; on Chicago as an art center 85–86; travel of, 96; and plan for University of Chicago, 118; and Addams, 126–27, 144; and Hull-House, 141; and opening of Art Institute to public, 156; relationship with Harper, 158–59; on Cliff Dwellers, 171; and Fuller, 175; and Herrick, 182; and public, 196, 205–6; on modern-

ism, 198–99; support of *Poetry* by, 203; sense of the Renaissance of, 207–8; as member of South Park Commission, 214; as president of American Federation of Arts, 219; and American Academy of Art, 220; as supporter of Chicago Plan, 223; death of, 226

Hutchinson, Frances Kinsley, 52, 144, 182

Ibsen, Henrik, 204

Idealism, 2–3; and Transcendentalism, 5; and Ruskin, 5–6; social implications of, 7; in Civil War, 11; German, 18; Hegelian, 18–19; as expressed by Bascom, 19; as expressed by Comfort, 22; and cultural institutions, 24–25; as expressed by Hutchinson, 74–79, 88–89, 91; Thomas on, 80; *Dial* on, 81; of pre-Raphaelites, 86; and sense of art as counterworld, 88; and science, 90; shared with eastern philanthropists, 97; as basis of cultural philanthropy, 97–98; and collections, 98–100; and building design, 113–16, 123–24; questioning of, by artists and writers, 193; and Chicago Plan, 221–23. *See also* Addams, Jane; Administrators; Art; Dewey, John; Fuller, Henry Blake; Herrick, Robert

Immigrants. *See* Ethnic groups

Imperialism, 68

Impressionists, 37, 86

Industrial education, 136–37, 141

Instrumentalism, 215–16

Insull, Samuel, 226

Inter-State Industrial Exposition, 37; art in, 37–38; art committee of, 38, 51–52; exhibit building of, 38–39, 40, 47

Iroquois Club, 56

Jackson, Huntington W., 232
Jackson Park, 116
Jarves, James Jackson, 9–10, 20, 22
Jay, John, 22
John Crerar Library. *See* Crerar Library
John G. Shedd Aquarium, 226
Jones, David B., 232
Jones, Jenkin Lloyd, 173

Keep, Chauncey, 232
Keith, Edson, 55, 232
Kieth, William, 201
Kinsley, Mrs., 184
Kohlsaat, Herman H., 45

Labor: and strife, 57, 62–63; attitudes toward, 66–67, 137
Laboratory School, 126
LaFarge, John, 86
Lake front development, 219, 223–24
Landscape architecture, 8
Lathrop, Bryan, 219, 232–33
Laufer, Bernard, 119
Lectures, 107, 109, 212
Legler, Henry E., 165, 215
Lenox Library (New York), 54
Liberal reformers, 13, 64, 65. *See also* Political reform
Librarians: as professional vanguard, 147; and desire for power, 148. *See also* Administrators
Libraries, establishment of, 20–21
Lincoln, Abraham, 15
Lincoln, Robert Todd, 72–73
Lincoln Park, 71–73
Lindsay, Vachel, 188, 190, 204
Literary Club, 146
Little Review, 191
Little Room, 170, 171, 181
Little Theater, 191, 201–2, 203–4
Lloyd, Henry Demarest, 152
Loan collections, 209, 210
Lovett, Robert Morss, 53
Lowden, Frank O., 233

Lowell, James Russell, 73
Loyal Publication Society, 15

McCagg, Ezra B., 35–36, 44, 46, 71–73
McCormick, Cyrus Hall, 29, 46, 59, 233
McCormick, Harold F., 202, 233
McCormick family, 53
McKim, Charles Follen, 220
McKim, Mead & White, 86–87
McMillan Commission, 89
MacVeagh, Franklin, 39, 55, 58, 64, 65, 73, 219, 233
Manierre, George, 55, 233
Manual Training School, 57
Mapes, Arthur, 203
Mark Twain, 18
Masters, Edgar Lee, 190, 204
Materialism, 2, 75, 86, 98, 117, 207. *See also* Idealism
Mathews, W. S. B., 103, 109, 134
Max Adler Planetarium, 226
Medieval art and architecture, 19–20
Medieval Italy: importance to Norton, 16–17
Medieval society, 6
Mergers, 59–60
Metropolitan Museum of Art (New York), 22–23, 25, 54, 87
Millet, Frank D., 106–7
Mitchell, John J., 45, 233
Modernism, 188–93, 195, 197–205
Monroe, Harriet, 115, 126, 170, 191, 200, 202–4
Moon-Calf, 188
Morgan, Anna, 170
Morris, Nelson, 61
Mugwumps, 13
Municipal Art Commission, 219
Municipal Art League, 211, 219
Municipal government, 143, 214
Municipal institutions, 32
Municipal Voters League, 63, 196
Murphy, J. Francis, 201

Museum extension, 159, 209–10
Museum of Fine Arts (Boston), 24, 25, 54, 74, 87
Museum of Science and Industry, 226
Museums. *See* Cultural institutions
Musical interest, 109, 110
Musical programs. *See* Collections and musical programs
Music schools, 33

Nation, 11, 13, 24
National Academy of Design, 7
Nationalism, 3, 4
Near North Side, 60
Neighborhood, 129, 130, 161
Neoclassicism, 3–4
Newberry, Walter, 35–36, 45
Newberry Library, 41, 45, 46, 52, 65, 66, 236; founded, 36; for elite, 71–73; architecture of, 87, 112; governance of, 94; and Crerar Library, 98–99, 103–4; and relation to public, 109; contrasted with Chicago Public Library, 121–22; first librarian of, 146–47; Poole's plan for, 152; and extension, 157
New England heritage, 55, 68, 146
New York City, 11, 17, 27, 58–59, 60; and cultural institutions, 7, 22–23; and Central Park, 8–9, 23
Noblesse oblige, 67
Norton, Charles Eliot, 9, 11, 14, 74, 177; and "ideal Chicago," 1, 26; as leader of Sanitary Commission, 11, 14; views on art of, 15–17, 20, 24, 70, 79

Ogden, W. B., 35–36
Olmsted, Frederick Law, 8–9, 10, 11, 13, 14, 15, 23, 71–72
One Woman's Life (Herrick), 187–88
Opera, 32–33, 202, 226–27
Orchestra Hall, 87, 110, 116, 169.

See also Chicago Symphony Orchestra
Orchestral Association, 64, 80, 103, 109–10. *See also* Chicago Symphony Orchestra
Orchestras, 20–21, 33, 97. *See also* Chicago Symphony Orchestra; Cultural institutions
Orpheus Gesangverein, 33–34
Orr, Arthur, 233
Otis, Philo A., 39, 41
Otis, W. A., 113

Pageants, 218–19
Palmer, Alice Freeman, 183
Palmer, George Herbert, 183
Palmer, Potter, 37
Patricians. *See* Elites and elitism
Patronage, 25, 90–91. *See also* Artist, role of; Artistic establishment; Endowment; Support for contemporary artists
Patterson, H. H., 45
Payne, William Morton, 84, 171
Peabody Institute (Baltimore), 151
Peck, Ferdinand W., 40, 42
Pennsylvania Academy (Philadelphia), 8
People's Concerts, 110
Perkins, C. C., 24
Philadelphia, Pa., 8, 11
Philanthropy, 51, 65. *See also* Cultural philanthropy
Philharmonic Society, 33
Pierce, John Irving, 37
Plan for Chicago. *See* Chicago Plan
Play festival, 218–19
Poetry, 191, 200, 202–4
Political machines, 12, 31, 61–62, 64
Political reform, 63–65, 142, 143, 196
Poole, William Frederick, 146–47, 150–52, 155, 157, 159–60
Popular demand. *See* Public
Post-Impressionist Show, 198–99
Pound, Ezra, 204

Powers, Johnny, 142
Prairie Avenue, 60
Pratt, Silas Gamaliel, 34
Pre-Raphaelites, 86
Programs. *See* Collections and musical programs; Public
Progressivism, defined, 194–95
Public: responsibility of elite's organizations to, 35–36, 45, 47, 65; defined as elite, 72; defined as middle class, 75–76, 104–5, 109–10, 114, 117, 120, 129; commitment to, 104–5; and museum techniques, 105–6; and World's Columbian Exposition, 106–7; and programs, 107–10; as extending beyond middle class, 108; and immigrants, 110–11; and buildings, 111–13; and Chicago Public Library, 120–24, 215–16; as seen by settlement house reformers, 128–29, 133, 140–41, 161–62, 196–97; as seen by administrators, 156–62, 196–97; as redefined to include urban masses, 195, 197, 206–7; Hutchinson's view of, 195–96, 205–6; new approaches to, 208–14, 217–20, 225–26; and Chicago Plan, 224–25. *See also* Buildings of cultural institutions; Collections and musical programs; Cultural institutions; *names of individual institutions*
Publications, 107–8
Public education, 157
Public Libraries, 160
Public parks, 140, 216–19. *See also* Central Park (New York); South Park system (Chicago)
Public School Art Society, 211
Pullman, George, 45, 46, 59
Pullman Company, 59

Realism, 18, 86
Ream, Norman, 45

Renaissance art and architecture, 19–20; and cultural institutions, 25, 87–90, 114–15, 123–24; as style of Boston Public Library, 26; as style of World's Columbian Exposition, 86–87, 115; expressive of art as counter-world, 87–88; and aesthetic collaboration, 89; as model for Chicago, 90, 207–8; eastern architects identified with, 112; meaning of, to younger artists, 190; and hope for social integration, 208; in Chicago Plan, 222
Rockefeller, John D., 41–42, 119
Romanesque architecture, 87, 112
Romanticism. *See* Idealism
Root, John Wellborn, 87, 112, 202
Rosenwald, Julius, 144, 195, 233
Ruskin, John, 5–6, 9, 14, 15, 24, 79, 89; influence of, on Addams and Starr, 127, 128, 134–37; and Dewey, 138; as impetus to reform, 141–42
Ryerson, Martin, 42, 45, 46, 53, 58, 73, 234; and Hutchinson, 52, 53; and idealistic thrust of science, 90; role of, at University of Chicago, 158–59; and Herrick, 182; death of, 226

St. Gaudens, Augustus, 86–87
Saint Louis, 28, 58
Sandburg, Carl, 190, 203, 204
Sanitary Commission, 10–13, 14–15; Northwestern branch of, 35–36; conscious elitism of national leadership of, 36
Scammon, J. Young, 34–36
Scandinavian community, 33
Scholarship, 25, 89–90, 156
Science, 25, 89–90
Science museums. *See* Cultural institutions
Settlement houses, 217. *See also*

Addams, Jane; Hull-House; Starr, Ellen Gates Settlement house reformers, issues of. *See* Chicago Plan; Ethnic groups; Neighborhood; Political reform
Shepley, Rutan and Coolidge, 112, 123
Singing groups, 33–34
Skiff, Frederick J. V., 90, 106, 149, 153
Skinner, Mark, 35–36
South Park Commission, 214, 222
South Park system, 217
Sprague, Albert A., 53, 55, 58, 234
Sprague, Albert A., II, 234
Sprague family, 53
Standards and popular taste, 80, 82–83, 86, 104–5, 124, 191. *See also* Public
Starr, Ellen Gates, 173, 211; and cultural idealism, 134; and Ruskinian vision of industrial society, 134–36, 141–42; and reform efforts, 142
Stedman, Edmund Clarence, 17
Sullivan, Louis, 40, 112
Sunday concerts, 110
Support for contemporary artists: level of, criticized by Chicago's artistic establishment, 173–74, 196; elitist implications of, 200; extended in Progressive period, 200–205. *See also* Artist, role of; Artistic establishment; Endowment; Patronage
Swift, Gustauvus, 46, 59
Swing, David, 74, 173
Symphony programs, 109. *See also* Collections and musical programs

Taft, Lorado, 170, 171–72, 200; dream museum of, 172
Taft, William Howard, 64
Tagore, Rabindranath, 204
Taylor, Bayard, 17

Taylor, Graham, 130, 215, 223
Temporary exhibitions, 108–9
Theater, 32–33, 184, 200–203
Theodore Thomas Orchestra, 39. *See also* Chicago Symphony Orchestra
Theory of the Leisure Class (Veblen), 162–65
Thomas, Theodore, 39, 74, 79, 95, 146; on art, 79–82; high standards of, 80, 85–86, 89; programs of, 102–3; and issue of the public, 110; and commitment to truth, 154–55. *See also* Chicago Symphony Orchestra
Tietjens, Eunice, 189
Toynbee Hall, 127, 131
Transcendentalism, 4–5, 77
Tree, Lambert, 62, 234
Trinity Church (Boston), 25–26, 54
Trustees, 23, 42, 45, 47, 55, 169; role and powers of, 93–96; and museum expeditions, 94; and acquisitions, 94, 101; and Newberry and Crerar libraries, 98–99, 109; and collections, 100–105; cooperation and independence of, 104; and commitment to the public, 105, 205–8; and programs, 108, 110; and buildings, 112; and downtown location of institutions, 117; business sense of, 117–20; and administrators, 145–46, 148–49; and institutions' relation to city, 195–97. *See also* Cultural institutions; Cultural philanthropists; Cultural philanthropy; Elites and elitism; *names of individual trustees*; *names of individual institutions*

Under the Skylights (Fuller), 180
Union League Club, 56
Union League clubs, 11, 12, 13, 22

Union Stock Yard, 29
University Club, 56
University of Chicago: founding of,
  41–43, 52, 57, 64, 65, 67,
  236–37; architecture of, 87, 113;
  and Ryerson, 90; relationship
  between president and trustees
  of, 95–96, 146, 150, 159; and
  effort to subsume cultural
  institutions, 104; publications
  program of, 108; speculation of,
  119; and Hull-House extension
  program, 113; and scholarship,
  156; extension program of,
  157–58, 159, 209; cultural
  impact of, 157; Herrick's role at,
  183–84. See also Harper,
  William Rainey
University of Chicago settlement,
  224
Upton, George P., 34
"Upward Movement in Chicago,
  The" (Fuller), 175
Urban planning, 87, 221
Utilitarian concerns, 150–54,
  215–16

Vaux, Calvert, 8–9
Veblen, Thorstein, 185–88; and
  Theory of the Leisure Class,
  162–65; on culture, 162; on
  cultural philanthropy, 163; on
  taste, 163; rejection of cultural
  idealism by, 164
Vincennes Gallery of Fine Arts
  (Chicago), 33
Voluntary associations, 65

Walsh, John, 45
Wealth, uses of, 21–22. See also
  Cultural philanthropy; Elites and
  elitism
Whistler, James McNeill, 200
White City. See World's
  Columbian Exposition
Whitman, Walt, 18
Williams, Norman, 82–83
Winsor, Justin, 147
With the Procession (Fuller),
  178–80
Women and culture, 55
World's Columbian Exposition, 1,
  2; and eastern reaction to
  Chicago as site of, 27–28;
  founding of, 41, 43; Directory of,
  43–44, 99, 111; commission of,
  43–44, 155; Fine Arts Department of, 52, 57, 85; Renaissance
  architecture of, 86–87, 115;
  Court of Honor of, 86–87,
  99–100, 106, 115; and role of
  Midway, 99; technological
  exhibits of, 100; anthropological
  exhibits of, 100; musical programs at, 103; and hucksterism,
  106–7; and Sunday closing, 111;
  visual impact of, 115–16; site of,
  116; overexpenditure of, 119;
  and Lorado Taft, 182
World War I as turning point of
  philanthropy, 226
Wright, Frank Lloyd, 164, 205

Yale University, 55
Young Men's Association, 34, 36

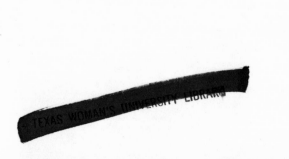